★★★★★★★★★

CORRUPTED CULTURE

★★★★★★★★★

Vincent Ryan Ruggiero

★ ★ ★ ★ ★ ★ ★ ★

CORRUPTED CULTURE

★ ★ ★ ★ ★ ★ ★ ★

Rediscovering America's
ENDURING PRINCIPLES, VALUES,
and COMMON SENSE

Prometheus Books

59 John Glenn Drive
Amherst, New York 14228–2119

Published 2013 by Prometheus Books

Prometheus Books recognizes the following registered trademarks, trademark, and service mark mentioned within the text: Celebrex®; Have it your way®; Just Do It™; No rules, just right℠; Play-Doh®.

Cover image © 2013 iStockphoto
Cover design by Nicole Sommer-Lecht

Inquiries should be addressed to
Prometheus Books
59 John Glenn Drive
Amherst, New York 14228-2119
VOICE: 716-691-0133
FAX: 716-691-0137
WWW.PROMETHEUSBOOKS.COM

17 16 15 14 13   5 4 3 2 1

Library of Congress Cataloging-in-Publication Data

Ruggiero, Vincent Ryan.
    Corrupted culture : rediscovering America's enduring principles, values, and common sense / by Vincent Ryan Ruggiero.
        pages cm
    Includes bibliographical references and index.
    ISBN 978-1-61614-749-5 (pbk)
    ISBN 978-1-61614-750-1 (ebook)
    1. United States—Social conditions—21st century. 2. United States—Civilization—21st century—Psychological aspects. 3. United States—Moral conditions. 4. Social values—United States. I. Title.

HN59.2.R839 2013
306.0973—dc23

                                                                    2013010075

Printed in the United States of America

To Barbara Kathleen Ruggiero
The sweetest and bravest person I know

CONTENTS

Introduction   9

1. The Legacy of Social Darwinism   15

2. Enter Humanistic Psychology   33

3. Meanings and Consequences   65

4. The Fallacies Exposed   95

5. More Vexing Questions   127

6. A Wiser Perspective   149

7. Human Nature Revisited   161

8. Reorienting Ourselves   179

9. Reforming the Culture   209

Notes   243

Index   283

INTRODUCTION

G. K. Chesterton once chided the thinkers of his day for analyzing the easy part of a problem, ignoring the hard part, then going home to their tea. Something similar has happened with the analysis of the social problems that have plagued America for the last half century. A common response is that they are related to the sexual revolution, feminism, the drug culture, and the antiwar movement that occurred during the 1960s. When asked to explain the relationship, however, analysts offer little more than vague references to a spirit of rebellion against authority and dissatisfaction with traditional views and values. That answer is not good enough. Before there can be any hope of solving the nation's problems, we must understand what *caused* the rebellion and dissatisfaction. We also need answers to a host of related questions, notably these:

★ Why did pride in American traditions and ideals give way to cynicism and contempt?

★ Why did success, especially financial success, become suspect?

★ Why did rights and entitlements become more important than responsibilities?

★ Why did self-esteem displace self-respect and self-assertion replace self-control as personal and social imperatives?

★ Why did the term *dysfunctional families*, a term that was virtually unknown in the 1950s, suddenly come into vogue?

★ Why did psychologists stop considering guilt and shame aids to personal development and begin classifying them as emotionally harmful?

★ Why did many churches shift their emphasis from leading a moral life to "feeling good" about oneself, and from liberation from sin to liberation from political oppression?

★ Why did many parents begin ignoring their parental responsibilities and allow their children to do as they wish?

★ Why did the divorce rate rise? Why did many divorced parents deny their children financial support?

★ Why did many young people treat parents and teachers with disrespect and contempt?

★ Why did academic performance continue to decline despite sizeable increases in education budgets?

★ Why did schools lower performance standards, inflate grades, relax discipline, and devalue excellence and achievement? Why did they shift from moral instruction to "values clarification"? Why do many educators impose their beliefs on their students?

★ Why did filmmakers begin glamorizing villains and ridiculing authority figures?

★ Why have television executives increased the sexual content of programs and made them more graphic and bizarre?

★ Why did many jurists begin sympathizing with convicted criminals, treating them as victims of society? Why do jurists and other government officials ignore the distinction between legal and illegal aliens?

★ Why do elected officials increasingly, and often blatantly, serve the desires of special interests rather than the good of their constituents?

★ Why have many journalists rejected the ideal of objectivity and the traditional distinction between fact and opinion?

★ Why has there been a dramatic rise in absurdity, particularly among social and governmental leaders—for example, claiming that a two-thousand-page bill must be passed before it can be understood?

More recently, America's social and political problems have been attributed to the resurgence of the early twentieth-century movement known as Progressivism rather than to "the Sixties." This newer viewpoint has promoted useful discussion of constitutional issues. Unfortunately, it has also shifted attention away from the unanswered questions about the Sixties. Moreover, it has raised—but left unanswered—additional questions, notably the following:

★ What caused the original Progressive movement to arise in the early 1900s?
★ Why did it appeal to many influential people of that time? Why were such people also attracted to the Eugenics movement?
★ What caused the resurgence of Progressivism toward the end of the twentieth century, after being long dormant?
★ Why were the works of radicals, notably Saul Alinsky's *Rules for Radicals*, so appealing to the new Progressives?
★ Why have many conservatives joined liberals in embracing Progressivism?

Corrupted Culture answers both sets of questions by demonstrating that virtually all our present social and political problems can be traced to two mistaken views of human nature.

The first view, which became prominent in the early twentieth century, was the pessimistic notion that biology is destiny, that most people are seriously deficient in intelligence, and that nothing can be done to alter their condition. This was a tenet of social Darwinism and it spawned the movement known as Hereditarianism, which led educators to stop teaching students *how* to think and to focus instead on telling them *what* to think. It also caused those in the business community to disparage workers' intelligence and deny their own companies a rich source of improvement and innovation.

In addition, the Hereditarian view that the average person is irremediably unintelligent provided the conceptual foundation for both Progressivism and the Eugenics movement. Progressives concluded that if people are incapable of running their own lives, government must do so; Eugenicists worried that uncontrolled reproduction by the unfit would "pollute" the gene pool and decided to use persuasion and force to prevent that outcome. (Most Eugenicists believed that, although evolution would eventually correct such problems, the process was too slow and therefore required their assistance.)

The second mistaken view of human nature was advanced in the mid-twentieth century by Humanistic Psychology, which taught that feelings are more reliable than reason, the locus of authority is within the individual, self-actualization is the greatest human need, and self-esteem is the key to achievement. In place of Hereditarianism's unfounded pessimism about human nature, the new psychology offered unfounded optimism. Almost overnight, the message changed from "people are uneducable morons" to "people are inherently wise, wonderful, and deserving of high self-esteem."

Although Humanistic Psychology's inflated notions of self revolutionized educational theory and practice, in some cases displacing traditional subject matter, they had little effect on the mind-stuffing regime established by Hereditarianism. Instead, it was only the content of the mind stuffing that changed—*telling* students to esteem themselves and trust their feelings replaced *telling* students about grammar, history, and science. One tragic effect of the elevation of emotion over reason was the suppression of one of the most important educational reforms of the twentieth century—that is, the Critical Thinking movement.

Both Hereditarianism and Humanistic Psychology have played important roles in the resurgence of Progressivism. The legacy of Hereditarianism in schools, business, and government has led modern Progressives, as it did their predecessors, to assert their intellectual superiority over the masses. The conditioning of Humanistic Psychology to regard themselves as exempt from rules, including those of logic, and to elevate their feelings over reason has made modern Progressives contemptuous of views that differ from their own. Meanwhile, as all this has been occurring, Hereditarianism has continued to deny the masses a meaningful education, and Humanistic Psychology has deprived them of their philosophical and moral heritage and conditioned them to self-absorption. Simply said, as the ruling class was being inspired to manipulate the masses, the masses were becoming increasingly vulnerable to manipulation.

Harvard philosopher George Santayana famously declared, "those who do not remember the past are condemned to repeat it." But it would be more accurate to say that those who do not *understand* the past are condemned to repeat it. Today's Progressives certainly remember their mentors Woodrow Wilson and Franklin Roosevelt. The problem is, they don't understand the errors of Progressivism. And neither they nor millions of other Americans understand the errors of Humanistic Psychology. That is precisely why the errors continue to create serious mischief and endanger America's future. This book first exposes these errors and demonstrates how they have corrupted our culture. Then it presents what I believe is a compelling case for restoring the traditional view of human nature and the principles and values associated with that view. Finally, it suggests what people can do to restore that perspective in their lives and in America's social institutions.

1

THE LEGACY OF SOCIAL DARWINISM

Judeo-Christian philosophy, as well as Platonic and Aristotelian virtue ethics, traditionally held that human nature consists of two dimensions, one material and the other immaterial, or more simply, the physical body and the metaphysical mind/soul. In other words, it classified a human being as not merely an animal but a very special kind of animal, one that in the Christian tradition is "created in the image and likeness of God," or in polytheistic cultures is molded by the gods. Such philosophies that focused upon our shared characteristics and qualities were the basis for the Enlightenment view that every human being, regardless of wealth or station, possesses an inherent dignity and certain "inalienable rights."

Then came Charles Darwin, who published *On the Origin of Species* in 1859, proposing that all species derive from a common ancestor through a process of natural selection in which the fit adapt to their environments and survive while the unfit perish. In this view, man was not divinely created but instead evolved from lower animal species. For some, human nature was seen as biological only—more advanced, to be sure, but not "higher." The implication, though not fully recognized in Darwin's day, was that humans possess no inherent dignity and no inalienable rights.

Darwinists regarded natural selection as having its own pace and progression and, therefore, needing no assistance from people, no matter how well-intentioned they might be. *Social* Darwinists, however, took a different view. This rather perverse adaptation of Darwin's views as applied to social existence held that unrestrained competition among social groups would lead to success for the more capable and imaginative while those less adept would and should fail. It was the natural order of things for the more intelligent, creative, and inventive individuals and groups to be rewarded financially and socially while those with less capability were destined to be laborers or survive by the charity of others.

Though these social Darwinists accepted in theory the idea that interfering with natural selection—for example, by helping the unfit through charity—was a mistake, in practice they were not content to wait, and so they sought ways to accelerate the process. Three distinct but overlapping forms of social Darwinism developed: Hereditarianism, Progressivism, and the Eugenics movement. All three forms had a powerful impact in the early twentieth century, but Hereditarianism was the most significant, not only in the scope and depth of its influence, but also in providing the rationale and the foundation for the other two.[1]

HEREDITARIANISM

The discipline of psychology began in the late 1800s.[2] Its pioneers were influenced by the research of physical anthropologists who believed that intelligence is inherited rather than acquired. The most influential of these individuals were Francis Galton, who published *Hereditary Genius* in 1869; Paul Broca, who argued that the size and weight of the brain were a true measure of the degree of a person's intelligence;[3] and Cesare Lombroso, who theorized that criminals are a throwback to savage apes and that certain physical characteristics, notably skull shape, are positively correlated with criminality.[4]

At the beginning of the twentieth century, France, like the United States, was wrestling with the challenge of providing mass education. In 1904 the Education Ministry commissioned Alfred Binet to devise a way to identify slow learners. Binet had been a disciple of Paul Broca and earlier had embraced Broca's theory of the correlation between head size and intelligence. By 1904, however, Binet had come to question that theory. He took a different approach and created what has since come to be known as the IQ test.[5] Binet warned that the test "[did] not permit the measure of the intelligence," and he worried that IQ scores could "give place to illusions" and cause teachers to give up on students with low scores. Moreover, he denounced the Hereditarian perspective that already was becoming influential in educational psychology. "Some recent thinkers," he wrote, "seem to . . . [affirm] that an individual's intelligence is a fixed quantity, a quantity that cannot be increased. We must protest and react against this brutal pessimism; we must try to demonstrate that it is founded upon nothing."[6]

Despite Binet's warning, a group of psychologists in the United States saw in his test a way both to prove and to disseminate their Hereditarian beliefs. One of the leaders of this group, H. H. Goddard, believed that "the intellectual level for each individual is determined by the kind of chromosomes that come together . . . [and] that it is but little affected by any later influences except such serious accidents as may destroy part of the mechanism." Goddard made no secret of his pessimistic view of the masses, writing: "There are great groups of men, laborers, who are but little above the child, who must be told what to do and shown how to do it; and who, if we would avoid disaster, must not be put into positions where they will have to act upon their own initiative or their own judgment. . . . There are only a few leaders, most must be followers." Goddard's view of government reflected the same pessimism: "Democracy means that the people rule by selecting the wisest, most intelligent and most human to *tell them what to do* [emphasis added] to be happy."[7]

Lewis Terman shared Goddard's Hereditarian views and activist inclinations. He affirmed that "the children of successful and cultured parents test higher than children from wretched and ignorant homes *for the simple reason that their heredity is better* [emphasis added]." Speaking of children with low IQs, Terman wrote:

> These boys are ineducable beyond the merest rudiments of training. No amount of school instruction will ever make them intelligent voters or capable citizens. . . . They represent the level of intelligence which is very, very common among Spanish-Indian and Mexican families of the Southwest and also among negroes. . . . Children of this group should be segregated in special classes and be given instruction which is concrete and practical. *They cannot master abstractions* [emphasis added], but they can often be made efficient workers, able to look out for themselves.[8]

A third Hereditarian psychologist, Edward Thorndike, argued that "if the mental and moral changes made in one generation are not transmitted by heredity to the next generation, the improvement of the race by direct transfer of acquisitions is a foolish, . . . futile aim."[9] A year later, he offered these thoughts on the nature of human intelligence:

> Nowhere more truly than in his mental capacities is man a part of nature. His instincts, that is, his inborn tendencies to feel and act in certain ways, show throughout marks of kinship with the lower animals, especially with our nearest relatives physically, the monkeys. His sense-powers show no new creation. His intellect we have seen to be a simple though extended variation from the general animal sort.[10]

Yet another Hereditarian, Harvard professor Robert Yerkes, invited Goddard, Terman, Thorndike, and others to join him in testing the intelligence of 1.75 million army recruits during World War I. The findings of these tests were that the average mental age of white American adults was 13 years and that, among immigrants, the average Russian's mental age was 11.34 years; the average Italian's, 11.01; the average Pole's, 10.74; and the average mental age of "Negroes," 10.41.[11] To appreciate how alarming these conclusions were to the average American, note that at the time of the test a "moron" was defined as an adult whose mental age was 12 or lower.

Although many were shocked by the "evidence" that the majority of nonwhites were mentally deficient, others were reinforced in their beliefs. After all, the institution of slavery was not long gone and many people still regarded blacks as inherently inferior. Also, contempt for immigrants had long been customary. In 1891, for example, Francis Walker of the US Census Bureau had issued this warning:

> So broad and straight now is the channel by which this immigration is being conducted to our shores, that there is no reason why every stagnant pool of European population, representing the utterest failures of civilization, the worst defeats in the struggle for existence, the lowest degradation of human nature, should not be completely drained off into the United States."[12]

Walker then proceeded to identify some of the people he had in mind: "Huns, and Poles, and Bohemians, and Russian Jews, and South Italians."

Many years would pass before the public learned how outrageously deficient the army testing process had been. Test explanations and procedures varied among test locations, some test takers were sitting too far back in the room to hear the directions, illiterate individuals were given test forms requiring reading, and recruits who could not speak English were given instructions only in English. As if these deficiencies were not enough, the test was culturally biased.

The interpretations and conclusions drawn by Yerkes and his associates were similarly wanting. Instead of acknowledging the obvious correlation between education and test scores, Yerkes concluded that "native intelligence is one of the most important conditioning factors in continuance in school." In addition, Yerkes professed amazement that so many black recruits had not attended school. (It was almost as if he had never heard of slavery and its aftermath, segregation.)[13]

How could individuals who claimed to be engaged in scientific investigation have failed to see the obvious correlations between the army recruits' poor performance and their lack of education and/or the inadequacies of the test? Stephen Jay Gould believes the explanation is that they were determined to make the data fit their Hereditarian biases.[14] Whatever the reason, the consequences of Hereditarianism have been, as we will see, disastrous and persistent.

PROGRESSIVISM

Progressivism may be defined in part as the belief that the US Constitution must be reconsidered in light of developments that the founding fathers could not have anticipated; or more specifically, that powers of government, particularly at the national level, must be expanded in order to deal with such developments. The rationale for Progressivism was that, "whereas the founders had posited what they held to be a permanent understanding of just government, based upon a permanent account of human nature

. . . the ends and scope of government [are] to be defined anew in each historical epoch."[15] In the justice system, Progressivism promoted judicial activism in which decisions are based on sources other than the Constitution, including the legal traditions of other countries and various theories from psychology, sociology, and anthropology.

There were several reasons that Progressivism took root in the early twentieth century, particularly during the presidencies of Theodore Roosevelt, Woodrow Wilson, and Franklin D. Roosevelt. One was that industrialization and immigration had swelled the size of many cities and caused housing and sanitation problems. Another was growing concern about child labor and unsafe working conditions for adults. Others were World War I, the depressions of 1920 and 1929, and World War II. Challenges of such magnitude were understandably seen as requiring the enlargement of government. Many of the safeguards we take for granted today were won by Progressive government officials, notably the Pure Food and Drug Act, laws restricting child labor, the regulation of business to protect consumers, the provision of workman's compensation, and requirements for safe working conditions.

A less positive impetus for Progressivism, however, was the Hereditarian belief that the masses are intellectually deficient and require either beneficent guidance from those who are better off, control by their intellectual superiors, or both. The publicizing of Yerkes's army-test findings intensified this Hereditarian view and prompted influential people to demand changes in America's immigration laws in order to keep out intellectually deficient people. Congress responded with the Immigration Act of 1917, which established a literacy test for immigrants and set minimum mental, moral, physical, and economic standards.

A quota system was added in 1921 and was made more restrictive several years later. As a result, northern Europe was favored over Russia (the home of many Jews), southern Europe, and Asia.[16] The restrictions on Jewish immigration no doubt also reflected the historic bias against Jews.[17] Historians believe that these restrictions, along with traditional anti-Semitism, played an important role in President Franklin D. Roosevelt's decision to refuse entry to the hundreds of Jewish exiles who fled Nazi

Germany on the steamship MS *St. Louis* in 1939.[18] Some historians argue that Roosevelt's decision reflected political reality rather than his personal viewpoint: a 1938 Elmer Roper poll revealed that 70 to 80 percent of Americans opposed lifting the restriction on Jewish immigration.[19] Given the impact of Yerkes's army tests and the subsequent denigration of southern and central Europeans, such widespread antipathy toward Jews (among others) was not surprising.

THE EUGENICS MOVEMENT

This movement was also spawned by Hereditarianism, but its program was much more ambitious than that of Progressivism. Eugenicists reasoned that the hordes of people who were deficient in intelligence posed a real and present danger to the human gene pool and should be institutionalized, sterilized, or both. Henry Goddard, one of the contributors to the army intelligence tests, expressed that fear in *The Kallikak Family: A Study in the Heredity of Feeble-Mindedness* and in *The Menace of Mental Deficiency from the Standpoint of Heredity*. In the latter book, he wrote, "We need to hunt them out in every possible place and take care of them, and see to it that they do not propagate and make the problem worse, and that those who are alive today do not entail loss of life and property and moral contagion in the community by the things they do because they are weak-minded."[20]

Many notable individuals supported the Eugenics movement. Among the delegates and/or officials of the First International Congress of Eugenics (1912) were Charles Darwin's son Leonard, Winston Churchill, and Lord Balfour. The Second Congress (1921) included Herbert Hoover as a member of the sponsoring committee and Alexander Graham Bell as the honorary president. The chairman of the New York Zoological Society at the time, Madison Grant, called for a "rigid system of selection" for the sterilization of "an ever widening circle of social discards, beginning always with the criminal, the diseased and the insane and extending gradually to types which may be called weaklings rather than defectives and perhaps ultimately to worthless racial types."[21] Theodore Roosevelt, an admirer of Grant, said that America should have "good breeders as well as good fighters." Planned Parenthood founder Margaret Sanger was an ardent proponent of eugenics and a critic of charitable institutions because, in her view, they enabled "defective" individuals to continue "breeding."[22] Others who spoke favorably of eugenics included Bertrand Russell, H. G. Wells, George Bernard Shaw (who proposed the use of gas chambers as early as 1910), and Woodrow Wilson.[23] Respected families such as the Harrimans, Carnegies, and Rockefellers provided financial support for the Race Betterment Society and the Eugenics Records Office.[24]

In the 1920s, even the Committee on Immigration and Naturalization of the US House of Representatives had a eugenics agent, H. H. Laughlin, who created the Model Eugenical Sterilization Law. Among those to be forcibly sterilized were the "feeble minded, insane, criminalistic (including the 'delinquent and wayward'), blind ('including those with seriously impaired vision'), deformed ('including the crippled') and dependent, including 'orphans,' 'ne'er do wells,' 'the homeless,' 'tramps' and 'paupers.'"[25]

Eventually, a majority of the states adopted these laws. In Virginia, however, Carrie Buck challenged the order for her sterilization. In time, her case (*Buck v. Bell*) reached the US Supreme Court, where Justice Oliver Wendell Holmes ruled that she should be sterilized, commenting: "It is better for all the world if . . . society can prevent those who are manifestly unfit from continuing their kind. . . . Three generations of imbeciles are enough."[26]

In the United States alone, the Eugenics movement was responsible for the "mercy killing" of defective infants, as well as 150,000 forced confinements and 66,000 forced sterilizations. As if that were not enough, the movement is well documented to have provided the model for the Nazi Holocaust that claimed the lives of six million Jews and three million other "undesirables."[27] That tragic event removed any credibility the Eugenics movement had enjoyed. Although some of its programs continued to exist in the United States until the early years of the twenty-first century,[28] and there are undoubtedly individuals who still cling to its premises, few dare express their support in public.

In contrast with the fading of the Eugenics movement, Progressivism has enjoyed a resurgence and is today more influential than it was a century ago. But the reasons for that resurgence are linked to the rise of Humanistic Psychology, which we will discuss in the next chapter. Before turning to that topic, however, it will be helpful to examine the impact of Hereditarianism on society.

HEREDITARIANISM AND EDUCATION

Toward the end of the nineteenth century, education authorities began consulting the new discipline of psychology for insights.[29] As a result, the Hereditarian view of intelligence began to shape curriculums, methods, and materials. In 1893, the Committee of Ten from the National Education Association (NEA) issued a report recommending that "every subject which is taught at all in a secondary school should be taught in the same way and to the same extent to every pupil so long as he pursues it, no matter what the probable destination of the pupil may be or at what point his education is to cease."[30] The committee also recommended that the emphasis should be on "training the powers of observation, memory, expression, and reasoning." The proposed curriculum was rigorous and included Latin, Greek, English, and other modern languages; mathematics; physics, astronomy, and chemistry; biology, including botany, zoology, and physiology; history, civil government, and political economy; and geography.

In 1903, however, oil magnate John D. Rockefeller established the General Education Board, later called the Rockefeller Foundation, which had a very different vision of what education should be. Its mission statement read in part:

> In our dreams . . . people yield themselves with perfect docility to our molding hands. The present educational conventions [intellectual and character education] fade from our minds, and unhampered by tradition we work our own good will upon a grateful and responsive folk. We shall not try to make these people or any of their children into philosophers or men of learning or men of science. We have not to raise up from among them authors, educators, poets or men of letters. We shall not search for embryo great artists, painters, musicians, nor lawyers, doctors, preachers,

politicians, statesmen, of whom we have ample supply. The task we set before ourselves is very simple . . . we will organize children . . . and teach them to do in a perfect way the things their fathers and mothers are doing in an imperfect way.[31]

Rockefeller here rejects the previous educational emphasis on teaching all students to think well and express their thoughts effectively. He also rejects the practice of offering every student a rigorous academic education. In place of these objectives he recommends vocational ones.

In 1911, another NEA group, the Committee of Nine, advocated a shift in the focus of instruction from the content and structures of the disciplines to the "laws" of learning and from the development of students' minds to the provision of training for citizenship. The committee claimed that traditional education was "responsible for leading tens of thousands of boys and girls away from the pursuits for which they are adapted and in which they are needed, to other pursuits for which they are not adapted and in which they are not needed. By means of exclusively bookish curricula false ideals of culture are developed."[32]

In 1918 the NEA's Commission on the Reorganization of Secondary Education published a report, titled "The Cardinal Principles of Education," declaring that a majority of students were incapable of mastering academic subjects and recommending that those students receive a vocational education instead of an academic one.[33] That view was shared by President Woodrow Wilson (himself a former professor and university president), who declared: "We want one class to have a liberal education, and we want another class, a very much larger class of necessity, to forego the privilege of a liberal education and fit themselves to perform specific difficult manual tasks."[34]

In that relatively brief span of time, IQ testing had provided the Hereditarians with the "scientific" proof they needed to persuade the public that the average American's mental age was barely above the "moronic" level and that the traditional goal of developing students' minds should therefore be replaced by training them for the workplace. A host of influential individuals joined the chorus. Lewis Terman, for example, warned that "laboring men . . . are ineducable beyond the merest rudiments of training. No amount of school instruction will ever make them intelligent voters or capable citizens,"[35] and argued that "educational reform [should] abandon, once and for all, the effort to bring all children up to grade."[36] In the early 1920s Terman and Robert Yerkes created the National Intelligence Test, which classified students according to ability and largely determined the course of study they could pursue. Soon after, another Hereditarian colleague, Princeton professor C. C. Brigham, created the Scholastic Aptitude Test (SAT) for the purpose of selecting college students, basing the new test on the army IQ test.[37]

The Hereditarians succeeded in making pessimism about intelligence the central principle of education. Traditional academic courses were replaced by new, more vocationally oriented ones. Between 1893 and 1941 the number of high school courses ballooned from 27 to 274, almost 80 percent of them nonacademic. Moreover, high school teachers were encouraged to develop individualized courses with little regard for the insights of scholars in the disciplines.[38] Instead of helping students learn *how* to think, teachers told them *what* to think. Textbooks were designed to be repositories of information rather than offering challenges to excite and encourage understanding. Academic excellence was measured in terms of the quantity of information possessed rather than the depth of understanding or the proficiency in applying knowledge to new situations. "Objective" tests (true or false, multiple choice, fill in the blank) replaced essay tests. Most important of all, teachers' colleges elevated these changes to educational doctrine, thereby ensuring the perpetuation of the changes through generations of teachers.

Over the next few decades, mindless education became a tradition resistant to reform, and the reigning pessimism received continuing reinforcement. In 1939, for example, Harvard professor Charles Prosser declared, "Nothing could be more certain than that science has proven false the doctrine of general education and its fundamental theory that memory or imagination or the reason or the will can be trained as a power." He added that "there are no general mental qualities to be developed; there are only specific things to be known."[39] In 1941, Benjamin Fine of the

New York Times praised New York City's experimental education program, noting that "instead of studying their reading, 'riting and 'rithmetic in the sedate traditional way, the children played and frolicked all day long. Gone were the agonizing hours spent on long division, on bounding the state of Maine, on grammar and composition."[40] And in 1951 a high school principal declared before the National Association of Secondary-School Principals, "When we come to the realization that not every child has to read, figure, write and spell . . . that many of them either cannot or will not master these chores . . . then we shall be on the road to improving the junior high school curriculum [ellipses in the original]."[41]

HEREDITARIANISM AND INDUSTRY

Hereditarianism had a profound effect on American industry. During the late nineteenth and early twentieth centuries, industrial growth was unparalleled. The completion of the transcontinental railroad in 1869 created new opportunities for commerce. Innumerable inventions revolutionized both the methods of production and the goods produced, in some cases creating entirely new industries. But even as the need for workers grew, management faced two significant challenges. One was that public opposition to child labor was increasing.[42] The other was that the workforce included large numbers of immigrants, most of whom were poor and uneducated. Business leaders were desperate for a way to train and manage these workers. In 1894, Frederick Taylor provided that way with his "scientific management" system.

Taylor shared the Hereditarian view that most workers were unequipped for thought and judgment, so his system assigned all decision making to executives and supervisory personnel. Workers were expected to leave the job of thinking to others and simply do as they were told. Scientific management also employed the principles and techniques of industrial engineering that had been developed by Frank and Lillian Gilbreth—notably, time and motion studies, which identified the fastest and least fatiguing ways to perform work tasks.[43]

Business leaders were quick to embrace Taylor's scientific management system and the Hereditarian assumptions on which it was based. For a time, scientific management produced some impressive results; for example, it increased the efficiency of operations and the productivity of workers, instituted "standard cost plans" that enabled industrial engineers to monitor the cost-effectiveness of departmental operations on a daily basis, and produced a simple and effective training method known as job instruction training (JIT).[44]

Unfortunately, the negative impact of scientific management was even more profound. Because the system was rooted in a pessimistic view of workers' intelligence, it prevented workers from contributing ideas and insights. The loss of such input might have been negligible in the beginning, a time when most workers were poorly educated, but as the education level of workers increased over the course of the next few decades, it became appreciable. This fact is best illustrated by the story of W. Edwards Deming.

In the 1940s Deming devised a new system of management called "quality control," which differed from scientific management chiefly in its emphasis on making *every employee* responsible for the improvement of the company.[45] Quality, in Deming's view, consisted of anticipating customers' expectations and constantly improving products and services to meet those expectations. Reasoning that the person in the company who is nearest to a problem or inefficiency is the best person to identify it, Deming concluded that workers should be encouraged to think about their tasks and produce ideas for improving their execution.[46] He therefore urged corporate executives to involve workers in problem solving and decision making and to create an atmosphere in which workers would develop pride in their work.

Deming presented his system of quality control to American business leaders after World War II, but their pessimism about workers' intelligence was deeply rooted and they rejected his ideas. Frustrated, he took his ideas to Japan, which was in the process of rebuilding its economy in the aftermath of its devastating defeat in the war. Unlike their American counterparts, Japanese business leaders were optimistic about the mental capacity of their citizens and accepted Deming's ideas enthusiastically. Over the next few decades, they not only rebuilt their economy but vaulted ahead of the United States in numerous industries. In 1985, W. Edwards Deming reflected on the unfortunate impact of the Hereditarian perspective on American business: "People are the most important asset of any company. . . . Failure to understand people is the devastation of western management."[47]

HEREDITARIANISM AND AMERICAN CULTURE

For millennia, culture was a local or regional phenomenon that reflected the ideas, attitudes, and values of home, school, and church. Then came a wave of inventions—notably radio, television, the personal computer, and the Internet—that made possible a new, homogeneous "mass culture." Disseminated by the communications and entertainment media, this new culture embodies a disparaging view of human intelligence. This view did not originate with the media, however; instead, it was borrowed from a related industry deeply influenced by Hereditarianism—that is, the advertising industry.

From the beginning, advertisers had little respect for the intelligence of the public, as evidenced by their exaggerations and irrational appeals.[48] However, when the principles of psychology were first applied to advertisements, this underlying disrespect matured into contempt. Psychologist Walter Dill Scott expressed the pessimistic perspective of the Hereditarians when he recommended that advertisements be based on suggestion rather than reason. "Today," he wrote, "we are finding that suggestion is of universal application to all persons, while reason is a process which is exceptional, even among the wisest. We reason rarely, but act under suggestion constantly."[49]

John Watson—founder of the psychological view known as Behaviorism, colleague of Robert Yerkes, and a respected consultant to the advertising industry—went even further than Scott. He denied the existence of a conscious mind and argued that human beings have neither intellect nor free will but simply respond to conditioning as animals do. Watson, perhaps more than any other individual, taught advertisers to manipulate people's emotions and make them crave things they neither needed nor could afford. Contemporary advertisers continue to perpetuate this insult to our intelligence, in some cases blatantly. For example, Nike's slogan "Just Do It" and Anheuser Busch's "Why ask why? Try Bud Dry" urge us to refrain from thinking and asking questions and, instead, to act on the impulse they have stimulated in us.

In the case of television, advertising's contempt for viewers' intelligence is demonstrated not only in the mindless content of commercials but also in their artificial pace. Over the last several decades, the length of an average commercial has decreased from one minute to thirty seconds and then to fifteen seconds. Today a typical television hour contains eleven commercial interruptions, each of which includes four commercials. That is not the worst of it, however. During a commercial break, the image on the screen changes much more frequently than during the program itself, often as many as two or three times per second. Thus, for every hour of television we watch, the commercials alone are forcing our attention to shift somewhere between one thousand and two thousand times.[50]

The artificial drama and pace of commercials have created pressure on TV programmers to maintain viewers' attention. Ever fearful that viewers will click their remotes, producers of dramas and comedies feel pressured to contrive similar sensory excitement. They responded initially by multiplying subplots as an excuse for scene shifts. Next they added car chases, explosions, and sexual innuendo. More recently, they have made the talk "more colorful," the couplings more graphic, and the violence more bizarre. The proliferation of crime-solving shows has enabled programmers to increase the assault on our senses by depicting both the crazed killer's assault and the forensic staff's scientific mutilation of the victim.

Since the advent of cable television, TV journalists have been forced to compete not only with one another but also with dramatic programming. Reporters have responded by shrinking content and streamlining their formats, shortening news segments, chopping newsmakers' statements into out-of-context but provocative sound bites, making frequent cuts to on-scene reporters, endlessly repeating film footage of sensational events, turning trivial stories into "news alerts," and airing numerous "teasers" for stories scheduled later in the program. Hosts of commentary and debate programs are often more concerned with the pace of discussion than with its coherence and meaningfulness. They demand yes-or-no answers to complex questions, interrupt guests who attempt to qualify or present a line of evidence, and permit all parties to talk at once, deluding themselves that the resulting cacophony constitutes spirited debate.

The print media have felt similar pressure from TV, as well as from the Internet. Fearing further declines in circulation, newspapers have followed the example of *USA Today* by thinning their content and shortening their stories. Nonfiction book publishers have increasingly shunned genuine scholars, whose writings require readers to expend intellectual effort, and have turned instead to people who know less about their subjects but offer strong "name recognition"—notably, journalists, TV and radio personalities, retired athletes, creators of scandal, and convicted felons.[51]

WHY PESSIMISM PREVAILED

By the 1970s, there were signs that the Hereditarian pessimism about human intelligence might be replaced by a more reasonable view. At that time, business leaders envious of the success of quality control in Japan and eager to hire problem solvers and decision makers began to demand that colleges include thinking instruction in their curriculums.[52] College administrators rushed to comply, and many institutions established special courses to provide such instruction. Such efforts had the potential to dramatically change textbooks, teaching methods, and testing, as well as make sound thinking habits and skills the focus of every academic discipline. Despite a flurry of national conferences and the widespread embrace of slogans, however, no such broader reform ever materialized for several reasons.

One reason was that the people leading the Critical Thinking movement were mainly professors of informal logic and/or composition. Some of these individuals were content to develop single courses in thinking and had no larger, cross-curricular vision. Those who did have such a vision were unable to create enthusiasm for it among the senior professors in their disciplines, who preferred the familiar approach of stuffing students' minds with facts over the unfamiliar one of teaching them how to think.

Another reason the reform never happened was that the educational psychologists who opposed Hereditarianism failed to challenge its central assumption—that intelligence is something people *possess*. Psychologist Robert Sternberg, for example, argued that intelligence consists of three capacities—analytical, creative, and practical ("street smarts")—all of which can be developed. He added that the capacities differ in strength, so that one person will have a greater capacity for analysis, a second for creativity, and a third for practical activity.

Developmental psychologist Howard Gardner differed with Sternberg, believing intelligence to be not one phenomenon with three divisions but rather multiple phenomena—specifically, nine (originally seven) separate intelligences.[53] Gardner acknowledged that what he chose to call "intelligences" could be called "talents" or "abilities," candidly remarking that "I am quite confident that if I had written a book called 'Seven Talents' it would not have received the attention that *Frames of Mind* received."[54] Similarly, he admitted that his theory does not account for "common sense, originality, or metaphoric capacity."[55] Sometimes he seemed to question his own theory; for example, when he wrote "it is helpful to think of the various intelligences chiefly as *sets of know-how*—procedures for doing things."[56]

In short, while Sternberg and Gardner both differed from the Hereditarians in some significant ways, most notably in rejecting the ideas that IQ tests can measure intelligence and that intelligence is fixed and unalterable, they shared the Hereditarians' central assumption that people *possess* intelligence. Educators were thus able to embrace Sternberg's and Gardner's theories without discarding the pedagogy of mind stuffing.

A third reason for the failure of the Critical Thinking movement to broadly reform education is that a group of influential educators foolishly opposed it. This group was led by E. D. Hirsch Jr., author of *Cultural Literacy*, which he defined as "[possessing] large amounts of specific information." He argued that "children can learn this information only by being taught it," and he lamented that school policies "have shrunk the body of information" and "caused our national literacy to decline." Hirsch further claimed, absurdly, that the very movement that sought to *overcome* the pessimism of the Hereditarians and to honor the mind—the Critical Thinking movement—was somehow *responsible* for undermining academic standards![57] Evidently he had not read the major study of one thousand secondary schools and twenty-seven thousand students published three years earlier, which concluded that though some schools talked about the importance of thinking skills, few classrooms in any discipline were doing anything to *develop* those skills. Instead, as the study demonstrated, the continuing emphasis was on the same kind of rote learning that Hirsch claimed was being neglected.[58]

Hirsch was also guilty of two glaring fallacies. The first was the idea that thinking instruction necessarily hinders subject-matter learning. In reality, it helps students learn to think well about subject matter in essentially the same way that composition instruction helps students write well about subject matter. The second fallacy was the idea that each academic discipline has its own unique, nontransferable thought patterns and skills. This is a transparently foolish notion considering that *the human mind created the various fields of study, not the other way around*.[59] The techniques and skills of thinking are eminently learnable, but students cannot learn them merely by reading textbooks or listening to lectures any more than they can learn how to drive a car by being a passenger or how to play a musical instrument or a sport by attending concerts or athletic contests. Students learn such things only by practice—ideally, practice done under the guidance of someone skilled in using them.

Despite these egregious errors, Hirsch gained the support of innumerable education officials, including the US secretary of education and the president of the American Federation of Teachers, and his book became a bestseller.

It is pleasant to imagine that, absent these obstacles, the Critical Thinking movement would have achieved its broader goal of establishing systematic instruction in thinking—that is, not just a course or two but an entire curriculum in which thinking instruction is central to *every* course and sequence—and that, as a result, a more favorable view of human intelligence would have displaced Hereditarian pessimism. Unfortunately, such outcomes would have been unlikely at best because a very different movement was already well underway, one that would replace unfounded pessimism about human nature with an absurd optimism that placed emotion above thought and self-esteem above learning. The movement was known as Humanistic Psychology.

2

ENTER HUMANISTIC PSYCHOLOGY

Humanistic Psychology was a reaction against the Hereditarian view that intelligence is inherited and nothing can be done to increase our allotted portion. It also challenged Sigmund Freud's claim that dark and often-sinister urges lie at the core of human nature and the Behaviorist denial of emotion, thought, free will, and human dignity. In contrast, Humanistic Psychology viewed human nature as inherently good and healthy rather than flawed by negative or evil tendencies. The fact that it was more positive and optimistic than any of the competing views of human nature helps to explain its rapid, widespread, and mostly uncritical acceptance.

Psychologists have generally substituted the term *self* for the philosophical term *human nature*. Unfortunately, *self* has always been so vague a term that it can mean almost anything. Consider, first, a sampling of definitions from people with no significant association with Humanistic Psychology:

A self is an actual person or individual: "The total, essential, or particular being of a person; the individual." —*American Heritage Dictionary*

A self is an apparent person or individual: "[Self] is the individual as he seems from his own vantage point." —Arthur Combs and Donald Snygg, personality theorists[1]

A self is an inner core that dominates: "[The self is a] 'kind of core in our being' that sometimes expands and seems to take command of all our behavior and consciousness" —Gordon Allport, personality psychologist[2]

A self is a person's behavior: "A self is a repertoire of behavior appropriate to a given set of contingencies." —B. F. Skinner, behavioral psychologist[3]

A self is a perceiver of things: "The self is that which perceives, thinks, wills, and performs divers[e] operations." —George Berkeley, philosopher[4]

A self is an object of perception: "The self is defined as the object of an individual's own perceptions." —*International Encyclopedia of Psychiatry, Psychology, Psychoanalysis, and Neurology*[5]

A self is something that grows: "The self is something that grows out of, and in relation to, its environment." —*Adult Pagan Action Essay Series*[6]

A self is a force that creates growth: The "real self" is a "central inner force, common to all human beings and yet unique in each, that is the deep source of growth." —Karen Horney, psychiatrist[7]

A self is a higher entity within a person: "A wizard exists in all of us; this wizard sees and knows everything [and] is beyond opposites of light and dark, good and evil, pleasure and pain." —Deepak Chopra, physician and author[8]

A self is divinity: "[The self is] Divine Consciousness residing in the individual" —*Siddhayoga*, a website dedicated to a particular form of yoga[9]

A self is two distinct entities in one: "There are two Selves in men—the Higher and the Lower, the Impersonal and the Personal Self. One is divine, the other semi-animal." —The Theosophical Society[10]

These definitions are not only very different from one another; each is directly in *conflict* with at least one other: A real human person *versus* an apparent person. An inner core that governs behavior *versus* behavior itself. A perceiver of things *versus* the thing that is perceived. That which grows *versus* the force that causes growth. A person *versus* an entity, such as a "wizard," *within* a person. One entity *versus* two entities (i.e., a "higher" and a "lower" one). The confusion does not end there. Some authors offer two or more definitions of *self* without explaining the difference. For example:

A self is both consciousness and identity: "[The self is] consciousness of [one's] own identity; a person considered as a unique individual." —WordNet[11]

A self is both an image and a principle: "The self is an image of the unity of the personality as a whole, a central ordering principle." —Garden of Life Temple[12]

A self is (a) an organizing function, (b) consciousness, (c) a capacity, and (d) a center of perception: "[The self is] the organizing function within the individual . . . ; consciousness of one's identity . . . ; not merely the sum of 'roles,' but the capacity by which one *knows* that he plays these roles; . . . the center from which one sees and is aware of these 'sides' of himself." —Rollo May, existential psychologist[13]

Given that self is central to Humanistic Psychology, it would be reasonable to expect the founders of that movement—Carl Rogers and Abraham Maslow—to be much clearer and more consistent in their definition than others had been. Yet if anything, they are *less* clear.

CARL ROGERS'S VIEW OF SELF

If there had been a prize for intellectual confusion, Rogers would have been a serious contender for it. He offered no fewer than *five* conflicting definitions of *self*:

A self is pattern of perceptions: "As a result of interaction with the environment, and particularly as a result of evaluational interaction with others, the structure of the self is formed—an organised, fluid but consistent conceptual pattern of perceptions of characteristics and relationships of the 'I' or the 'me,' together with values attached to these concepts."[14]

A self is the product of experience: "The self and personality emerge *from* experience rather than experience being translated or twisted to fit pre-conceived self-structure."[15]

A self is (a) a participant in and (b) an observer of experience: "One becomes a participant in and an observer of the ongoing process of organismic experience, rather than being in control of it."[16]

A self is what one truly is and cannot escape being: "One must be that self which one truly is."[17]

Rogers deepened the confusion in his famous book, *On Becoming a Person*, by conjoining the terms *self* and *person*, arguing that becoming a person means accepting ourselves as we are.[18] Yes, you read that right: according to Rogers, becoming what we are *not* is accomplished by accepting what we already *are*. That's somewhat like saying we complete a journey by staying home or climb a mountain by standing at the bottom and congratulating ourselves. The obvious question is, "If one truly *is* oneself, and cannot be anything else, what sense does it make to speak of *becoming* that self?" The answer, of course, is no sense at all.

Despite his profound confusion about self, Rogers made many pronouncements about the powers of the self. In his view, the self does not discover reality—it *determines* reality. In an early book, he remarked that "it seems unnecessary to posit or try to explain any concept of 'true' reality. For purposes of understanding psychological phenomena, reality is, for the individual, his perceptions."[19]

This was not a slip of the pen. Many years later he repeated the claim, declaring that objective reality "clearly does not exist in the objects we see and feel and hold. . . . The only reality I can possibly know is the world as I perceive and experience it at this moment." To reinforce the point, he wrote, "Can we today afford the luxury of having 'a' reality? Can we still preserve the belief that there is a 'real world' upon whose definition we all agree? I am convinced that this is a luxury we cannot afford, a myth we dare not maintain."[20]

Rogers also argued that feelings are more dependable than reason. "When an activity *feels* as though it *is* valuable or worth doing," he wrote, "it is worth doing. . . . I have learned that my total organismic sensing of a situation is more trustworthy than my intellect." This he offered not merely as his personal perspective but as a universal principle, asserting that, for *anyone*, "doing what 'feels right' proves to be a competent and trustworthy guide to behavior which is truly satisfying," and that a person's "own deep impulses are not destructive or catastrophic."[21] Two decades later, he repeated these views even more forcefully:

> I have come to prize each emerging facet of my experience, of myself. I
> would like to treasure the feelings of anger and tenderness and shame and
> hurt and love and anxiety and giving and fear. . . . I would like to trea-
> sure the ideas that emerge—foolish, creative, bizarre, sound, trivial . . . I
> like the behavioral impulses—appropriate, crazy, achievement-oriented,
> sexual, murderous. I want to accept all of these feelings, ideas, and
> impulses as an enriching part of me. . . . The criteria for making value
> judgments come more and more to lie in the person, not in a book, a
> teacher, or a set of dogmas. The locus of evaluation is in the person, not
> outside.[22]

William Coulson, a close associate of Rogers, notes that to Rogers (and Maslow) this devotion to feelings was not merely an intellectual exercise but a guide to behavior. Rogers believed that self-actualization required "unstinting satisfaction of desires—bodily or otherwise" and that people should prove their "personhood by having sex in as unconstrained and uncivilized a way as possible." Coulson points in particular to a series of writings in which Rogers wrote approvingly of, in Rogers's words, "living in sin, committing adultery, lewd and lascivious conduct, fornication, homosexuality, ingesting illegal drugs, even soliciting."[23]

For Rogers, then, the self is the source of truth and reality, its "deepest impulses" are always admirable, and its feelings are a trustworthy guide to behavior.

ABRAHAM MASLOW'S VIEW OF SELF

The cofounder of Humanistic Psychology, Abraham Maslow, held a similarly murky view of self. On one occasion, he claimed that "to talk of self-actualization implies that there is a self to be actualized," adding that "what

I have sometimes referred to as 'listening to the impulse voices' means letting the self emerge."[24] On another occasion, he spoke of an "inner core, or self," that "grows" partly through discovery and partly through creation.[25] He also spoke of the "urge to complete oneself, to be, to become fully human" and of "the real self that you will discover within yourself," explaining that "one must somehow love one's ideal self and at the same time one's current actual self . . . so that one can be and become simultaneously."[26]

These ideas raise some obvious questions:

Are the "impulse voices" Maslow speaks of synonymous with the "inner core, or self" that "grows," or are they merely something that speaks to that core or self? If they *are* the self, how can listening to them cause the self to "emerge"? If they are not that core, what is their source?

Maslow's reference to the "urge to complete oneself, to be, to become fully human" implies that in its original state the self is *incomplete* and only *partly human*. If so, in what way? Also, can there be an *urge* "to be" in any meaningful sense? (Common sense suggests that it is necessary to be before experiencing any urge.)

His phrase "the real self . . . within yourself" implies that there are two selves and that the outer one is *unreal*. In what sense could the self be unreal?

If the "current actual self" is not yet "fully human," and is in that sense inferior to the "ideal self," why should anyone attempt to "be and become simultaneously," even if that were possible? Wouldn't it make more sense to *cease* being the inferior self and become, instead, the superior, ideal self? Isn't that transition the essence of self-improvement?

Given that the major focus of Maslow's work was the self and that he repeatedly used the term as a prefix—notably in *self*-esteem and *self*-actualization—his failure to address these questions and to define the term more precisely is baffling.

Similar lack of reflection is also evident in Maslow's theory of human motivation, with its famous hierarchy of human needs, first introduced in two 1943 scholarly articles[27] and later expanded on in several books.[28] The hierarchy, which Maslow and others modified over the years,[29] was originally expressed as follows:

Self-Actualization

Achievement, fulfillment

Esteem Needs

Self-esteem, esteem of others

Love Needs

Affection, friendship, sense of belonging

Safety Needs

A stable, orderly, unthreatening environment

Physiological Needs

These include food, drink, warmth, shelter, and sex

A central premise in Maslow's theory is that *before any need shown in the diagram can be met, those under it must first be met.*[30] This premise clearly implies that celibates (whose sex needs remain unmet) cannot love other people or feel a sense of belonging, that people from poor or unstable families cannot feel good about themselves, and that people who do not esteem themselves cannot accomplish anything or experience fulfillment.

Not only was this premise uncharacteristically rigid (for Maslow); it also lacked evidentiary support. Moreover, everyday experience contradicts it. Celibates have been models of loving kindness—St. Francis of Assisi and Mother Teresa of Calcutta come readily to mind. Starving people on the verge of death—for example, prisoners in Nazi concentration camps—have demonstrated nobility of spirit.[31] And people with little or no self-esteem have been outstanding achievers. The most dramatic example is the many Asian students who measure far below average in self-esteem tests yet are above average academically and professionally.

Maslow's conception of *needs* is even more confused than his conception of *self*. On one occasion, he equates *needs* with *goals*.[32] On another, he refers to needs as "a hierarchy of values which are to be found in the very essence of human nature itself."[33] On still other occasions, he uses *needs* and *desires* interchangeably.[34] Yet these terms cannot reasonably be considered interchangeable—the differences among them are too significant. *Needs* are requirements of health or welfare. In contrast, *values* are assessments of the worth of things, *desires* are wants, and *goals* are pursuits. There is nothing *necessary* about a value, a desire, or a goal. (Had Maslow reflected on the differences among these terms, he might have considered calling his model a hierarchy of *aspirations* or *challenges* instead of a hierarchy of needs.)

Although Maslow was less explicit than Rogers in favoring emotion over reason, his view is essentially the same. Maslow describes self-actualized people—those who have fulfilled the highest human need—as "relatively spontaneous in behavior and far more spontaneous than that in their inner life, thoughts, impulses, etc."[35] He also holds that "pure spontaneity consists of free, uninhibited, uncontrolled, trusting, unpremeditated expression of the self, i.e., of the psychic forces, *with minimal interference by consciousness* [emphasis added]."[36]

THE CHALLENGE TO TRADITION

Given Rogers's multiple, conflicting definitions of self, his rejection of objective truth and reality, and his exaltation of emotion over intellect, it would have been understandable for his associates to refer him to a mental-health clinic. Given the carelessness of Maslow's inquiries into human nature and of the construction of his hierarchy,[37] one might expect peer reviewers to have scoffed and publishers to have issued rejection letters.

If this assessment seems extravagant, imagine a person from any other profession—for example, law, medicine, engineering, or accounting—announcing, "I can't define my subject. It could have any number of con-flicting meanings. Nevertheless, I am going to write books, give lectures, and create programs telling people all about it anyway." (A first-year college student wouldn't get away with that approach to a simple composition.) The sensible reaction to such a declaration is, "Wait a minute. Until you know what you are talking about, you have no business talking about it."

Surprisingly, that was not the reaction Rogers and Maslow received. On the contrary, both men gained the respect and admiration of the intellectual establishment and the unquestioning devotion of leaders in education, the arts, religion, and government. Before long, Rogers's and Maslow's muddled conceptions of *self* dominated psychological discourse. Over the next few decades, these muddled conceptions rose to the level of dogma, permeating mass culture, and spreading throughout America and most of the Western world.

By the 1950s, psychologists began providing more and more of the therapeutic services formerly reserved to psychiatrists, and the ranks of related professionals—marriage and family counselors, school guidance counselors, career counselors, and clinical social workers—began to swell.[38] Over the next few decades the number of clinical psychologists and related professionals increased dramatically. By 1990, those professionals outnumbered psychiatrists more than five to one.[39]

With so many influential people available to disseminate Rogers's and Maslow's ideas, it is not surprising that these ideas reached a wide audience.[40] What is more difficult to understand, however, is that in the space of a few decades, they effectively *replaced* the general public's traditional views of human nature. After all, those ideas were diametrically opposed to the beliefs that had prevailed for millennia:

> In the traditional view, human nature is flawed—that is, we have within us an irrational component and so we have the capacity for both good and evil. In Rogers's and Maslow's view, *it is inherently wise and good*.
>
> In the traditional view, the self needs to be disciplined and mastered. In Rogers's and Maslow's view, *it needs to be actualized*.
>
> In the traditional view, self-esteem (like pride), when excessive, is an obstacle to achievement. In Rogers's and Maslow's view, *it is prerequisite to achievement*.

In the traditional view, truth and reality are objective; they exist inde-
pendently of the human mind. In Rogers's and Maslow's view, *truth
and reality are created by the human mind*. Similarly, in the traditional
view, morality is objective and transpersonal; basic moral values
transcend individuals and cultures.[41] In Rogers's and Maslow's
view, *morality is subjective and personal*.

In the traditional view, feelings are capricious and must be tested before
being trusted. In Rogers's and Maslow's view, *feelings are reliable and
should be followed*.

In the traditional view, sexual expression should be coupled with a
mutual commitment between the parties. In Rogers's and Maslow's
view, *all sexual expression is both natural and wholesome*.[42]

One reason for the widespread acceptance of Rogers's and Maslow's
ideas, as noted earlier, is that they were more optimistic and encouraging
than the ideas of Freudianism and Behaviorism. They also seemed to offer
an antidote to what was perceived as the gloomy, atheistic existentialism
popular in intellectual circles at the time.

When Rogers speaks of "human potential" and Maslow of "peak
experiences," as they often do, they seem to be promoting traditional
spiritual values. In reality, however, they were doing the opposite. Rogers
believed that human beings had no need of outside authority, social rules,
or moral guidelines, whatever their origin.[43] And Maslow was well aware
that his ideas were incompatible with many if not all religious perspectives.
For example, after giving a talk to hundreds of Catholics, he made the
following entry in his journal: "They shouldn't applaud me—they should
attack. If they were fully aware of what I was doing, they would."[44]

An even more important reason for the remarkable success of Rogers's
and Maslow's ideas was that they came at the beginning of a series of
revolutionary changes in communications technology. Before tracing these
changes, however, we will consider a third individual who shared Rogers's
and Maslow's view of human nature and whose ideas about sexuality were
believed to provide scientific documentation of theirs—the biologist Alfred
Kinsey.

ALFRED KINSEY'S CONTRIBUTION

Until the late 1940s, the traditional view of sexuality was normative in America. This view, derived mainly from the Judeo-Christian moral code, held that sexual acts are appropriate only between spouses and, therefore, that premarital and extramarital sex are morally wrong.[45] Then, in 1948 and 1950, respectively, Alfred Kinsey published his twin studies, *Sexuality in the Human Male* and *Sexuality in the Human Female*, in which he claimed that homosexuality, adult-child contact, and even bestiality are all as normal as heterosexuality.[46]

Further, he argued that incest can be satisfying and enriching and that the only reason children get upset by adult sexual advances is the prudishness of parents and legal authorities.[47] The sexual prohibitions that had been accepted for hundreds of years were, in Kinsey's view, not only unjustified but also harmful.

Kinsey has been widely regarded as an honest scientist, but a number of researchers have presented evidence that he was, at best, very careless in his research and, at worst, consciously dishonest. A particularly revealing example occurred in his relationship with Abraham Maslow. Maslow told Kinsey that he believed Kinsey's use of volunteers in his sex studies distorted his findings because the volunteers tended to be atypical. They agreed to a test in which Kinsey interviewed students in five of Maslow's classes. The result of the test confirmed Maslow's contention. As he put it: "As I expected, the volunteer error was proven and the whole basis for Kinsey's statistics was proven to be shaky." Kinsey not only refused to publish the results of the test; he thereafter deleted from his own books all reference to Maslow's works.[48]

Another example of Kinsey's dishonesty is offered by Sociology professor Diana Russell. She points out that though *the majority of cases* on incest in Kinsey's study of women involved uncles, fathers, and grandfathers, Kinsey claimed that "the most frequent incestuous contacts are between pre-adolescent children, but the number of such cases among adolescent or older males is very small."[49]

Kinsey's books were so ponderous and dull that they might have had little impact outside academe, and perhaps even within it, except for two facts: they purported to represent genuine *scientific* findings; and they were promoted by a clever entrepreneur who packaged their message in a highly visual vehicle aimed at adolescent males and older males whose adolescent fantasies were still intact. The entrepreneur was Hugh Hefner and the vehicle was *Playboy* magazine.

For the next several decades, *Playboy* and its imitators popularized Kinsey's message through nude photographs, advice columns, illustrations, and cartoons. Judith Reisman, visiting professor at Liberty University School of Law, analyzed thirty years of *Playboy* and its clones *Hustler* and *Penthouse*. She found that, though much of it was designed with humorous intentions, the magazine included not only glamorization of the seduction and rape of adults but also 6,004 *child* scenes, of which 1,675 were associated with nudity, 1,225 with genital acts, 989 with adult sex acts, 592 with force, 267 with sex with animals or objects.[50] The unrelenting theme in these magazines since their inception has been that all forms of sex are healthy and it's a good thing for men to deflower women. Reisman offers this quote from a *Playboy* Advisor column: "Most men realize that virginity is an unpleasant little matter to be disposed of early in life . . . you are actually doing the girl a service."[51]

Realizing that sex was selling, the editors of mainstream magazines followed Hefner's lead. From the 1960s to the 1980s, magazine articles about sexual functioning tripled and references to sexual terms increased sixfold. Moreover, the focus changed from sexual morality to the quality of sex and the liberal perspective of sex outside marriage.[52] (The development of contraceptive pills and devices and the legalization of abortion also diminished fear of pregnancy, which historically had provided an argument for sexual restraint.)

THE BIRTH OF MASS CULTURE

At the same time that Rogers, Maslow, and Kinsey were publishing their ideas,[53] a revolution in communications technology was beginning. In previous decades, people could *read* or *hear* news and literature at home, but to *see* them, they had to go to movie theaters. Now television brought visual presentations into the nation's living rooms. (The number of homes with TV sets rose from 0.5 percent in 1946 to 55.7 percent in 1954, and then to 90 percent in 1962.[54]) Subsequent decades would bring many other innovations that expanded and enhanced the visual experience, including cable and satellite television, video games, DVDs, computers, and the Internet.

From the outset, the communications revolution not only changed the means by which information and entertainment were transmitted, it also changed *the sources and content of the ideas* that were transmitted. For millennia, parents had been the primary bearers of culture from generation to generation. By precept and example, they and a small circle of trusted delegates—relatives, neighbors, teachers, religious leaders, and social role models—imparted to their children the beliefs, attitudes, and values they regarded as worthy. This task was made easier by the fact that the producers of information—journalists and the authors of imaginative literature—generally held values similar to those of most parents.

At the beginning of the communications revolution, parents understandably expected television broadcasters to continue mirroring traditional ideas and values as newspapers and radio had done.[55] Accordingly, most parents welcomed TV into their homes. The new medium was more accessible than printed matter and, because it required neither reading skill nor imagination, could be enjoyed with little or no intellectual effort.

For a time, TV and the other entertainment and communications media were still reinforcing the lessons of home, school, church, and other moral exemplars. Then the situation began to change. Instead of continuing to represent the traditional values, the media became the purveyors of the views of Rogers, Maslow, and Kinsey. This change was not the result of any media conspiracy but simply the natural outcome of the following sequence of events:

★ From the late 1950s on, the ideas of Rogers, Maslow, and Kinsey received considerable media attention. Supermarket tabloids, men's and women's magazines, newspaper columns, and books advised people to accept and esteem themselves, cast off their inhibitions, get in touch with their feelings, and banish guilt and shame. Over the years, hundreds of books promoted these ideas. Sample titles include: *Looking Out for #1*, *Getting What You Want*, *Feeling Good*, *Learning to Love Yourself*, *Your Sacred Self*, *Ten Days to Self-Esteem*, *Goodbye to Guilt*, *The Joy of Sex*, and *Sex without Guilt*.[56]

★ In time, the message became hyperbolic. Psychologist Matthew McKay and coauthor Patrick Fanning complained that parental rewards and punishment create an inner "pathological critic" in children, a "tyranny of the shoulds" that blocks self-esteem.[57] Education professor and prolific author Wayne Dyer announced, "You are sacred, and in order to know it you must transcend the old belief system you've adopted," and "You are a divine being called to know your sacred self by mastering the keys to higher awareness."[58] Deepak Chopra rhapsodized, "A wizard exists in all of us; this wizard sees and knows everything [and] is beyond opposites of light and dark, good and evil, pleasure and pain. . . . Human order is made of rules; the wizard's order has no rules—it flows with the nature of life. . . . Wizards never condemn desire; it was by following their desires that they became wizards."[59] Author Peter McWilliams termed traditional beliefs "learned junk" inflicted by authority figures. Science-fiction author Ray Bradbury declared, "We are God giving himself a reason for being."[60] Psychiatrist M. Scott Peck advised, "To put it plainly our unconscious is God. God is within us."[61] Psychiatrist David Burns proposed a "*cognitive* therapy that had nothing to do with cognition (thought processes) but was all about *feeling*—that is, all about 'understanding your moods,' 'feeling good about yourself,' 'feeling confident,' and 'feeling good together.'"[62]

★ As technological advancements made it possible for TV stations to be on air for longer periods of time, TV programmers were challenged to find material for a variety of new situation comedies, dramas, documentaries, and talk shows. They understandably looked to the most popular ideas of the day—the ideas of Rogers, Maslow, Kinsey, and their followers—for topics and themes.

★ Television (and movie) producers combined Rogers's denigration of mind and celebration of sensory experience with Kinsey's anything-goes sexuality to produce mindless dramas filled with chase scenes and spectacular explosions punctuated by steamy couplings and gory demises. They also abandoned the traditional distinctions between good and evil, hero and villain, and depicted a world of moral grays, often treating criminals more sympathetically than victims, even to the point of telling stories from the perpetrator's point of view.

★ Producers of situation comedies narrowed their focus from the broad range of human blunders and foibles to sexuality and self-absorption, driving leering and double entendres to new lows and reflecting the themes of Rogers, Maslow, and Kinsey.

★ Since the Romantic period of the late eighteenth and nineteenth centuries, the arts had been associated with the bizarre, the undisciplined, the iconoclastic. That association continued in the twentieth century with the Bohemian and the Beat Generations. In one way, the "hippie" generation was an extension of that association. In two other ways, however, it was very different. First, the reigning psychology, Humanistic Psychology, encouraged and validated it by asserting that feelings are a better guide to behavior than reason and encouraging liberation from social norms. Then, too, mass culture made it more public and therefore influential than its forbears. In frenetic celebration of the senses, rock musicians pranced across the stage screaming ungrammatical tributes to drugs and raunch, and rappers violated meter and rhyme in vile insults to women and authority figures, notably the police. Artists celebrated the subjectivity of reality, and proceeded to express their artistic vision with blank or dung-spattered canvases, toilets claimed from the junk heap, or smelly garbage cans borrowed from a nearby alley. Most significantly, television kept these people in the spotlight.

★ Talk-show producers, whose success depended on the "relevance" of their programming, gave self-help authors, movie and TV stars, and musicians and artists a forum to discuss not only their crafts but also their feelings and opinions on subjects beyond their competency. On the rare occasions when hosts or other guests were bold enough to challenge what they said, the typical response was "Well, that's my *opinion*" in a tone reminiscent of the cry of "sanctuary" uttered by miscreants who sought safety in medieval cathedrals.

★ As television viewing grew in popularity, reading declined and the publishing industry was seriously affected. Small, "quality" publishers that specialized in serious works by qualified but not necessarily well-known authors were especially affected by this trend, and many went out of business. Self-help books remained profitable, however, and many of the remaining publishers either expanded their offerings in that genre or made celebrity the main criterion for offering book contracts.

★ Encouraged by the success of talk shows, television executives transformed morning news programs into chat sessions with celebrities and authors of self-help books, often the same people who appeared on the talk shows. (This scheduling also served a business purpose because by this time the networks and the guests' publishers were often owned by the same conglomerates.) As competition for audiences increased, the line between fame and infamy was blurred and sensationalism displaced newsworthiness as the criterion for selecting guests.

★ While all these developments were occurring, the advertising industry, ever alert for ways to influence audiences, was turning Rogers's, Maslow's, and Kinsey's ideas to their financial advantage by creating commercials that used self-absorption, pursuit of pleasure, and exaltation of feelings to sell goods and services. Slogans such as "You deserve it," "Just do it," "Have it your way," "No rules, just right™," and "Why ask why? Try Bud Dry" are just a few examples of such appeals.[63]

The constant repetition and dramatization of the ideas of Rogers, Maslow, and Kinsey in the communications and entertainment media over several decades created a new "mass culture" that reviled what traditional culture honored and honored what traditional culture reviled.[64]

IMPACT ON SOCIETY

This new culture not only displaced the old; it also transformed the principal guardians of the old culture—parents—into objects of scorn and derision. More importantly, it became the means by which the ideas of Rogers, Maslow, and Kinsey profoundly affected every social institution.[65]

EDUCATION

In chapter 1, we noted that Hereditarianism had a profound effect on education. Because the masses were considered intellectually handicapped, the emphasis was placed on telling students what to think rather than teaching them how to think. Textbooks provided information to be remembered, and objective tests measured recall rather than students' ability to understand or apply knowledge. By the 1960s the most needed reforms were to restore trust in students' intellectual potential, raise academic standards, and replace mind stuffing with mind building.

In the 1970s and 1980s the Critical Thinking movement offered these needed reforms. But the intellectual tide favored the opposing views of Rogers, Maslow, and Kinsey,[66] who believed that students should be indulged rather than challenged, notably by emphasizing emotion rather than thought and encouraging them to create rather than discover truth— that is, to form beliefs that matched their desires and preferences and then regard them as true without further inquiry.

These ideas were welcomed in psychology courses and textbooks—not just in advanced college courses for psychology majors, but also in introductory courses recommended or required for all students. Moreover, high school counselors were guided by these ideas (having learned them in undergraduate and graduate psychology courses), and college student-personnel staffs and dormitory resident assistants offered noncredit courses and discussion groups based on them. It was not uncommon for college students to be *unlearning* in the dormitory the principles and techniques of *thinking* that they were learning in the classroom. For example, students would leave classrooms devoted to reasoned judgment about objective reality and return to dormitory discussion groups where they learned to ignore reason and create their "personal reality."

Soon the ideas of Rogers, Maslow, and Kinsey began to influence teaching methods across the curriculum. English teachers found these ideas especially appealing because they seemed uniquely compatible with the spontaneity, creativity, and freedom they associated with literature. Accordingly, many English faculties changed their approach to teaching writing, dispensing with the formalities of substance, style, and organization and instead emphasizing free, unfettered expression. Some colleges eliminated the composition requirement altogether. Teacher-training programs urged sensitivity to students' learning "styles." At all levels of education, undemanding elective courses were substituted for rigorous required ones and grading standards were relaxed so as not to damage students' self-esteem. Carl Rogers set the standard for such permissiveness in his own psychology classes. He downplayed subject matter, set no expectations, left issues unresolved, and let students choose their own readings, decide the direction(s) of class discussion, and even grade themselves![67]

The initiatives that most clearly reflected the premises of Humanistic Psychology were "values clarification" and self-esteem programs. Designed by educator Louis Raths, among others, values clarification sharply contrasted with the traditional study of ethics or moral judgment.[68] Among its central premises were that there are no absolutes and therefore all values are relative, that individuals decide for themselves what their values are, that what an individual decides cannot be wrong, and that teachers should never pass judgment on the values students choose.[69]

Self-esteem programs, originally derived from Abraham Maslow's contention that self-esteem is required for achievement, were made popular by Canadian psychotherapist Nathaniel Branden, who argued that low self-esteem leads to pathology. Most of these programs included exercises designed to make students feel good about themselves regardless of their academic performance. They also forbade teachers from any criticism or discipline that might reduce students' self-regard. Educational researcher Alfie Kohn describes one such school, which considered itself a "showcase" for self-esteem training. He notes that every classroom emphasized building students' self-esteem. Slogans such as "You are beautiful" were posted on bulletin boards. Students were required to begin each day by saying "I am somebody" and to applaud one another's presentations. Teachers reminded students that "You can do anything."[70] Researcher Joshua Michael Aronson points out that "a proliferation of self-esteem kits, programs, and gimmicks" has encouraged and supported such classroom practices.[71]

RELIGION

We have seen how the ideas of Rogers, Maslow, and Kinsey quickly penetrated the field of psychology and became central precepts in counseling. The obvious result was that those ideas became working principles for students in the various counseling professions, such as school guidance counseling and marriage and family counseling. What is often overlooked is that members of the clergy, who provided *spiritual* counseling, generally enrolled in the same graduate courses as secular counselors and therefore were exposed to the same ideas. Those members of the clergy were thus led to question the religious and moral teachings of the religion they were pledged to profess to their congregations. They wondered:

"Is human nature really flawed? Perhaps it is instead, as Rogers and Maslow claim, inherently good."

"Could what I learned in the seminary about pride be wrong? Could pride, understood as self-esteem, be a virtue rather than a vice? If so, what implications does this have for self-abnegation and self-sacrifice?"

"Are Rogers, Maslow, and Kinsey correct in their conclusion that there are no moral absolutes and that right and wrong are subjective matters? Is the concept of sin, especially sexual sin, outmoded?"

If Rogers, Maslow, and Kinsey had been more explicit in their opposition to religion, fewer members of the clergy would have entertained such speculation. But Rogers and Maslow spoke in ways that implied respect for religion, so many clergy were able to regard their own speculation as healthy and supportive of their faith. More significantly, if they decided that the new psychology was right and their religion was wrong, they were able to reject the teachings of their church without leaving the church. In their minds, there was no reason to leave because they were not apostates but reformers.

One influential evangelical preacher, Robert Schuller, was so enthralled with the concept of self-esteem that he made it the lens through which he read the Bible. Schuller wrote: that "the 'will to self-love' is the deepest of all human desires," that the message Jesus really intended to deliver was "stop putting yourself down," that "the core of original sin . . . could be considered an innate inability to adequately value ourselves," that what Christ meant when he said "deliver us from evil" was deliver us from "a negative self-image, a lack of self-esteem," and that "man's deepest need [is] the 'will to self worth.'"[72]

Less dramatic but equally reflective of the influence of Humanistic Psychology is the appearance of Rogers's and Maslow's ideas (and sometimes their terminology) in homilies. For example, many preachers changed their preference from "peace on earth to men of good will" to "peace on earth, good will to men," suggesting clearly that, with respect to their religious doctrine, it is not necessary to be of good will to receive God's blessings.[73] Also, instead of sermonizing on Christ's admonition to "love your neighbor as yourself," many spoke of "the necessity of *loving oneself* before loving others." I recently heard a pastor, in reciting the Lord's Prayer, say "forgive us our trespasses *that we may forgive* those who trespass against us." This phrasing not only has no support in biblical scholarship, but it also, and more significantly, completely reverses Christ's stated meaning— instead of *I must forgive before I will be forgiven*, it says *I must be forgiven before I can forgive*. (This is the same kind of reversal that Humanistic Psychology made in changing *achievement makes you feel good about yourself* to *you must feel good about yourself before you can achieve*.)

A more subtle example is the increasing preference for the singular word *sin* over the plural word *sins*. Because *sin* is broader and vaguer, its use conveyed Humanistic Psychology's idea that society rather than the individual is responsible for evil.[74] Today, in all but the most conservative denominations, the message is typically that God loves us no matter what we do rather than on the spiritual peril of disobeying God's laws.

Nowhere was the new psychology's impact on religion more dramatic than in Carl Rogers's work with Catholic religious orders. In one case, Rogers, his close associate William Coulson, and a large group of facilitators conducted a series of encounter groups with the Catholic Sisters of the Immaculate Heart of Mary (IHM). The grant called for three years of encounters but the project was suspended after two years because, as Coulson recalls, "we were alarmed about the results. We thought we could make the [IHMs] better than they were; and we destroyed them," adding that "we provoked an epidemic of sexual misconduct among clergy and therapists." Coulson's summary of the outcome of the sessions underscores the devastating impact of Rogers's ideas: "The [IHMs] had some 60 schools when we started; at the end, they had one. There were some 615 nuns when we began. Within a year after our first interventions, 300 of them were petitioning Rome to get out of their vows. They did not want to be under anyone's authority, except the authority of their imperial inner selves. . . . The college campus was sold. There is no more Immaculate Heart College."[75]

The IHM sisters were not the only case of an entire order being transformed by the new psychology. Rogers ran encounter groups with "dozens of Catholic religious organizations," including the Mercy Sisters, the Franciscans, the Sisters of the Providence of Charity, and the Society of Jesus (Jesuits).[76] The Jesuits' case is perhaps more illustrative than any other of the power of the ideas central to Humanistic Psychology because that transformation entailed casting aside the order's legendary commitment to intellectual excellence.

According to Jesuit historian Malachi Martin, Humanistic Psychology's view that humans are inherently good and that society is to blame for evil was evident at General Council 31 (GC31) of the Society of Jesus in 1964.

That council also embraced the new psychology's view that the purpose of sexuality was merely pleasure to which everyone had a right, urged that priests be allowed to have intimate relations with women outside marriage, and encouraged them to enroll in "professionally directed sensitivity lessons."[77] Martin says flatly that a major factor in the radical transformation of the Society of Jesus at the time was the substitution of Humanistic Psychology for the beliefs and ideals of its founder, St. Ignatius. As a result, at GC31 and GC32 (in 1975), there was no evidence of "a religious and supernatural analysis of any aspect of the human condition." The emphasis was on sociopolitical matters such as employment, housing, pollution, and civil rights.[78]

Another Jesuit historian, Joseph Becker, documents the influence of Humanistic Psychology in the everyday lives of Jesuits between 1965 and 1975.

Those in charge of novices "began attending psycho-religious institutes, sensitivity sessions, and similar activities of humanistic psychology" and bought popular-psychology books for their libraries. A new model of formation was introduced based on the new psychology's notions that the "traditional religious lifestyle" can lead to being "psychologically deprived," and that "a healthy psyche result[s] not from passive conformity to a preexisting pattern but from active responsibility for creating one's own pattern." Proposed changes to the Spiritual Exercises included adding "I am worthwhile," and "creation is for me," as well as the healing of one's negative self-image, becoming "in touch with" oneself, and finding one's personal truth about theology.[79]

Given the influence of mass culture, the endorsement of Humanistic Psychology by many priests and theologians,[80] and the continuing secularization of Catholic colleges,[81] it is understandable that many Catholics felt justified in "creating their own truth" about religious belief and morality. One result has been "cafeteria religion," in which people choose what they believe much as they would the food in a cafeteria, accepting what appeals to them and rejecting what does not.[82] Another has been the idea that it is intellectually honest to act in ways that deny our beliefs. Former New York governor Mario Cuomo popularized this idea when he advocated that politicians put aside their personal moral views and the views of their religion when they determine public policy on abortion.[83] Adopting Cuomo's perspective, many Catholic politicians embraced views they professed to condemn, notably abortion and the harvesting of stem cells from aborted fetuses.

Not surprisingly, there has been a dramatic decline in Catholics' use of the sacrament of reconciliation (also known as "penance" or "confession") since the 1960s. Evidently, many Catholics accept Rogers's idea that the locus of authority is within themselves rather than in the Church *or in God*, and that feeling an action is right makes it right.

THE FAMILY

The impact of Rogers's, Maslow's, and Kinsey's ideas on families was both significant and detrimental. Parenting in the 1930s, 1940s, and early 1950s was much the same as parenting had been in the previous hundred or so years. Parents set and enforced the rules, and children were expected to obey them. For the most part the rules were based on some accepted religious foundation and the principles of civic virtue. The school and the church could generally be relied on to support and reinforce the lessons learned in the home.

In contrast, from the late 1950s on, the influence of parents was diminishing. Not only were the entertainment and communications media disseminating the views of Rogers, Maslow, and Kinsey; the schools and churches were increasingly echoing those views. As a result, children were being taught to disrespect their parents and to regard the traditional values of their parents as outmoded and obstructive of their individuality.[84] If parents counseled delaying sexual activity, teenagers could claim that "science" gave the opposite advice. If parents said "Think before you act," children could reply, "We've been taught to follow our feelings." If parents taught standards of conduct based on their own experience or on religious convictions, children could say "Those standards may be true for you, but they aren't necessarily true for us—our truth lies within us." Given this resistance, many parents succumbed to the pressure of mass culture and became more permissive with their children.

Also, because *parents themselves* were encountering the ideas of Rogers, Maslow, and Kinsey, many of them began questioning the values they learned in their youth. "How do we know that *our* parents were right?" they asked. "Maybe they were misinformed, as the experts now say. Maybe by adhering to their standards, we've deprived ourselves of valuable experiences and missed a great deal of pleasure and personal fulfillment. Perhaps it's not too late for us." At best, such questioning made parents less committed to setting standards for their children. At worst, it led to behavior very much like that of the IHM nuns in Rogers's encounter program— neglect of obligation and a frantic pursuit of personal fulfillment.

Legions of parents began following the advice of the self-help literature—looking out for number one, putting self-actualization above marital and parental obligations, experimenting with drugs, and seeking the joy of guilt-free sex. The result was an epidemic of infidelity, marital discord, and divorce. The greatest victims were children, who were not only deprived of stable homes and parental guidance, but were often denied financial support by "deadbeat" dads. Many divorced parents remarried or cohabited, increasing their children's sense of alienation and risk of sexual molestation.[85] Understandably, many children reacted to these stressful circumstances by becoming inattentive and rebellious in school and seeking escape in alcohol, drugs, and sexual promiscuity. These behaviors led to a rise in the school drop-out rate and the incidence of addiction, sexually transmitted disease, teen pregnancy, and abortion.[86]

The ideas of Rogers and Maslow not only led to these problems in the family, they also hindered efforts to find solutions. Family members followed their feelings, which typically said, "I must be right, so when things go wrong, others must be to blame—parents, spouses, or siblings." Having been taught to regard truth as subjective, they distorted their memories to corroborate their feelings. For further ego-support, they portrayed their families—that is, all members except themselves—as "dysfunctional," a term conveniently provided by the therapy industry. Finally, if a feeling of guilt or shame managed to penetrate these defenses, they suppressed it, lest they lower their self-esteem.

GOVERNMENT

It is common to think of government as an abstract entity untouched by the culture that influences people. That notion is false. Government is composed of *individuals* elected or appointed to legislate in the collective interest of their fellow citizens. Those individuals are as subject to cultural influences as anyone else, and since the late 1950s they, like others, have been increasingly influenced by the ideas of Rogers, Maslow, and Kinsey. This influence is manifest in many of their programs, legislative views, and judicial opinions.

President Lyndon Johnson's Great Society program, for example, accomplished some good, particularly in the area of civil rights, but its "war on poverty" led not only to assistance to the desperately poor (a laudable consequence) but also, in some cases, to a "welfare mentality" and a sense of victimization and entitlement.[87] The creators of the program did not anticipate these negative consequences because they accepted Rogers's and Maslow's assumption that human nature is inherently good rather than flawed. To this day, more than a trillion dollars later with little if any progress on poverty, the advocates of the agencies spawned by Great Society continue to deny that something-for-nothing programs often bring out the worst in people.

The influence of Rogers and Maslow and Kinsey on legislators is most clearly revealed in the radical shift of Democratic members of Congress from a pro-life to a pro-choice position on abortion. For example, in 1971 Senator Edward Kennedy wrote this to a constituent:

> While the deep concern of a woman bearing an unwanted child merits consideration and sympathy, it is my personal feeling that the legalization of abortion on demand is not in accordance with the value which our civilization places on human life. Wanted or unwanted, I believe that human life, even at its earliest stages, has certain rights which must be recognized—the right to be born, the right to love, the right to grow old. . . . When history looks back to this era, it should recognize this generation as one which cared about human beings enough . . . to fulfill its responsibility to its children from the very moment of conception.[88]

Not long afterward, Kennedy became the leading *opponent* of the position he so enthusiastically endorsed in the letter. For the remainder of his long career, the National Abortion Rights Action League (NARAL) gave him a 100 percent rating as a supporter of its abortion agenda.

Many other Democrats (and some liberal Republicans) behaved similarly. Until 1987, Al Gore still called abortion "the taking of a human life"; in 2000, however, he declared, "My position has changed. I strongly support a woman's right to choose."[89] Senator Dick Durban was against abortion until 1989, when he reversed his position.[90] Senator Joseph Biden originally believed there is no constitutional right to abortion and still believes that life begins at conception, but he refuses to let his belief inform his voting.[91] Former president Bill Clinton famously declared that "abortion should not only be safe and legal, it should be rare"[92] but seems never to have asked the obvious questions: Why should it be rare? Is there something objectionable about it? If so, is the objection serious enough to warrant the classification of illegal?

Former Massachusetts senator John Kerry's position on abortion, while not changing so dramatically, is nevertheless as contradictory as his famous statement on the Iraq War—"I voted for it before I voted against it." At a 2003 NARAL meeting, Kerry said: "I think that tonight we have to make it clear that we are not going to turn back the clock. There is no overturning of *Roe v. Wade*. . . . We need to speak up and be proud of what we stand for."[93] This seems unambiguous—he is pro-choice and proud of it. But a year later, during the third Bush-Kerry presidential debate, the fog rolled in. Kerry said, "I am a Catholic. And I grew up learning how to respect those views. But I disagree with them, as do many. I can't legislate or transfer to another American citizen my article of faith. I believe that choice is a woman's choice."[94] In other words, he's Catholic but he disagrees with the Catholic view on abortion, yet the view that he disagrees with remains an "article of faith" for him. It seems that for Kerry (as for Carl Rogers), logic is optional and reality is whatever he wants it to be.

When elected officials dramatically shift their positions on important issues (or appear to hold contradictory positions), they owe their constituents a reasonable explanation. Yet the explanations typically offered in the case of abortion are anything but reasonable. One such explanation is "I now believe a fetus is a potential human being but not an actual one." This begs the question: What evidence caused you to abandon your earlier conviction that a fetus *is* a human being? (Certainly not science. All scientific evidence confirms that a fetus is a human being.) Another explanation is, "It would be wrong of me to base my legislative decision about an issue like abortion on my personal beliefs." This is absurd—*both* legislative decisions *and* personal beliefs should be based on careful judgments about the evidence. No public servant should vote *against* what he believes is right and true in matters of human life. (One may, of course, vote against one's personal beliefs in less grave matters when one's beliefs differ from those of one's constituents. The repeal of Prohibition comes to mind.) In any case, elected officials should offer their constituents a meaningful rationale for their views.

Another dramatic example of Rogers's and Maslow's influence was present in the financial crisis that occurred in October 2008. That crisis was a complex event with a number of contributing factors.[95] But there is general agreement that one main factor was established in the Carter administration and continued by succeeding administrations (hence, by both political parties). That trend was for government to pressure the banking industry to set aside banking standards and extend home loans to people who could not afford to repay them. This policy ran counter to common sense and centuries, if not millennia, of sound banking practice. In demanding this change, elected officials were guided by *feelings* (as Rogers advocated) rather than reason—specifically, feelings of compassion for those who could not afford to own homes.[96]

The "toxic" loans that resulted cost hundreds of billions of dollars and ruined the economy. Then, as if they had not done enough harm, elected officials *blamed the banking industry* and hastily devised first a "bailout" and then a "stimulus package," that included wasteful spending unrelated to the crisis and omitted meaningful controls on the distribution and use of the money. These plans were so complex and detailed that most members of Congress were forced to vote on them before they read them. Rather than demand more time to evaluate the plans, they approved them.

Think about that for a moment. Congress voted on the largest expenditure in the history of the world—an expenditure that has the potential of destroying the financial stability of the country—*without reading its provisions*. Many economists were so appalled at the irrationality of this behavior that they wondered aloud whether members of Congress were living in an alternative universe.

LAW

Rogers's views on self and authority are mirrored in what is known as judicial activism—that is, the inclination of judges to ignore the Constitution and legal precedent and instead assert their own views.[97] Rogers held that "the criteria for making value judgments come more and more to lie in the person, not in a book, a teacher, or a set of dogmas. The locus of evaluation is in the person, not outside." Also, that "We are wiser than our intellects . . . [and] our organisms as a whole have a wisdom and purposiveness which goes beyond our conscious thought." This wisdom, he continued, warrants our "rejecting the view of one single, culture-approved reality."[98]

Examples of judicial activism could be cited at every level of state and federal judiciaries. Here is a representative sampling from the Supreme Court:

Brown v. Board of Education (1954) ordered the desegregation of public schools.

Griswold v. Connecticut (1965) asserted a constitutional right to possess, distribute, and use contraception.

Tinker v. Des Moines School District (1969), ruled that students have a free-speech right to wear black armbands in school, and school authorities may not discipline them for doing so.

Miranda v. Arizona (1966) offered protection for those accused of crimes by stipulating that nothing elicited from a defendant would be admissible in court unless he was apprised of his rights, including the right to remain silent and to have an attorney present during questioning.[99]

Coolidge v. New Hampshire (1971) validated the exclusionary rule by which evidence can be excluded from a trial if the manner in which it was obtained was inappropriate.[100]

Roe v. Wade (1973) established a constitutional right to abortion any time before birth.[101]

Planned Parenthood v. Casey (1992) ruled that fathers, including husbands, have no rights when it comes to abortion; mothers alone decide.

Sternberg v. Carhart (2000) legalized partial-birth abortion.

Lawrence v. Texas (2003) established a constitutional right to sodomy.

Kelo v. City of New London (2005) expanded "eminent domain" to give state and local governments the right to force one private owner to sell his land to another private owner for private (rather than public) purposes.

Constitutional scholar Mark Levin calls decisions such as these "mind-boggling." He calls specific attention to the Supreme Court's inconsistencies in the application of the First Amendment to the Constitution:

> What was once unthinkable is now law. Your right to free speech—especially political speech—is being suppressed with the active support of the courts. So absurd and dangerous has the Supreme Court's view of free speech become that it struck down an anti-virtual child pornography statute as a violation of the First Amendment, but upheld prohibitions against running a political ad during the month before a federal general election as criminal. Indeed, you can burn an American flag as a form of protest, but you can't distribute pro-life leaflets within one hundred feet of an abortion clinic. When students wear armbands to school, they are engaging in free speech, but mentioning God at a commencement ceremony is unconstitutional.[102]

None of this suggests that the influence of Rogers is recognized by jurists or that they are less than conscientious in their deliberations and decisions.[103] It suggests only that, like the rest of us, jurists have been influenced by the *zeitgeist*—that is, the values and attitudes of Humanistic Psychology that have permeated our culture.

JOURNALISM

To understand how dramatically the ideas of Rogers and Maslow affected journalism,[104] one need only compare the standards of the early twentieth century with the standards of today. In 1923 the American Society of Newspaper Editors advised journalists: "Sound practice makes [a] clear distinction between news reports and expressions of opinion. News reports should be free from opinion or bias of any kind."[105] A journalism textbook published in the same year declared that "a news article should tell what happened in the simplest, briefest, most attractive and accurate manner possible; it should draw no conclusions, make no gratuitous associations, indulge in no speculation, give no opinion."[106]

That standard of objective reporting of facts, with opinions confined to the editorial pages and clearly labeled, prevailed until Rogers's and Maslow's ideas began to displace traditional norms. Journalists, like others, were exposed to the mass culture that popularized those ideas—that individuals create their own truth, that their feelings are more important than facts and evidence, and that the demands of self-esteem and self-actualization trump the requirements of any code, including the code of journalism. It is therefore not surprising that many journalists ignored the traditional standards of their profession, notably the 1923 statement of standards described above.

How widespread are these changes? At the beginning of the twenty-first century, a group of scholars conducted forums and surveys of over 1,200 journalists and concluded that "being impartial or neutral is not a core principle of [contemporary] journalism."[107] A journalism textbook published at about the same time declared: "Rule Number 1 makes it clear that if any rules or policies have to exist, they can be broken—crushed whenever the news requires it."[108]

The abandonment of traditional reporting standards is not limited to individual journalists. It can be observed in entire news organizations, including the once-venerable *New York Times* (*NYT*), as attorney Bob Kohn has impressively documented. He cites innumerable examples of *NYT*'s "journalistic fraud," under more than a dozen headings, including:

slanting headlines and lead paragraphs, distorting facts and statistics, interviewing only people who agree with them, omitting news and opinions that placed the favored viewpoint in a bad light, and using labels and loaded language to evoke the desired response from readers.[109] The practices of the *NYT* are especially significant because it owns fifteen large-circulation regional newspapers, including the *Boston Globe*, and because hundreds of other print- and broadcast-news organizations rely on the New York Times News Service for their national and international reporting.

The effect of journalism's embrace of the ideas of Rogers and Maslow has been profound.[110] By offering biased and oversimplified information, journalists make it difficult, if not impossible, for people to make sound judgments about important issues. As James Fallows, national correspondent for the *Atlantic* and National Book Award winner, has noted, this negative effect has been intensified by the fact that although "journalists are not required to have any systematic training in history, the liberal arts, natural sciences, or sociological and economic analysis . . . they have largely displaced the scholars" as interpreters of events for the general public.[111]

The previous chapter and this one described the general impact of Hereditarianism and Humanistic Psychology on American culture. The next chapter will look more closely at that impact by examining specific meanings and consequences.

3

MEANINGS AND CONSEQUENCES

We have seen how, over the course of the twentieth century, two extreme views of human nature displaced time-honored values and beliefs and became the basis for a new mass culture that changed individual lives and social institutions. Close examination of these views is the key to understanding the social, political, and economic problems and issues that continue to plague us. Unfortunately, social commentators have seldom attempted such examination, settling instead for vague references to the "legacy of the Sixties" and ignoring the earlier developments altogether.

Why have commentators neglected these matters? Mainly because they assume that cause-and-effect relationships do not exist in the realm of ideas—in other words, that people are uninfluenced by the ideas that dominate their culture. (This assumption derives in large part from Rogers's notion that each person creates his or her own truth.) Before addressing that assumption, let us examine cause and effect as it is commonly understood and then explain how it also applies to ideas, albeit in a different sense.

CAUSE AND EFFECT AS COMMONLY UNDERSTOOD

In science, *cause and effect* refers to the influence of one physical force or object on another. For example, a lightning bolt striking a house and the house catching fire and burning. Or a flower pot falling off a window ledge and shattering on the ground. Or a speeding car failing to negotiate a curve, careening off the highway, and crashing into a tree. In such cases, a scientific principle or law applies—combustion, gravity, inertia—and the effect is certain or, at the very least, highly predictable.

When dealing with a *chain* of events, sorting out causes and effects can be especially difficult, in that the effect of one event becomes the cause of the next event—for example, when a squirrel crosses a road, forcing a driver to swerve and hit another car that then careens onto the sidewalk and kills a pedestrian. Also, causes can be classified in several ways: *moral* versus *physical* (if I tell you to throw a rock through a window and you obey, I am the moral cause of the damage and you are the physical cause); *principal* versus *instrumental* (if John fires a gun and shoots someone, John is the principal cause and the gun is the instrumental cause); *proximate* versus *remote* (if a baseball player hits a ball and it goes over the fence and breaks a car window, the ball is the proximate cause of the shattered window and the player is the remote cause). Further, some causes are *necessary* (something tossed in the air returning to earth from the pull of gravity) and others are *free* (ordering a pizza, absent coercion). Finally, it is easy to be mistaken in identifying causes: for example, one event might seem to have caused another merely because it happened to precede it, much as an innocent person might be accused of a crime merely because he was present shortly before it occurred.

The difficulty of identifying some cause and effect relationships is underscored by the "butterfly effect," described by meteorologist Edward Lorenz and later expanded into "chaos theory." Lorenz noted that a small change in one time and place (the flapping of a butterfly's wings) can make a large difference later in another place (a storm in a faraway place). The butterfly effect is similar to someone dropping a stone in a pond and causing ripples that are at first large and perceptible but become smaller and imperceptible; or on a larger scale, an earthquake erupting at sea and setting in motion a wave that becomes a tsunami. But the stone's and quake's effects are measurable, whereas the butterfly effect is difficult or impossible to measure or predict.[1]

CAUSE AND EFFECT AMONG IDEAS[2]

The physical phenomena just discussed are helpful in understanding the *effect of ideas on human behavior.* Here is a rough analogy: as the flapping of the butterfly's wings creates a tiny air movement that impacts larger air currents, and the dropping of the stone and the erupting of the quake create a movement that affects the condition of the water, so also the expression (and more especially, the *repetition*) of an idea creates a reaction in the minds of those who receive it that can alter both their thinking about the subject and their subsequent actions.

To explain somewhat differently, the expression of the idea is like the flapping of the wings, the dropping of the stone, or the eruption of the seafloor. The impact of the idea on the mind is like the movement of the air or water. And the altered thinking about the subject is like the small or large environmental changes resulting from the storm, the ripples, or the tsunami wave.

Of course, people's thinking and acting are very different from scientific effects in the material world, and ideas are very different from butterflies, stones, and earthquakes.

In the realm of ideas, *cause and effect* refers to the influence of an idea on the thoughts and/or actions of those who embrace it.[3] For example, being exposed to the values and attitudes of our parents, both in word and in deed, and then exhibiting them later in our own lives. Or learning a problem-solving strategy and applying it. Or hearing a point of view expressed by others so often that it gains the status of familiarity, and then mistaking familiarity for evidence and embracing it ourselves.

Both physical cause and effect and ideational cause and effect involve one thing influencing another. The main difference between them is in the kind of influence exerted. In science, the cause may be said to *force* the effect to occur; in the realm of ideas, the cause *invites, encourages,* or *inspires* the effect. Scientific analysis, we might say, is concerned with *hard* causation; human-affairs analysis, with *soft* causation. Columnist George Will no doubt had the latter view of causation in mind when he responded to the argument that "no one has ever dropped dead from viewing 'Natural Born

Killers,' or listening to gangster rap records." Will responded by saying that, "No one ever dropped dead reading 'Der Sturmer,' the Nazi anti-Semitic newspaper, but the culture it served caused six million Jews to drop dead."[4] The principal difference between hard and soft causation is that in the latter—that is, in the realm of ideas—people have the choice of surrendering to the influence or resisting it.[5]

Unfortunately, although everyone has the power to choose, many people do not exercise that power because doing so requires conscious mental effort. It is much easier to remain in the default mental state of mindless acceptance. This state reflects years of teachers telling us what to think rather than teaching us how to think, as well as entertainment media conditioning us to receive ideas passively. Whenever we are in this state, either through habit or mental lapse, we are especially vulnerable to the influence of whatever ideas come our way. Here is how that influence typically occurs:

We encounter an idea explicitly stated in an article or a book, suggested in an advertisement, or embedded as a thematic element in a movie or a TV drama.

Although more or less aware of the idea's presence, we do not wonder about it or ask probing questions.

Later we encounter the idea again, and, because it is familiar, we feel comfortable with it.[6] The more frequently we encounter it, the more comfortable we feel.

In time, the idea settles into our memory. There it mingles with the beliefs we have formed more carefully, by evaluation and judgment.

Thereafter, whenever we recall the idea, we assume that because it is in our mind, it is our idea. It therefore evokes the same protective intellectual and emotional responses as do our other ideas. In other words, we devise arguments to support it, and to defend it when it is challenged. Moreover, we *act* in ways that are consistent with the idea.

The more often this sequence occurs, especially when the idea is expressed by people we respect and admire, the more attached to it we become. After hundreds or thousands of encounters with an idea in articles, books, movies, talk shows and TV dramas, it is not surprising that we regard it as a profound insight and are surprised, even offended, when others do not share it.

An example of an idea that has had such influence is "Talking out anger gets rid of it—or at least makes you feel less angry." As psychologist Carol Tavris notes in *Anger: The Misunderstood Emotion*, this idea became popular during the 1960s and 1970s to the point where it enjoyed the status of folk wisdom. And yet, when subjected to testing in research studies, it was proved false. In fact, as she documented, expressing anger is more likely to intensify it than to ventilate and dissipate it.[7]

In brief, cause and effect in the realm of ideas is probable rather than certain, *but no less real or significant for that fact*.[8] To disqualify it because it is not exactly the same as scientific cause and effect is as illogical as denying the designation "tree" to every variety other than an oak, or arguing that because a poodle is not a beagle, it cannot be a dog.

HOW IDEAS MULTIPLY

The mind is not just an idea warehouse but also an intellectual factory that processes the ideas it has stored. In other words, it perceives implications and makes connections with other, related ideas. In its more active moments, the mind also forms conclusions, devises new, imaginative ways of expressing the initial ideas, and creates new ideas. These tasks are carried out regardless of whether the ideas were obtained by passive acceptance or thoughtful consideration.

To realize how ideas impact our lives and institutions, we need to understand that ideas have meaning, and not just obvious, literal meaning but also associated—that is, implied, logically related—meanings. *The consequences of an idea flow both from its obvious meaning and also from its associated meanings, and the latter can be numerous and varied.* We might say that ideas are related in ways analogous to family relationships among humans—some ideas are as close as siblings; others are more like cousins; still others, like in-laws. Ideas, of course, are related *in meaning* rather than genetically. Thus, when one idea is expressed, closely related ideas are simultaneously conveyed, logically and inescapably, and less closely related ideas are implied.[9] In logic, this kinship is expressed by the term *sequitur*, Latin for "it follows"; or conversely, *non sequitur*, "it does not follow."[10]

The reason for being aware of the "kinship" among ideas is that such understanding enables us to think more effectively. As noted author and theologian David Elton Trueblood rightly observed: "The basic rule of philosophy is . . . [that] it is not intellectually honest to hold a position after it is known that the position leads inevitably to other positions which are recognized as false."[11]

Our behavior is influenced not only by the ideas we have consciously or unconsciously embraced, but also by all the related ideas that follow logically from them or are implied by them. Noted English lexicographer Samuel Johnson was alluding to such influences when he remarked about an acquaintance: "But if he does really think that there is no distinction between virtue and vice, why, Sir, when he leaves our houses let us count our spoons." And again, when he wrote, "He that overvalues himself will undervalue others, and he that undervalues others will oppress them."

UNINTENDED CONSEQUENCES

When we act upon our ideas, the consequences are sometimes exactly as we intend them to be. But not always. Many consequences are very different from what we intend. A dramatic example is the case of television advertising. When TV executives began selling commercial time, they believed they were benefiting everyone—they would gain financially, advertisers would be able to promote their products, and viewers would be informed about helpful goods and services. It would have been virtually impossible for the executives to foresee the dramatic consequences that would occur to their industry, to the culture, and to millions of individuals.

In the beginning, commercial interruptions were one minute in length and consisted of people detailing the wonders of a detergent and proclaiming how it had transformed their lives. Eventually, network executives realized they could increase their profits by splitting each commercial break in half and selling time to two sponsors. Later the commercial minute was halved again to accommodate *four* separate commercials. By this time, advertisers had devised more sophisticated visual and auditory presentations, featuring a dozen or more shifts in image and camera angle within each fifteen-second commercial. Meanwhile, television executives had hit upon the idea of adding network promotions in the form of newsbreaks and program announcements.[12]

When the commercial interruptions became more exciting than the programs they were interrupting, program producers had to find ways to maintain their audiences' attention. Game shows added more noise and flashing lights; situation comedies quickened the banter and enhanced the laugh tracks; dramas increased the sex, violence, or both; news shows selected more sensational stories and abbreviated them to speed the pace; talk-show hosts pressed guests to give shorter, more simplified answers.

The most obvious effect of all these advertising and programming practices has been to force viewers to shift their attention hundreds of times an hour. People who watch television regularly—and many do so three or more hours a day—are almost certain to suffer a shortened attention span. In other words, they are likely to become impatient with the comparatively slow and unexciting pace of everyday affairs, to lose attention frequently, and as a result, to experience a decline in performance in school or at work. It is not unreasonable to wonder whether the relatively new medical condition known as attention deficit/hyperactivity disorder (ADHD) is aggravated, and perhaps even caused by, television's forced attention shifts. A less obvious but equally significant effect of these advertising and programming practices has been to create a vicious circle in which forced attention shifts shorten the audience's attention span, thus making them more impatient with the existing pace, and therefore requiring programmers to add more attention shifts.

Another example of unintended consequences is the decline of quality in movies and television programs. In applying Humanistic Psychology's model of human nature and breaking traditional taboos, moviemakers and TV programmers intended to raise their art to a higher level. Yet as more and more taboos have been broken, subject matter and themes have gotten more predictable, plots more formulaic and disjointed, and character development more superficial.[13]

The lesson in the decline of movie and TV quality, which media people continue to miss, is that not all constraints impede artistry; some, in fact, stimulate it because, as G. K. Chesterton noted, "The essence of the picture is the frame." A good example of this effect is the modern beer commercial. When advertisers were forbidden to show people actually drinking beer, they had to find other ways to make viewers thirst for their product. Their creative responses to the challenge have stimulated salivation more than depictions of people swilling pitchers of suds ever would have.

Yet another example of unintended consequences occurred when TV journalists applied Humanistic Psychology's perspective to news broadcasts and commentary shows. Embracing the notion that truth is relative and personal, they ignored the distinction between fact and opinion, as documented in chapter 2. But instead of achieving more meaningful presentations, they produced biased, agenda-driven journalism.[14] (This is not to ignore that irresponsible, "yellow" journalism existed in the past. But the journalists responsible for those lapses did not deny the validity of journalism standards—they simply ignored them. The journalists I am speaking of here deny the standards.)

Similarly, talk-show discourse degenerated from meaningful dialogue into serial sound bites or, worse, dueling monologues characterized by shouting and interrupting. Even when hosts deplore such cacophony, they are forced to engage in it in order to compete with the fast-paced stories simultaneously featured on reality, news magazine, and courtroom shows, as well as the copulation, explosions, and violence on dramatic programs.

THE LEGACY OF HEREDITARIANISM

Having established how cause and effect operates in the realm of ideas, let's consider how it operates in the specific case of the central idea of Hereditarianism discussed at length in chapter 1. We will first identify its expanded meanings—that is, the related ideas that it implies, encourages, or invites—and then identify the actual events that are logically related to that "family" of ideas. It is important to keep in mind that expanded meanings are the logical extensions of an idea and that they exist *whether or not they are expressed and whether or not the person expressing the original idea is conscious of them.*

IDEA

Intelligence is genetically determined, unequally distributed, and impossible to increase.

EXPANDED MEANINGS

Members of families have similar intelligence levels.

Efforts to raise intelligence are pointless.

No one can be trained to think.

Education should be suited to students' intelligence levels.

Tests are needed to determine people's intelligence levels. *(After the Army Tests during World War I "proved" that the average mental age of adult Americans ranged from 10.41 to 13 depending on race and ethnic group, the meaning was expanded further.)*

Some races and ethnic groups are genetically favored.

Unfavored groups should be barred from immigration.

Few students can profit from an academic education.

Most students should receive vocational education.

Unfavored people should be discouraged/barred from reproducing.

CONSEQUENCES

Curriculums changed from academic to vocational.

School administrators gained control over classroom activities.[15]

The goal of education changed from developing minds to presenting information.

Instruction focused on stuffing minds with facts rather than developing thinking skills.

Skills related to thinking, notably communication skills, were neglected.

Business leaders, distrustful of workers' mental capacities, turned to "Scientific Management," which assigned all thinking to executive elites, notably industrial engineers.

Progressivism gained influence; government grew larger and more paternalistic.

Legislators revised immigration laws to favor "superior" groups, notably Northern Europeans.

Jurists began to emphasize social agendas rather than the Constitution.

The Eugenics movement gained influence.

Contraception was urged for the lower classes.

Sterilization of the unfit was encouraged.

Enmity and discrimination against blacks and similarly "deficient" ethnic groups increased.

Am I speaking of the above consequences in the "hard" (scientific) sense of virtual certainty? No, because though force could have been present (as in the case where the government mandated that a person be sterilized), it was generally not present; for example, nothing forced educators to change curriculums from academic to vocational. Rather, in most of these cases I am referring to consequences in the "soft" sense of ideas *influencing* behavior. In that sense, Hereditarianism can be said to have caused the specified events.

THE LEGACY OF HUMANISTIC PSYCHOLOGY

The format here is the same as in the previous section: we examine, in turn, each of the core ideas of Humanistic Psychology, first identifying its expanded meanings—that is, the related ideas that it implies, encourages, or invites—and then identifying the actual events that are logically related to that "family" of ideas. (For the sake of conciseness, where the meanings and consequences are numerous and varied, I have added examples and clarifying comments in the endnotes.) Here, as with our examination of Hereditarianism, it is important to keep in mind that expanded meanings are the logical extensions of an idea and that they exist *whether or not they are expressed and whether or not the person expressing the original idea is conscious of them.*

IDEA

Human nature is inherently wise and good.

EXPANDED MEANINGS

Foolishness and evil reside outside the person. (If we are inherently wise and good, the clear implication is that foolishness and/or badness cannot reside within us.)

When something goes wrong for a person, the fault must lie in outside events or people, for example, parents, teachers, or other authority figures.[16]

All knowledge worth possessing lies within. (If we inherently wise, we possess the knowledge upon which wisdom rests; and if we already possess that knowledge, it follows that we have no need of seeking it in school or elsewhere.)

The center of authority is within each person rather than in society, religion or, for that matter, God. (This is clearly implied in the idea that human nature is inherently wise and good: if we have that kind of insight within us, it is worthy of being regarded as our authority. But Rogers did not leave this at the level of implication. As noted in chapter 2, he expressed it directly: "The locus of evaluation is in the person, not outside."[17])

Individuality is automatic and requires no effort. (This idea is not *implied* by the belief that we are inherently wise and good but instead *invited* by it. Our view of individuality is intimately related to our view of human nature, so believing in our inner completeness encourages belief that we needn't strive for individuality.)

There is no need for "salvation" and therefore no need for religion. (*Salvation* is a religious term based on the belief that we stand in need of deliverance from sin. If we are inherently good, however, we are incapable of sin and therefore have no need of salvation or of the institution that purports to offer it.)

External standards, expectations, and norms are irrelevant. (If wisdom and goodness lie within us and they are worthy to serve as our locus of authority, then it follows that outside kinds of authority are unnecessary.)

There is no need for guilt or shame or apology for one's actions.[18]

CONSEQUENCES

Social scientists deflected responsibility from individuals by devising terms such as *dysfunctional family* and lengthening the list of "compulsive" behaviors and emotional "disorders" for which people are assumed to have little or no responsibility.[19]

Since the 1960s there has been an increase in students rejecting parental guidance and becoming inattentive, insubordinate, and truant from school. Also, academic achievement has declined, as evidenced by the poor performance of American students in international comparisons.

Since the 1960s, many young adults have tended to be alienated from their elders, suspicious of authorities, hostile toward their own country and its traditions,[20] and supportive of alternative political systems.[21]

Members of religious communities rebelled against their leaders and their churches' doctrines.[22]

The focus of theology shifted from liberation from sin to liberation from political oppression—hence "Liberation theology."

"Social justice" was transformed from a religious idea to a socialist program.[23]

Politicians embraced the idea of "redistributing wealth."(The concept of redistributing wealth did not originate with Humanistic

Psychology's idea that human nature is inherently wise and good, but rather the political program for such redistribution has been *encouraged* by the idea. The operative rationale is, if all people are wise and good, differences in financial success are most likely attributable to social injustice rather than individual achievement and should therefore be remedied.)

Government entitlement programs such as Aid to Dependent Children, Community Action Programs, Medicaid, and Food Stamps were created or expanded since the 1960s; political correctness created new categories of grievance, such as college rules that forbid speech or actions that someone may feel are offensive.

Numerous judges regarded criminals in general as victims of society and reduced their sentences to account for what the judges perceived as society's role in causing or exacerbating criminal behavior.

Humility declined, arrogance increased, and more and more people felt aggrieved over minor (or imagined) offenses;[24] litigiousness increased significantly. (The relationship between the belief that human nature is inherently wise and good and lack of humility and arrogance is expressed effectively, though not scholarly, in the country song, "O Lord, It's Hard to Be Humble [if you're already perfect].")

IDEA

Self-actualization is the highest human need.[25]

EXPANDED MEANINGS

An individual's most important focus is on self-actualization—that is, on identifying, nurturing, and expressing one's "real self." (This is not only implied by Humanistic Psychology. It was made explicit by Rogers when he spoke of "get[ting] in touch with this real self, underlying all my surface behavior" and averred that "the only question that matters is, "Am I living in a way which . . . truly expresses me?"")[26]

Restraint is an obstacle to self-fulfillment.[27] (This, too, is not only implied in the idea that self-actualization is the highest human need. Rogers also made it explicit in his writings. For example, he wrote that "positive development" as a person occurs when one discovers that he can trust his own feelings and reactions—"that his own deep impulses are not destructive or catastrophic, and that he himself need not be guarded, but can meet life on a real basis." Rogers's chief associate, William Coulson, notes that "unstinting satisfaction of desires—bodily or otherwise—was implicit" in the idea of self-actualization.[28])

Other people's needs are less important than one's own needs. (The emphasis on self-actualization, as well as on self-esteem, rather than, say, working for others, clearly implies that self must come first.)

Obligations to others (rather than to self), including those of marriage, parenthood, and employment, are less important than self-interest. (When one believes obligations to self take precedence, it follows logically that obligations to others become less important.)

CONSEQUENCES

Self-centeredness and inattention to, or disdain for, the rules of civility increased.

Marital discord increased, as did infidelity, separation, divorce, and neglect of children and the elderly.[29]

People began to speak of needs as rights—for example, the need for self-esteem became a right to self-esteem—and to demand that they be honored even when doing so violated others' rights. (A notable example of this demand is the creation of campus speech codes that elevated one person's "right" not to feel offended over other people's rights to free speech.)

Among elected officials, self-aggrandizement and putting their own aspirations above constituents' interests increased.[30] (The continuing polarization of the political parties and the resulting gridlock is an example of this increased tendency.)

In business, adherence to codes of ethics diminished and, accordingly, neglect of obligations such as customer service increased.[31]

Workers' loyalty to employers diminished, as did employers' loyalty to workers, customers, and stockholders. (These developments have a number of causes, notably the changing nature of business, the increased frequency with which employees changed jobs, and the growth of larger, more impersonal corporations. But the tendency to focus on self more than on others certainly contributed to the developments.)

Greed became more evident among corporate executives, often on a scale that undermined the welfare of companies, their employees, and stockholders. (Among the causes of the 2008 financial crisis, a federal inquiry revealed, was inordinate risk taking without regard for the possible impact on people and institutions.[32])

At this point, it is helpful to recall the format of the analyses we have been conducting in this chapter. First, a *core idea* that was explained at some length in chapter 2 is stated. Then its *expanded meanings* are presented. Expanded meanings are the ideas that the core idea implies, encourages, or invites—in other words, the logical extensions of the core idea. Finally, the *consequences* of the core idea and its expanded meanings are indicated. It is important to note that the term *consequences*, as used here, refers to actual events and developments whose occurrence has been influenced (rather than formally caused) by the core idea and its "family" of related ideas. This same format is employed in the following analyses.

IDEA

Self-esteem is a prerequisite to achievement.

EXPANDED MEANINGS

The higher one's self-esteem, the greater one's potential for achievement.

Low self-esteem is responsible for failure and social maladjustment, as in delinquency and crime.

People should strive to feel good about themselves, unconditionally.

Difficult goals and expectations are risky and should be avoided.

Whatever diminishes self-esteem, notably discipline and criticism (including self-discipline and self-criticism) thwarts achievement.

Whatever raises self-esteem, notably praise and affirmation (including self-affirmation), enhances achievement.

CONSEQUENCES

Scholars and authors emphasized self-indulgence over self-control, self-approval over self-improvement, self-assertion over self-restraint. (Carl Rogers's associate William Coulson explained this consequence in this comment: "When we implied to people that they could trust their impulses, they also understood us to mean that they could trust their evil impulses, that they weren't really evil."[33])

Many parents criticized children less, excused their inappropriate behavior, and defended them from criticism in school, the community, and the courts.

Many schools made self-esteem a prominent part of the curriculum. (Researcher Roy Baumeister points out that the self-esteem movement, barely known before the 1960s, became the focus of much research in the 1970s and became a "national buzzword" and was adopted in a "staggering variety" of educational settings thereafter.[34])

Teachers lowered performance standards (by giving higher grades for lesser performance), relaxed discipline, and thereby devalued excellence and achievement.[35]

Children exposed to self-esteem instruction tended to become used to teachers' unconditional affirmation and praise and avoidance of criticism and, thus, came to expect such treatment from others outside education. (Author Samantha Cleaver identifies this effect of self-esteem instruction, among others, in *Scholastic Online*.[36])

Social behavior previously considered "deviant" became acceptable. (As Daniel Patrick Moynihan pointed out in his famous essay, "Defining Deviancy Down," when crime, out-of-wedlock pregnancies, the breakdown of the traditional family, homosexual lifestyle, and communal living increased, there was little if any alarm expressed; instead, these behaviors were redefined as the new "normal."[37] There is no clear consensus on *why* the phenomenon Moynihan describes occurred, but it is plausible that the idea that self-esteem is deserved despite one's behavior was a contributing factor.)

Courts became more open to "low self-esteem" defenses in criminal cases. Robert W. Reasoner of the International Council for Self-Esteem, in his review of self-esteem research, argues that most problematic behaviors, including crime, are attributable to low self-esteem. Though he acknowledges that a number of researchers challenge his view, he rests his case on nine researchers who share it.[38] Reasoner's view has influenced the thinking of a number of jurists.[39]

Print and broadcast media extolled self-contentment, self-indulgence, self-assertion, even self-worship, and ignored or denigrated self-criticism, self-denial, self-discipline, self-control, and self-sacrifice.[40]

The learning gap with other countries widened. (Research psychologists Harold W. Stevenson and James M. Stigler examined the learning gap in the 1970s and then updated their research fifteen years later, noting little had changed. In their search for causes, they focused on how American approaches to education differed from

Chinese and Japanese approaches. Among the numerous differences they found was whereas American educators avoid dealing with students' errors lest they damage students' self-esteem, Asian educators "regard mistakes as an index of what still needs to be learned." As a result, Asian educators focus on mistakes and teach students to overcome and profit from them.[41])

The high school graduation rate in the United States, which had risen during the 1950s and 1960s, fell incrementally or significantly in each of the next three decades and showed "a sharp drop during the first half of the 1990s."[42]

Workers who received an education stressing self-esteem brought a sense of entitlement to the workplace. (Paul Harvey, professor of management at the University of New Hampshire, found that such workers scored 25 percent higher in "entitlement and narcissism" than their parents' generation and 50 percent higher than their grandparents' generation. "Even if they fail miserably at a job, they still think they're great at it," notes Harvey. Another study by Stacy Campbell and Jean Twenge supports Harvey's findings.[43])

IDEA

People create their own truth and reality.

EXPANDED MEANINGS

Whatever a person believes to be true is true.

Changing one's mind changes truth/reality. (If we create our own reality and whatever we believe to be true is true, it follows logically that when we change our minds, truth/reality changes accordingly.)

Opinions have the force of fact. (An opinion is a statement of belief. If a belief is always true by the mere fact of our believing it, then opinions are not open to challenge. Such thinking underlies the common response to the question "Why do you believe that?" The response is "Well, it's my opinion," with the implication that no further explanation is necessary.)

No opinion is better than any other.[44] (If everyone creates his or her own truth and reality, everyone's opinion has the force of fact, and no one's opinion is open to challenge because all opinions have equal merit.)

Encyclopedias and other works, including philosophical and religious works, mean whatever we want them to mean.[45] (Such works are descriptions and interpretations of truth/reality. If we create our own truth and reality, then we also, logically, create the meaning of such works.)

Morality is subjective and personal. (This is an inescapable implication of the idea that we create our own truth/reality. To say that morality is objective and impersonal—in other words, that in a given situation an action would be right or wrong irrespective of who performed it—would mean, as intellectual tradition asserts, that we do *not* create truth/reality.)

The rules of logic are arbitrary and nonbinding. (The purpose of logic is to guide us to sound conclusions, or in a related sense, to test conclusions for soundness. If we create truth/reality, then our conclusions are necessarily sound and therefore we have no need of logic.)

CONSEQUENCES

Curriculums substituted "values clarification" for moral education[46] and introduced concepts such as *multiculturalism, diversity*, and *tolerance*, which discouraged criticisms of other people's beliefs and behavior.[47] (As noted in chapter 2, "values clarification" was created on the premise that people create their own values, as they create their own truth/reality.)

Many students lost the motivation to learn and their knowledge and skills decreased.[48] (The decrease in knowledge and skills has been well documented and publicized in studies of comparative achievement among first-world countries. The decline of student motivation to learn, and of employee motivation in the workplace, has been addressed by a number of authors. Adam Smith attributes the loss of motivation to a more general decline of the work ethic.[49] Stevenson and Stigler concur, documenting that Japanese and Chinese students' superior performance is due largely to their conviction, often lacking in American students, that success is directly related to effort. The notion that truth is created rather than discovered, through effort, surely contributes to American students' motivation problems.[50])

In business and the professions (as well as in education), cheating, including plagiarism and résumé fraud, increased.

Dictionary makers changed from a prescriptive to a descriptive philosophy, and presented all usage as equally correct.[51]

With morality considered subjective, some fiction writers and filmmakers tended to ignore the moral implications of dramatic action for their characters and, in some cases, replaced traditional heroes with antiheroes.[52]

Many legislators began to ignore or consciously reject basic distinctions in lawmaking, notably the distinction between legal and illegal immigration.

Numerous jurists began ignoring their pledge to uphold the Constitution, arguing that it is a "living document" that can be revised to reflect changing realities. (This view is at the very least reinforced, if not directly influenced, by the idea that reality changes from individual to individual.)

Many journalists disdained objectivity and the distinction between fact and opinion, notably by mixing opinion and fact. (Bob Kohn has comprehensively documented this practice in his study of the changing culture at the *New York Times*.[53])

People began taking a "cafeteria approach" to religious belief—that is, an approach that selects from a religion the beliefs that one likes and rejects other, sometimes more fundamental, beliefs. (This approach reflects the view that truth is fashioned to one's personal specifications rather than discovered.)

Some historians began omitting or distorting facts unflattering to their personal views, such as facts about the limited success of the war on poverty or about Saddam Hussein's reported possession of weapons of mass destruction.[54]

Some documentary filmmakers substituted wishful thinking for fact. (For example, Oliver Stone argued that his ignoring of fact in his film *JFK* was justified because it expressed "an inner truth.")[55]

Some TV talk shows replaced dialogue with serial monologue; guests and hosts increasingly violated common courtesy by interrupting one another.

IDEA

Feelings are more reliable than reason.

EXPANDED MEANINGS

Emotion is more relevant to everyday living than reason.

There is no need to consider alternative actions, or to weigh consequences, before acting. (Considering and weighing are all functions of reason, so if feelings are more reliable than reason, these are not necessary.)

Whatever feels good is good, whatever feels bad is bad. (Not only is this implied in Humanistic Psychology's idea that feelings are more reliable than reason, but Carl Rogers actually stated it: "When an activity *feels* as though it is valuable or worth doing, it *is* worth doing. Put another way, I have learned that my total organismic sensing of a situation is more trustworthy than my intellect."[56])

Spontaneity is desirable; emotional restraint is repressive. (Spontaneity is a characteristic of feelings and involves an immediate response to a situation. Emotional restraint, such as necessitated by reasoned consideration, hinders immediate reaction and is therefore repressive.)

Impressions, intuitions, and hunches are trustworthy. (Although some researchers would argue that all three kinds of responses to experience have a cognitive component, most tend to agree that they are more associated with feelings than with reason. The statement that they are trustworthy is therefore implied by the idea that feelings are trustworthy.)

Words and actions based on feelings need not be explained or apologized for. (It is axiomatic in philosophy that feelings, like other matters of taste, are not open to dispute: *de gustibus non disputandum est*. So the argument that feelings are superior to reason implies that behavior based on feelings need not be explained. (Carl Rogers cited approvingly what one of his clients remarked, after therapy: "I finally felt that I simply had to begin doing what I wanted to do, not what I thought I should do, and regardless of what other people feel I should do."[57])

CONSEQUENCES

As the case for feelings trumping reason became widely publicized, people became less inclined to practice reflection and restraint and more inclined to respond to situations impulsively.

Traditional morality was replaced, for many, with a feelings-based "New Morality." (Traditional morality is largely based on affirmations or prohibitions of behavior set by religious tenet or philosophic—that is, *reasoned*—insight. It emphasizes what we should or should not do. When feelings became ascendant, it is not surprising that, as Irving Babbitt noted about Romanticism in general, morality tended to become "a matter of mood."[58])

People who accepted the idea that feelings are more reliable than thinking became less inclined to be discriminating and to avoid potentially dangerous behavior; as a result, the incidence of problem gambling, alcohol and drug abuse, and eating disorders became more common.

Social scientists regarded a number of behaviors traditionally associated with lack of will power as compulsive disorders.[59]

Reports of sexual harassment, discrimination, and hate crimes increased. (This may have been due, at least in part, to a greater awareness of the offensiveness of such behavior and, accordingly, increased motivation to report it. But to the extent that there was an actual increase in such behavior, it was surely invited by the belief that one's own feelings are more important than other people's.)

Impulsive behavior such as shoplifting, rape, assault, and road rage became more prevalent.

Spousal abuse, marital infidelity, child abuse, and divorce increased.

Traditional taboos against incest and the sexual molestation of children were more likely to be ignored.[60]

Public discourse was coarsened; insult and personal attack frequently replaced analysis of ideas. (In some ways the most troubling example of this tendency is the demonization of opponents practiced by both political parties. Name-calling and stereotyping are, of course, as old as politics itself, but until recent decades they had been retired after campaign season so that the nation's business could be attended to. Today there is an increasing tendency for the demonizing to continue and therefore to prevent honest dialogue and meaningful action from taking place. I would argue that the reason for this troubling change is the embracing of feelings over reason popularized by Humanistic Psychology.)

IDEA

All sexual expression is natural and wholesome.

EXPANDED MEANINGS

(Such meanings, remember, are the logical extensions of an idea. They exist whether or not they are expressed. The person expressing the idea may or may not be conscious of its implied meanings.)

The distinction between love and lust is meaningless.

There are no general standards governing sexual behavior. (If all such behavior is natural and wholesome, it follows that whatever anyone chooses to do is acceptable.)

Traditional rules about sexual behavior, notably religious rules, are mistaken and should be ignored. (Traditional rules, especially religious ones, are characteristically proscriptive—that is, they classify some behaviors as unnatural or unwholesome and are incompatible with the idea that any sexual behavior is acceptable.)

Delaying initiation into sexual activity is unnecessary and unreasonable.

Any sex act or partner one chooses is by that very fact acceptable.[61]

No one should feel guilt or shame over his or her sexual behavior. (If all sexual behavior is permissible, then no behavior is wrong; therefore, there is no basis for guilt or shame.)

Laws based on traditional taboos are oppressive and should be repealed. (If all forms of sexuality are natural and wholesome, taboos make no sense and laws that enforce them violate people's rights.)

CONSEQUENCES

(Here, as in the previous sections, the consequences are the *actual developments* that have occurred since the advent of Humanistic Psychology and are related to the idea that all sexual expression is natural and wholesome and its associated meanings.)

As all sexual behavior was becoming accepted as natural and wholesome, sexual behavior was more frequently and graphically depicted in media and the arts.

The distinction between love and lust was increasingly denied or ignored.

People became more accepting of pornography, prostitution (including child prostitution), and sadomasochism.

Laws proscribing certain sexual behaviors, notably homosexual behavior, were relaxed or overturned; gay marriage gained more supporters.

Sex education in schools was expanded and made more graphic; youthful sexual experimentation was encouraged rather than discouraged.

Sexual experimentation among preteens and teenagers increased.

The incidence of promiscuity, infidelity, incest, adult-child liaisons,[62] and sexual assault increased.

The rates of abortion and sexually transmitted disease increased.

Jurists became more lenient in their treatment of sexual offenders, including rapists and teachers who have sex with students.[63]

It is worth noting that each of the six ideas of Humanistic Psychology produce similar, in some cases identical, consequences. One example is that all the ideas undermine parent-child relationships. "You are inherently wise and good" and "You create your own truth and reality" convey the message that children have no need of guidance. "Your feelings are more reliable than reason" suggests that parental arguments for or against something are irrelevant. In addition, the emphasis on self-actualization and self-esteem creates an absorption with self that makes relationships with others, including family members, more difficult. And the idea that all sexual expression is wholesome creates a barrier to parental advice and counseling on the subject of sex.

Some readers may be inclined to reject the connections that I have claimed exist between the original ideas and the alleged consequences on the basis that what I call a connection is really *coincidental*. My response is that the connections are too obvious and logical to be so easily dismissed. For example, believing oneself inherently wise and good obviously inclines one to reject the advice of parents and teachers;[64] believing one can *create* truth logically diminishes one's interest in careful analysis; and believing that feelings are more reliable than reason is a powerful, if not a necessary, motivation to behaving impulsively. Once again, we are speaking here not of hard causation but of soft causation, in which ideas *invite, encourage,* or *inspire* the behavior that produces the consequences. In this sense, we can say with confidence that ideas have consequences.

ROGERS AND MASLOW REFLECT

Even Rogers and Maslow eventually grew concerned about the implications and consequences of their ideas. When Rogers ended the encounter group experiment with the Immaculate Heart of Mary (IHM) nuns discussed in chapter 2, he was shocked that it turned out so differently than he had expected. (As we noted, within a year after conducting the "Encounter Groups" that introduced the nuns to the ideas of Humanistic Psychology, 300 of the 615 nuns had left the order and the sixty schools they had run were reduced to one.) Rogers explained his reaction in a 1976 tape recording: "I left there feeling, Well, I started this damned thing, and look where it's taking us; I don't even know where it's taking me. I don't have any idea what's going to happen next. And I woke up the next morning feeling so depressed, that I could hardly stand it. And then I realized what was wrong. Yes, I started this thing, and now look where it's carrying us. Where is it going to carry us? And did I start something that is in some fundamental way mistaken, and will lead us off into paths that we will regret?"[65]

Maslow was equally concerned about the consequences of his own and Rogers's work, and much more reflective than Rogers was about what had gone wrong, as these examples demonstrate:

★ Maslow came to understand that self-esteem is "stable" and "healthy" only when it is "deserved."[66] Also, that "the relation between self-esteem [and] work is closer" than he had thought, and that achievement is more necessary for self-esteem than he had previously acknowledged.[67]

★ After remarking that one of the characteristics of self-actualization is *selflessness*, he went on to lament that "our youngsters suffer from too little selflessness and too much self-consciousness [and] self-awareness."[68] (It is not clear in this passage whether he realized that his hierarchy of needs, notably the self-esteem factor, led people to the very attitude and behavior he was lamenting.)

★ He became uncomfortable with the idea that the child is by nature good because he had too often seen the effects of overindulgence, specifically, inability "to delay, to work hard [and] long, to tolerate frustration or punishment." He went on to speculate that young people might profit from "training in hardship, frustration, delay, mortification, overcoming [*sic*]."[69]

★ He criticized "liberals, humanists" and others—citing Rogers in particular—for rejecting the idea that evil exists, "as if there were no sons-of-bitches or paranoids or psychopaths or true believers in the world to crap things up." Moreover, he claimed that such people "don't really know right from wrong" because of their "Rousseauistic Utopianism."[70] (Maslow had previously held views on good and evil similar to those of Rogers, though not as extreme or, for that matter, definite. He once wrote that "[People are not] evil intrinsically at the deepest levels of biological self." Then, years later, he decided that they are "not exactly 'good' either," but more like "neutral." His confusion is perhaps traceable to his failure to distinguish between the physical brain and the metaphysical mind.)

★ He added a significant qualification to his earlier claim that "the internal voice of the real self [is] the Supreme Court where the values are found." The qualification: that what seems to be the inner voice may be something less than that and may lead us into error. To guard against being misled, he counsels "empirical validation" of the message.[71] How that validation would occur, he doesn't say. Neither does he identify what might constitute the "something less than" the inner voice. Nor, for that matter, does he entertain the possibility that there may be no "internal voice of the real self" at all. Moreover, the "Supreme Court" metaphor is at best confusing—the high Court does not create laws or values; it merely evaluates the constitutionality of what legislatures create. (The point that should be noted in all this is not that he has overcome the shortcoming of his earlier viewpoint—because he hasn't—but only that he is acknowledging that it needs overcoming.)

★ He admitted that an absolute code of values is possible and that such a code refers to "real right [and] wrong, good [and] bad, healthy [and] sick. And this is what the wobbly liberals can't swallow. They're still with cultural [and] ethical relativism."[72]

★ He acknowledged the significance of *transcending* basic needs, identity, self, and even the need to be loved.[73] (This acknowledgment is important because, as we will see in chapter 6, Maslow's contemporary Viktor Frankl had long emphasized that self-transcendence rather than self-actualization is the highest human need. In effect, Maslow is here yielding to Frankl's insight.)

★ He rejected the idea that the "impulse of the moment should be the only determinant of behavior" and emphasized that the "older apostles" of impulse (such as Rogers) possessed discipline and self-control that young people lack and need.[74] (Maslow realized at this point that those "older apostles" had failed to realize how important the more traditional mental habits and attitudes they rejected had been to their own development. Also, that by rejecting them, they had deprived their own students and disciples of the qualities needed for their own development.)

★ He lamented his previous failure to recognize that self-gratification, though good in its place, can be overdone to the point of "pathology." He defined this "pathology of gratification" as a condition wherein gratification of basic needs brings, not contentment, but "boredom, aimlessness, anomie and the like."[75] (This is no small failure. The very structure of his hierarchy of needs is based on the idea that the needs are in the form of a ladder, each rung of that ladder must be attained before the next is attempted, and the final rung is self-actualization—that is, ultimate achievement, fulfillment as a person, or the term he uses here, "self-gratification."

To state, as he does here, that the process and/or the final outcome can be "overdone," is to raise serious and fundamental questions about the process. Unfortunately, he does not seem to realize that fact.)

It is not easy to acknowledge serious shortcomings in one's lifework and it is a mark of integrity that Maslow was able to do so. But it should also be noted that even after gaining these insights, he failed to renounce the underlying error that human nature is inherently good and to revise his hierarchy of needs. (The next chapter will demonstrate that error.) Of course, even if he had done these things and more, it would have been too late to undo the harm that Humanistic Psychology had already done.

4

THE FALLACIES EXPOSED

We have seen that Hereditarianism and Humanistic Psychology have ruined lives and undermined social institutions. That revelation alone would persuade many people that their central ideas deserve to be rejected. But more extensive and damning evidence is available. And it is worth close examination, particularly for those who are reluctant to put aside beliefs that have promised so much and to which our age has become so deeply committed. So let us examine the ideas further and consider the evidence against them.

IS INTELLIGENCE FIXED AND UNALTERABLE?

Even as Hereditarians were proclaiming that intelligence cannot be increased, other authors were demonstrating the contrary. These authors argued that the essence of intelligence is sound, effective thinking, and they identified the specific principles, strategies, and patterns involved in such thinking. One of the earliest demonstrations, ironically, was *Hereditarian* psychologist Charles Spearman's 1904 finding that, although some aspects of intelligence are inherited, others are learned. Over the next several decades, other scholars added support to Spearman's finding by providing evidence that an essential element of intelligence—critical/analytical thinking—can, in fact, be taught and learned.[1]

English social psychologist Graham Wallas wrote in 1926: "An art of thought exists, that the practice of that art is one of the most important activities of human society, that training in that art should be part of the education of the future thinker, and that . . . a complete separation between teaching and doing will be fatal to the art itself."[2] Ernest Dimnet, a French priest, argued that "education is nothing if it is not the methodical creation of the habit of thinking," and he charged educators of the day with the error of neglecting that ideal.[3] Noted American philosopher John Dewey stated that, "upon its intellectual side education consists in the formation of wide-awake, careful, thorough habits of thinking." A central feature of effective thinking, he explained, is the habit of basing beliefs on evidence rather than on whim and of being critical about one's own ideas as well as other peoples'. As a means of developing students' thinking skills, Dewey urged teachers to ask questions that provoked the exploration of ideas rather than questions that elicited rote responses.[4] In 1939, psychologists Harold Skeels and Harold Dye demonstrated that children's intelligence increased or decreased significantly depending on the quality of the care and nurture they received from adults.[5]

In 1940 educational psychologists Goodwin Watson and Edward Glaser created the Watson-Glaser Critical Thinking Test, which continues to be used today to assess critical thinking and decision-making abilities. A year later Glaser published *An Experiment in the Development of Critical Thinking*, which argued persuasively for thinking instruction to be central to education at every level. The book cited over three hundred sources—from fields including science, mathematics, English, logic, and social studies—that demonstrated that "almost any subject or project can be so taught as to put pupils on guard against generalization, contradictory assertions, and the uncritical acceptance of authority." From his research, Glaser concluded that "if the objective is to develop in pupils an attitude of 'reasonableness' and regard for the weight of evidence and to develop [the] ability to think critically about controversial problems, then the component attitudes and abilities involved in thinking critically about such problems must be set up as *definite goals of instruction* [emphasis added]."[6]

Some of the strongest evidence that intelligence can be learned came from Israeli psychologist Reuven Feuerstein's work with mentally challenged children and adults or persons who were at the time labeled "retarded."[7] He found that a central feature of their cognitive deficiency was an "episodic grasp of reality"—that is, the habit of seeing every object or event "in isolation without any attempt to relate or link it to previous or anticipated experiences in space and time." The problem was not that such individuals lacked the capacity for thinking, he concluded, but that the way they saw the world and themselves disabled their thought processes. Feuerstein's program of "instrumental enrichment" set six specific goals for its students: (1) correcting cognitive deficiencies, notably the episodic grasp of reality; (2) acquiring basic mental concepts and operations; (3) developing positive and productive habits of mind; (4) learning to avoid impulsive reactions and instead to be reflective; (5) finding pleasure in difficult tasks such as thinking and thereby strengthening motivation; and (6) seeing themselves as producers of ideas and not merely as passive receivers of information.[8] The continuing success of Feuerstein's program provides irrefutable evidence that, in his words, "intelligence is not a static structure, but an open, dynamic system that can continue to develop throughout life!"[9]

Eventually, it became clear that even features exclusively associated with genius—such as creativity—were learnable. In 1950 American psychologist J. P. Guilford discovered that there was virtually no psychological research on creativity. He found this deficiency "appalling" because he believed that education's "main objective [is] to teach students how to think." Accordingly, Guilford conducted his own research and identified a number of specific characteristics possessed by creative people, notably "sensitivity to problems, ideational fluency, flexibility of set, ideational novelty, synthesizing ability, analyzing ability, reorganizing or redefining ability, span of ideational structure, and evaluating ability."[10] In less technical terms, Guilford found that creative people are quicker than others in recognizing problems, able to produce more ideas and more imaginative ones than others, and more skilled in identifying the best ideas and combining them in interesting and useful ways. (Many of these qualities had been noted decades earlier in research on *critical* thinking, but Guilford seems to have been unaware of that research.[11])

Over the next several years, Guilford developed his structure of intellect (SOI) model, which identified 150 "factors" in intelligence.[12] Subsequently, Guilford's associate, Mary Meeker, demonstrated that IQ tests do not measure inherited knowledge, as Hereditarians had long claimed, but instead measure *acquired* knowledge, particularly verbal knowledge. She also demonstrated that when students' knowledge increases, their IQ scores increase comparably.[13] Educational psychologist E. Paul Torrance, the author of numerous books on the teaching of creative thinking, "invented the benchmark method for quantifying creativity and arguably created the platform for all research on the subject since."[14]

In the early 1970s, Ilma Brewer, professor of biology at the University of Sydney, Australia, began a ten-year experiment during which she gradually changed her goals for students from simply recalling information to applying what they had learned to solve problems. Her tests changed accordingly, containing no application questions at the outset and 80 percent application questions at the end. Despite the fact that the tests were more demanding, the number of students who scored 80 or above (out of 100) rose from 2 percent at the outset to 31 percent at the end of the ten years. The mean grade score increased from 60.7 to 72.9.[15] Brewer's painstaking experiment provides strong evidence that systematic training in thinking skills leads students to respond more intelligently to challenges.

At about the same time Brewer was conducting her study, medical researchers Howard Barrows and Robyn Tamblyn were investigating the effectiveness of medical school education. Their study was unique in that it focused on individuals who had already completed grade school, high school, and college and had taken the most demanding courses and received the highest grade point averages. Moreover, the medical students' motivation to learn was far above average, and they were in the habit of devoting long hours to study. If anyone could be expected to validate the mind-stuffing approach of telling students what to think, it was these students. Yet the study produced just the opposite conclusion, demonstrating that after the medical students had succeeded in passing their grueling examinations, they quickly forgot most of what they had learned, including the knowledge of basic anatomy and physiology that was essential to their role as physicians.[16]

The research of Barrows and Tamblyn led a number of medical schools, notably Canada's McMaster University School of Medicine, to make dramatic changes in their teaching methods. The essential change was to replace information-based learning with what Barrows and Tamblyn called problem-based learning (PBL). Instead of attending mass lectures and memorizing what professors (and textbook authors) told them, students worked in small groups to address specific medical problems in the form of cases carefully chosen and sequenced. Working with a real or a simulated case, students conducted their own analysis, identified the symptoms, did the necessary research, and prescribed treatment.[17] As their case experience expanded, so did their mastery of the principles, concepts, thought patterns, and procedures of medicine.

The experience of McMaster and other medical schools has demonstrated the superiority of active, thinking-based instruction over information-based instruction. After conducting his research into medical education, Barrows wondered: If PBL was more effective with the academically elite than mind stuffing, might it not be at least as effective with average and below-average learners? His subsequent work in high schools proved that it was.[18]

Taken together, these research findings make abundantly clear that the Hereditarian claim that intelligence is fixed and unalterable is patently false.

IS HUMAN NATURE INHERENTLY WISE AND GOOD?

Essayist and social critic G. K. Chesterton once noted the difficulty of proving that civilization is superior to barbarism. The problem, he explained, is not a lack of evidence but an overabundance, the sheer volume of it leaving one wondering where to begin. Challenging the notion that we are inherently wise and good poses a similar difficulty.

We could begin by listing everyday examples of our imperfection: our struggle to learn math, science, or a foreign language; our difficulties in saying exactly what we mean (and meaning what we say); our gullibility and vulnerability to deception; our inability to find our car keys, balance our checkbooks, be consistent in our golf swing or tennis strokes, and maintain concentration in meetings; our inclination to smoke, drink to excess, ingest drugs, eat unhealthful foods, and buy things we don't need and can't afford; our proneness to treating others in ways we would never allow ourselves to be treated; our difficulty seeing ourselves as others see us and admitting our faults.

The point is not that we, and people in general, *never* act wisely—it is that we are not *inherently* wise. To be wise takes effort; to be foolish is embarrassingly easy. The same can be said for being good. Pick up the newspaper or turn on a TV newscast and you're sure to find reports of stalking, harassment, slander, drunken driving, malfeasance, theft, perjury, infidelity, child neglect, spousal abuse, rape, and murder. Even if we allow for the probability that journalists prefer to report bad behavior because it is more sensational ("if it bleeds, it leads"), we must admit that they don't have to exert much effort to find such stories. There is plenty of bad behavior to be found, and not just in other people. We all know how easily the temptation to behave badly can overcome the desire to behave well.

In addition to our personal experience of human imperfection and the evidence in current events, there is the more expansive testimony of history and literature. When the historical record is considered in all its warfare and strife, the most striking impression is not human goodness but what Scottish poet Robert Burns famously termed "man's inhumanity to man." The earliest literature, the play, was cast as either comedy or tragedy, and human flaws were central to both.[19] In modern literature, no less than in the past, wisdom and goodness may make a dramatic appearance, but it is foolishness or evil that drives the story. Indeed, as Nigerian poet and novelist Ben Okri observed, "Where there is perfection there is no story to tell."[20]

Imperfection (fallibility) is not limited to one component of human nature but is characteristic of all. To begin with, *perception* is imperfect. One study showed that people can perceive that their view of an issue is unchanging when, in reality, it changes from pro to con and back again, as they hear persuasive presentations of contrary views and the corroborative evidence for each.[21] Another shows that teachers may perceive that they are grading essays on content when they are actually grading them on far more superficial grounds, such as penmanship.[22] A similar study showed that the same response with a man's name attached will get a higher grade than with a woman's name.[23]

Even our perceptions of *self* are often flawed. As Seymour Epstein explains: "People who are highly competent sometimes feel deeply inadequate; people who are inferior feel superior; people with an ordinary appearance feel beautiful; and people who are attractive feel ugly. More impressive yet, some people who have lived exemplary lives are torn with severe guilt to the point they no longer wish to live, while others who have committed horrendous crimes suffer not a twinge of conscience."[24]

Abundant research demonstrates that our *observation* is also imperfect. Rather than see what is before our eyes, we sometimes see what we *want* or *expect* to see, and even when we see accurately, our focus may be limited. In watching a football game, for example, we tend to follow the ball and miss what is happening elsewhere on the field; in attending a meeting, we tend to look at the person speaking and miss the reactions of the others in the room. A famous experiment conducted in a university classroom, and widely replicated in other settings, involved a drama in which actors engaged in a mock quarrel that quickly escalated to a mock shooting. When it was over, the actors left the room and the professor directed the class to record as accurately as possible what they had just seen. Their accounts differed considerably, not just in minor details, but in major ones, including the sequence of events, the descriptions of the actors, the angry words they exchanged, which actor made each statement, and the "weapon" that was used. (Auditory perception is as imperfect as visual. Researchers estimate that people grasp about *half* of what they hear.[25])

Memory, too, is far from perfect, popular notions notwithstanding. The popular conception of memory is that it is a precise mental recording of information and events, much like the tape recording of a conversation or a DVD of a movie. In this view, a person may forget or suppress what was received but the memory still exists, unchanged, in the unconscious mind. Research on eyewitness testimony has demolished that notion. We now know that memory can be altered by subsequent events, new information, and changing points of view. Experiments have proven that people can be influenced to alter the details of their memories and even to remember events that never occurred. Thus, "experimental psychologists think of memory as being an integrative process—a constructive and creative process—rather than a passive recording process such as a videotape."[26] A great deal of the difficulty of resolving disputes is the self-serving, albeit unconscious, distortion of memory by imagination and desire.[27]

The imperfection of human *judgment* has been recognized since ancient times. The Greek philosopher Aristotle identified thirteen common reasoning errors. Over the centuries, the list has grown to over one hundred specific errors. Moreover, despite the efforts of logicians to teach ways of avoiding such errors, the danger of committing them remains present any time people think or speak. Overgeneralizations, oversimplifications, unwarranted assumptions, hasty conclusions, rationalizations, and *non sequiturs* are as common in discourse as clouds in the sky. Their commonness helps to explain why solutions to problems often create new problems and why many controversies remained unresolved for decades, centuries, and even millennia.[28]

Errors in reasoning do not just happen—our underlying tendencies invite them to happen. Studies show that we tend to form beliefs on the basis of first impressions rather than careful analysis.[29] Moreover, an abundance of evidence shows that once we form a belief, we go to great lengths to select the evidence that supports it and ignore what opposes it.[30] In some cases we do this even when the belief is without foundation. Since the Middle Ages, gentiles have condemned Jews for being too interested in matters related to money despite the shameful fact that in the Middle Ages Jews were forbidden to engage in few other occupations.[31] A similar absurdity is white people's having prevented black children from becoming educated and then disparaging black adults for being uneducated.

Perhaps the most ironic example of the imperfection of human judgment is our belief about the quality of our judgments. As psychologist Janet Metcalfe reported, research reveals that

> people think they will be able to solve problems when they won't; they are highly confident that they are on the verge of producing the correct answer when they are, in fact, about to produce a mistake; they think

they have solved problems when they haven't; they think they know the answers to information questions when they don't; they think they have the answer on the tip of their tongue when there is no answer; they think they produced the correct answer when they didn't, and furthermore, they say they knew it all along; they believe they have mastered learning material when they haven't; they think they have understood, even though demonstrably they are still in the dark.[32]

The individuals who established our social institutions did so with clear understanding of the range of human imperfection. Traditional education was founded on the idea that wisdom and goodness are not inborn but learned, and the purpose of every traditional course and curriculum was, in principle if not always in practice, to provide knowledge, skills, and habits that foster wisdom and goodness. Democratic government was based not only on the belief that people have inalienable rights, but also on the presumption that those rights require protection from individuals who—through *lack of* wisdom or goodness—might violate them. If human beings were inherently wise and good, we would have no need of schools, legislators, police departments, or courts.[33]

For most Americans, the most familiar brief for human imperfection is the story of Adam and Eve in the Old Testament book of Genesis. That story is the basis of what Christianity calls "original sin," which for centuries was understood to result in a clouding of the intellect and a weakening of the will, not just in our first parents but in all their progeny up to and including ourselves. From this perspective, the "stain" of original sin has *deprived* human beings of the fullness of their mental and spiritual faculties.[34]

However, Judaism and Christianity are not the only religions to affirm human imperfection. Although Hinduism has many forms,[35] one belief is central to all: that humans must overcome their inclination to selfishness before they can achieve illumination. Confucianism considers imperfection the natural human condition—an ancient Chinese proverb counsels that "gold cannot be pure, and people cannot be perfect"—and urges its followers to strive for *jen*, benevolence toward others. Buddhism teaches that the highest goal is to achieve "freedom from human imperfection." (Interestingly, the Buddha claimed that human beings are characterized by innate moral laziness, a concept that, as the literary critic Irving Babbitt has noted, "works out in practice very much like the original sin of the Christian theologian."[36]) Islam teaches that to be human is to be imperfect and that wisdom and goodness are achieved only through dependence on Allah.

Secularists may disagree with religionists over the origin of human imperfection—claiming, for example, an evolutionary design flaw or a universal genetic defect rather than original sin—but they are in agreement about the *fact* of that imperfection.

Throughout the centuries, respected thinkers and writers have underscored the human propensity for foolishness and unacceptable behavior. Shakespeare declared "what fools these mortals be." In his *An Essay on Man*, Alexander Pope described humanity as:

> Chaos of thought and passion, all confused;
> Still by himself abused, or disabused;
> Created half to rise, and half to fall;
> Great lord of all things, yet a prey to all;
> Sole judge of truth, in endless error hurled;
> The glory, jest, and riddle of the world.

Mark Twain observed that of all creatures, "[man] is the most detestable. Of the entire brood he is the only one—the solitary one—that possesses malice. That is the basest of all instincts, passions, vices—the most hateful. . . . He is the only creature that inflicts pain for sport, knowing it to be pain."[37] Albert Einstein maintained that "it is easier to denature plutonium than to denature the evil spirit of man."[38] Havelock Ellis declared that "a sublime faith in human imbecility has seldom led those who cherish it astray."[39]

Before ending our discussion of the idea that people are inherently wise and good, it is helpful to consider the companion idea that crime is the fault of society rather than the criminal. Like many other individuals, criminologist Stanton Samenow initially accepted this view. Then he became an associate in the longest in-depth clinical study of the criminal personality ever conducted in North America. Thousands of case studies and his extensive private counseling convinced him that society is not to blame for crime—*criminals are*. As he later explained, "I had to unlearn nearly everything that I had learned in graduate school." Here are a few of his research findings concerning career criminals:[40]

Crimes may differ, but criminals "are carbon copies of one another in their view of themselves and the world." They lie, they have an "inflated self-image," and they think they are "special and superior" and that other people should indulge their wishes.

Criminals know right from wrong and their problem is not deprivation or compulsion but bad habits. They commit crimes not because they are ignorant of the law or because they can't tell right from wrong, but merely because they think that law and morality don't apply to them.

Criminals are not forced into crime—they choose it. The groundwork for that choice is laid in childhood. As children, criminals often adopt a contemptuous attitude toward their parents, no matter how good, kind, and responsible the parents might be.

The goal of rehabilitating criminals is based on a "total misconception" because the verb "to rehabilitate" presupposes a former healthy condition that never existed in the criminal. This fact, he believes, explains why providing criminals with career planning, a nurturing environment, and opportunities for success seldom makes a difference. Thus, the popular view that poverty causes crime serves only to provide criminals with an excuse for past crimes and encouragement for future ones.

Against the near-universal evidence of human imperfection, what evidence is offered by those who claim that human beings are inherently wise and good?

None, only wishful thinking and wild imagining. The only possible evidence would be that of individuals who for years had no contact with other humans and, when discovered, were fonts of wisdom and paragons of virtue. In fact, the tragic literature of feral children reveals that they have lived in every respect like animals.[41] In light of all these facts, the notion that humans are inherently wise and good is absurd.[42]

IS SELF-ACTUALIZATION THE HIGHEST HUMAN NEED?

Self-actualization holds the same place in Humanistic Psychology as sex in Freudian psychology and power in Adlerian psychology—as the central force or urge in human affairs. This formulation, perhaps more than any other, reveals Rogers's and Maslow's laudable intention of elevating psychology's view of humanity. But a good intention was insufficient to rescue their treatment of self-actualization from shallowness and error.[43]

As Professor Maurice Friedman points out, Maslow first conceived of self-actualization as a beneficial *consequence* of effort.[44] That formulation— hard work actualizes potentiality—was and remains unobjectionable. Eventually, however, Maslow expanded this view, placing self-actualization at the pinnacle of his hierarchy of needs and thereby making it the highest of goals, something to be pursued with zeal.[45] Moreover, he did so with characteristic carelessness, leaving unclear whether what would be actualized was talents or potentialities or values or mystical experiences, or some combination of these.[46] Whatever the choice, the goal came to be considered so important and urgent that any means of achieving it seemed justified. As Michael Daniels puts it, with Maslow the end becomes "a commodity to be purchased at any cost or sought using whatever means may seem effective," one that induces "a state of permanent dissatisfaction, even desperation."[47]

Because the focus of self-actualization is so vague, it can easily take the form of self-indulgence and even narcissism. And pursuit of it can result in a state of anxiousness about achievement in which one constantly asks, "Am I actualizing myself in this activity?" To appreciate how such a question *impedes* rather than enhances achievement, imagine a runner or a racecar driver asking it while competing, a singer asking it in the midst of performing, or a scholar in delivering a lecture. Paradoxically, the best way to realize one's potential is to forget about it altogether and devote oneself to the task at hand.

Another error in Maslow's (and Rogers's) conception of self-actualization is that it confuses psychological and philosophical issues, notably by treating questions about the purpose of life and how life ought to be lived as mental-health questions.[48] But philosophical questions are not reducible to psychological terms; they require some grasp of the epistemological, metaphysical, and ethical dialogue that has gone on over the centuries. Lacking that, Maslow (and Rogers) were unable to escape oversimplification.

The most glaring example of oversimplification is the flimsy foundation on which Maslow built his self-actualization model. His selection criterion was "positive evidence of self-actualization," which he explained "may be loosely described as the full use and exploitation of talents, capacities, potentialities, etc." His approach was to choose people that *he believed* fit this criterion and then to determine the personal characteristics that *he believed* contributed to their self-actualization. The determination was made through biographical study or, where possible, by interview. The main group consisted of such famous people as Abraham Lincoln, Thomas Jefferson, Albert Einstein, Eleanor Roosevelt, Jane Addams, William James, Albert Schweitzer, Benedict Spinoza, and Alduous Huxley; also twelve people whose identity he had agreed not to divulge.[49]

Years after Maslow published his self-actualization model, he acknowledged that it was in some ways biased and that the data on which he had based it did not meet the usual scientific standards of reliability, validity, and sampling. Also, he admitted that some of the individuals he had offered as prime examples of self-actualization did not fit neatly into that paradigm.[50] And he confesses to being confused about whether there is a correlation between self-esteem, self-actualization, and "full humanness." His decision: "not necessarily."[51] An even more troubling admission was this: "Maybe what I've written applies only to this elite [group of positive successful people]. If so, then [I] should have revised the paradigm because it clearly doesn't fit the majority of men."[52] How many did it fit? Elsewhere Maslow admits, "less than 1% of the adult population."[53] Despite that fact and his realization that he should have revised the paradigm, he did not do so.

The most definitive and devastating criticism of Maslow's claims concerning self-actualization was made by the famous Austrian psychiatrist Viktor Frankl, who demonstrated that self-actualization cannot be successfully pursued—it can never be more than a by-product of self-transcendence. Because Frankl's work is of special significance to the theme of this book—rediscovering lost insights about human nature—an entire chapter (chapter 6) is devoted to it.

IS SELF-ESTEEM PREREQUISITE TO ACHIEVEMENT?

The belief is widespread that people must have self-esteem before they can hope to achieve anything. Moreover, that the higher one's self-esteem, the greater one's success in life; and the lower one's self-esteem, the greater the chance of social maladjustment and criminal behavior. So strong is this belief that the schools have given self-esteem training a central place in their curriculums and parents have been persuaded to praise their children unreservedly, regardless of the quality of their behavior. The apparent goal and observable effect has been to keep everyone "in perpetual adoration before the holy sacrament of himself."[54]

What is particularly odd about society's embrace of self-esteem theory is that it occurred with little or no critical analysis, despite the fact that it contradicts a consensus that had spanned continents and cultures and persisted for over two thousand years.

Socrates led his followers to wisdom not by praising them but by exposing their ignorance and teaching them to question their own perceptions and thoughts. (He also practiced what he preached by publicly acknowledging his own ignorance.) In a similar vein, Samuel Johnson, one of the most learned men of the eighteenth century, wrote: "It is . . . certain that no estimate is more in danger of erroneous calculations than those by which a man computes the force of his own genius." He also made clear the consequences of excessive regard for self:

> Such is the consequence of too high an opinion of our own powers and knowledge; it makes us in youth negligent, and in age useless; it teaches us too soon to be satisfied with our attainments; or it makes our attainments unpleasing, unpopular, and ineffectual; it neither suffers us to learn, nor to teach; but withholds us from those, by whom we might be instructed, and drives those from us, whom we might instruct."[55]

Arnold Toynbee, the distinguished British historian, was convinced that "man's fundamental problem is his human egocentricity."[56] He also pointed out the "unanimity" of Jesus, Zarathustra, the Buddha, and Mohammed in "calling for self-conquest and self-surrender."[57]American psychiatrist Karl

Menninger argued that "vanity, egocentricity, hubris, arrogance, self-adoration, selfishness, self love, and narcissism" are "synonyms for pride," and that "to transcend one's own self-centeredness is not a virtue; it is a saving necessity."[58] Thus, whereas traditional wisdom held that esteeming oneself is more likely to corrupt than to elevate, modern self-esteem theory makes the opposite claim.[59] The question is, does research support this revolutionary claim?

As Alfie Kohn has noted, in 1990 a University of California–based group of scholars, many of them *favorably* disposed to self-esteem theory, addressed that very question. After reviewing the research on self-esteem, they found, in the words of their colleague, sociologist Neil Smelser, "the associations between self-esteem and its expected consequences are mixed, insignificant, or absent." In light of this finding, Kohn concluded that "the whole enterprise [of teaching self-esteem] could be said to encourage a self-absorption bordering on narcissism."[60] And there is evidence that this self-absorption can lead to other consequences. Martin Seligman has examined the issue of why a prosperous nation should produce so many cases of depression. He cites the rise of the self-esteem movement as one of the causes. "Depression," he explains, "stems partly from an over commitment to the self and an under commitment to the common good."[61]

When researchers tested the academic skills of elementary school students in Japan, Taiwan, China, and the United States, the Asian students easily outperformed their American counterparts. But taking the research a bit further, the researchers asked the same students how they felt about their subject skills. The Americans exhibited a significantly higher self-evaluation of their academic prowess. In other words, they *combined a poor performance with a high sense of self-esteem.*[62] This should not be surprising. Studies have shown that rather than self-esteem leading to accomplishment, it's the other way around.[63]

Several years later, a team of scholars led by Roy Baumeister undertook an even more ambitious, interdisciplinary review of the issue of alleged connection between low self-esteem and antisocial activity.[64] After reviewing nearly two hundred independent studies, they reached the following conclusions:

★ People with *high* self-esteem have a greater desire for self-enhancement and are both more sensitive to criticism than others and more likely to blame others rather than accept responsibility when things go wrong.

★ "The implication is that unrealistically positive self-appraisals will increase the frequency with which external ego threats are encountered. Inflated views of self should therefore *increase* the frequency of violence."

★ Aggression, crime, and violence are *not* caused by low self-esteem but by "threatened egotism." And those with "inflated, unstable, or tentative beliefs in the self's superiority" are most susceptible to threats.

★ Narcissism is correlated with disregard for others and this "contributes to willingness to behave violently."

★ "In general . . . men are more violent than women, and they also have higher self-esteem. This finding is most consistent with our hypothesis that *high self-esteem is a cause of violence* [emphasis added]."

★ Juvenile delinquents have not lower but *higher* than average self-esteem.

★ Rapists have an inflated sense of their superiority, and the *higher* a man's self-esteem, the more likely he is to commit rape and other violent crimes. (The researchers caution that high self-esteem by itself does not necessarily make one violent.)

★ Psychopaths do not suffer from low self-esteem but instead have an *inflated* sense of their own abilities and are highly reactive to perceived insults.

★ White oppression of blacks is attributable to high rather than low self-esteem.

★ People are more inclined to torture others if they have high rather than low self-esteem. (The researchers note that the training of torturers therefore aims at *increasing* their self-esteem and sense of superiority.)

★ "Rapists, murderers, wife beaters, professional hit men, tyrants, torturers, and others . . . are often violent precisely because they already believe themselves to be superior beings." The researchers conclude that therapy should not aim at raising self-esteem but instead at instilling self-control, modesty, and humility.

Proponents of self-esteem building believe that most people tend to think of themselves as inferior to others and therefore need to bolster their self-image. Studies show the reality is exactly the opposite—that is, that most people tend to think they are superior to others. "One of the most documented findings in psychology," writes psychologist Thomas Gilovich, "is that the average person purports to believe extremely flattering things about him or herself—beliefs that do not stand up to objective reality." He further notes that "a large majority of the general public thinks that they are more intelligent, more fair-minded, [and] less prejudiced . . . than the average person."

Along with other evidence, Gilovich cites a survey of one million high school students in which 70 percent rated themselves above average in leadership ability and only 2 percent rated themselves below average. In addition, 100 percent rated themselves above average in ability to get along with others, with 60 percent claiming to be in the top 10 percent and 25 percent claiming to be in the top 1 percent. Another study found that 94 percent of university professors thought themselves better at their jobs than their colleagues.[65] Yet another researcher cites a study of British motorists in which 95 percent rated themselves better drivers than the average person.[66]

In brief, research reveals that there is no correlation between self-esteem and achievement. Moreover, given the fact that most people have *too favorable* a view of their capacities and qualities, the most sensible approach is to *reign in* self-esteem rather than to enhance or indulge it.

DO PEOPLE CREATE THEIR OWN TRUTH AND REALITY?

Although Rogers and Maslow drew their ideas about truth and reality mainly from Jean Jacques Rousseau and the Romantic movement, they were also influenced by contemporary physics, in particular by Albert Einstein's theories of relativity and Walter Heisenberg's uncertainty principle. These ideas had been carelessly applied to history, anthropology, sociology, and ethics.[67] Ultimately, practitioners of these disciplines came to understand Bertrand Russell's earlier observation that "if everything were relative, there would be nothing for it to be relative to."[68] They also realized that they were inconsistent in claiming for their pronouncements the legitimacy they denied to other people's ideas; that is, they were offering their denouncement of absolute truth as an absolute truth! Moreover, they came to understand that by denying the existence of truth, they were undermining the very basis for their own scholarly investigations, the *pursuit* of truth.[69] Rogers and Maslow, however, did not achieve these insights. Neither did their disciples who created mass culture.

The fundamental test of any idea is whether it can be applied without creating insurmountable difficulties and contradictions. At the start of such a test, we need to be clear about the idea's meaning. The idea that people create their own truth and reality (also known as relativism) means that there is no requirement to which anyone's created truth and reality must conform; in other words, that whatever anyone *decides is true* will by that very fact *be true*, at least for that person. That, in turn, means that no one's truth is better than anyone else's, so no one can ever be wrong about anything. In other words, more than everyone having a right to an opinion, everyone's opinion is necessarily right![70]

This absurd view of truth has led to one of the greatest educational crimes of our time, telling legions of schoolchildren that they can be anything they want to be and do anything they want to do, that there are no limits except those they impose on themselves. Teachers who impart this nonsense have obviously never pondered the odds of a tone-deaf man singing lead tenor at the Met or a five-foot woman playing center for the Los Angeles Lakers. (Note to those unfamiliar with basketball: it is virtually a requirement that centers be in the neighborhood of seven feet tall.) No matter how pure the intentions of such teachers, they are perpetrating lunacy, and cruel lunacy at that. Life itself imposes all kinds of restrictions on us all, and the earlier in life we learn it, the less traumatic the realization will be. Some of us are positively overflowing with musical potential; others couldn't carry a tune with the combined assistance of Pavarotti, Domingo, and Carreras. Some have impressive mechanical aptitude; others couldn't program a VCR if their lives depended on it. And so on down the long list of capacities.[71]

The notion that we can create our own truth and reality ignores one of the most fundamental principles of thought, the principle of contradiction: *an idea may not be both true and false at the same time and in the same way*. Because experts in every field disagree about many issues, including fundamental ones, we need a way to make progress in our thinking, some principle or approach to give us a grip in much the same way that studded tires keep a car's wheels from spinning on ice. The principle of contradiction is such a principle. It helps us identify times when we must choose between alternative views (because both cannot be true) and those when we can profitably look to synthesize competing views. True contradictory statements are mutually exclusive.[72]

The most obvious fact about the idea that we can create our own truth and reality is that it has no application to everyday experience. If we wish to take a trip to an unfamiliar place, we don't close our eyes and imagine the route—we get a map. If our car breaks down, we don't create our own truth about what is wrong—we have a mechanic inspect it and determine what is actually wrong. If we become ill, we don't look inward for a diagnosis—we go to a physician; and if our condition is not evident, we don't settle for the physician making up *her truth* about it—we expect her to order lab work, an x-ray, or an MRI and find out *the* truth.

If relativism doesn't work in our personal lives, it's not hard to imagine the mischief it would cause in social institutions, including the following, that affect the lives of everyone.

Law. If relativism were carried to its logical conclusion, we could no longer have laws specifying that certain acts are criminal. All acts would be a matter of interpretation and therefore binding only on people who shared the interpretation. The concepts of guilt and innocence would no longer be meaningful because everyone (except, perhaps, masochists) would declare themselves innocent and that declaration would be considered unassailable. The only oath possible for witnesses in court would be to tell "*my* personal truth, *my* whole truth, and nothing but *my* truth," in which case the very idea of the oath would be meaningless because no one's truth would be false. Without an objective standard (established facts) against which to measure testimony, perjury would be impossible and cross-examination of witnesses futile.

Science. Traditionally, the aim of scholarly research has been to determine which answer to a question best fits objective reality. The general scholarly method of making this determination has been to identify a problem or issue, accumulate relevant data, interpret and analyze the data, and frame the logical conclusion. The "scientific method" varies only slightly from this general pattern, by adding a second step of framing a hypothesis and later, during the analysis phase, confirming or disconfirming it. If relativism were practiced, the traditional aim of research would be pointless and the scientific method a complete waste of time. Any notion about anatomy and physiology or the causes and cures of disease would be as good as any other; for example, bloodletting would be as acceptable a treatment for infection as administering antibiotics. And the technical equipment used to acquire objective data—microscopes, telescopes, space probes, and so on—would be consigned to the junk heap. Armchair wisdom would have no need of it.

Logic. Logic is not just another field of study—it is, as one scholar put it, "the interchangeable handle" of inquiry in all fields of study. It also is uniquely dependent on the concept of objective reality. This dependency is clearly reflected in the terminology associated with logic, in particular, and reasoned inquiry, in general.[73] *Reality* is defined as "real existence," as opposed to imagined or presumed existence; *fact* means "something that has really occurred or is actually the case"; *truth* is "conformity with fact, agreement with reality; accuracy, correctness, verity (of statement or thought)." Similarly, *dialectic* consists of "critical examination into the truth of an opinion," and *fallacy, illusion,* and *delusion* all refer to deception by false ideas and/or impressions. *Discernment* is "discrimination, judgment; keenness of intellectual perception; penetration, insight." *Wisdom* is the "capacity of judging rightly in matters relating to life and conduct; soundness of judgment in the choice of means and ends." All these definitions have meaning only in the context of a reality that exists apart from people's perceptions or beliefs. In denying such a reality, relativism rejects these definitions and thus opposes the very foundation and function of logical inquiry.

Public discussion and debate. Traditionally, these activities have been employed to dispel confusion, overcome misunderstanding, and provide a basis for resolving controversies. Such purposes are meaningful in the context of objective reality and discovered truth. However, if each person constructs his or her own reality and truth, as relativism holds, there can be no error, no confusion, and no misunderstanding. Fact and opinion are no longer clearly differentiated—indeed, opinions *become* facts if people believe them to be so; and more subtle classifications of ideas, notably *irony* and *paradox*, lose their meaning entirely. In this context, people are encouraged to view controversy as a healthy manifestation of diversity rather than as an opportunity for intellectual cooperation. Moreover, since each person is thought to have his or her own truth, other people's viewpoints are by definition irrelevant. At best, relativism replaces dialogue with serial monologue; at worst, it provides a rationale for shouting down and interrupting others.

Education. We needn't speculate what would happen if relativism were applied; we can sample the actual record. In 1970, educational psychologist William Perry argued that relativism is a normal (indeed, a higher) stage of intellectual development.[74] Others applied Perry's notion and made relativism a central tenet of teaching and learning. For example, Maxine Hairston, a college professor and author, declared, "We teach not to give students truths but to make it possible for them to discover their own."[75] A textbook titled *The Production of Reality* argues that reality "will vary across time, across cultures, and from one person to the next"; that "there is no single truth; no simple, non-contradictory reality and no single version of justice and authority"; and that "it takes insight, courage and responsibility to engage in the mindful production of reality."[76] Sociologist David Newman claims that "reality is always a product of the culture and historical period in which it exists. If we change the culture or time frame, fundamental truths also change."[77] One literary scholar, Stanley Fish, argues that all readings of a work of literature are *right*; another, Harold Bloom, argues that all readings of a work of literature are *wrong*.[78]

Similar applications of relativism produced the cafeteria-style curriculum that lets students decide what courses are "relevant" to their personal reality; the demise of grammar instruction; the transformation of history (which aims to illuminate the truth of human experience) into "social studies" (which explores cultural diversity);[79] and the shift in focus from academic substance to individual "learning styles." Most significantly, relativism has led to the substitution of "unconditional self-acceptance" for the traditional educational aim of leading students from ignorance to knowledge.

Not surprisingly, the effect of educators' embrace of relativism has been to undermine students' natural curiosity and destroy their motivation to learn. After all, if whatever one believes has the status of truth, why read textbooks and listen to lectures? And if embracing whatever notion happens to float through one's mind is as efficacious as wondering, investigating, analyzing, interpreting, and reasoning, why devote time to those difficult activities?

For centuries the great majority of people believed in objective reality and in the power of the human mind to apprehend it—for example, by digging in the ground for artifacts of past civilizations, poring over old documents in the library, conducting laboratory experiments, or simply consulting everyday experience. Most people also understood that the aim of such efforts is to discover *the* truth—that is, the most accurate representation of the reality in question. If their search produced conflicting answers, they were confident that careful analysis would reveal the right answer. This traditional view of truth is certainly more reasonable than the relativistic view that regards truth as a designer product styled according to individual tastes and reality as a kind of cosmic Play-Doh that can be molded into pleasing shapes.

ARE FEELINGS MORE RELIABLE THAN REASON?

The emphasis on feelings is not original to Humanistic Psychology but was instead borrowed from the Romantic movement that began in the seventeenth century. Moreover, the current emphasis confuses more than it clarifies.[80] As Arthur Reber explains in *The Penguin Dictionary of Psychology*, the term *feelings* is used so differently from one psychologist to another that it is difficult to find a single agreed-upon meaning. And of its near-synonym *emotion*, Reber writes, "Probably no other term in psychology shares [this term's] nondefinability with its frequency of use," adding that "it is unfortunate that a term of such importance is used in such loose subjective fashion."[81]

Despite the differences in usage, it is fair to say that the term *feelings* is virtually interchangeable with the term *emotion* and that both terms exclude the idea of reflective thought or reasoned judgment.[82] Thinking is essentially under our control; feelings are not.

To say that feelings are a natural part of our human makeup, perfectly wholesome in their own way, is unobjectionable. Passion for a righteous cause—for example, for justice or human rights—can inspire us to noble actions and sustain us in difficult moments. To say that feelings are more reliable than reason, however, is to overlook their many shortcomings.

Feelings are capricious. They can be prompted by any number of internal and/or external factors, many of which we cannot control. Internal factors such our physical and mental condition—whether we are sick or well, tired or rested, anxious or calm, apprehensive or confident. External factors such as weather outdoors, the temperature and humidity indoors, light/ darkness, background noise, the demeanor and behavior of the people around us. Even a single factor can prompt an inappropriate response; a combination of factors can compound the problem.

Feelings are often contradictory. We may simultaneously feel conflicting feelings. For example, after a heated discussion with someone, we may feel both offended at what they said and ashamed of what we said. When a loved one has escaped mortal danger caused by foolishness, we may feel both anger and relief. If a friend is convicted of a crime, we may feel both pity and contempt toward him. In such cases, the advice "follow your feelings" makes no sense because they are pulling us in different directions. We must choose between them and the basis for choosing must be something other than the feelings themselves.

Feelings can distort perception. When we feel depressed, afraid, angry, or suspicious, the world appears negative and threatening. We expect the worst rather than the best from people—vice rather than virtue, hostility rather than good will, obstruction rather than cooperation. Conversely, when we are elated or euphoric, everyone and everything seems positive and every person trustworthy. In either case, mood is an unreliable measure of reality.[83]

Feelings are easily manipulated. Hucksters, propagandists, and the creators of advertisements know this very well. That is why they use emotional appeals that short-circuit thought and make us desire the product or service. By keeping us feeling rather than thinking, they discourage questions such as

"How valid are the claims for this product or service?" "How does it compare with competing products or services?" "Do I really need it?" "Can I afford it?" and "Can I get it cheaper elsewhere?" In recent years propagandists have come to realize that this approach can be as effective in selling their social and political agendas as it is in selling goods and services. For example, they use test groups to discover which words or phrases evoke the feelings they want from their audience, and then fill their presentations with those words.

Following feelings invites self-deception. When guided by reason, we have a way to assess our behavior by deciding whether our evidence was sufficient and our interpretation and judgment were sound. We can therefore determine whether we are responsible for unfortunate consequences. In contrast, when guided by feelings, we have no way to determine whether we are at fault. We are therefore led to denial or shifting blame to others. (Consider how many people deny that smoking, sunbathing without sunscreen, and unprotected promiscuous sex are dangerous, and how many others blame their obesity on fast-food restaurants.) This tendency to self-deception is also present both in the heralded category of feelings known as "intuition"[84] and in matters of morality.[85]

Following feelings reinforces prejudice. We may arrive at a prejudiced view either by thought or emotion. Because thinking-based prejudice is based on faulty reasoning, it is open to correction by reason—for example, by being shown that the judgment about *all* members of the group fits only *some* members and is therefore unreasonable. However, emotion-based prejudice is unresponsive to reason because it is not based on reason. That is why people who trust their feelings tend to maintain their prejudices.

Following feelings leads to impulsiveness. Reasoning is a deliberate process involving examining, interpreting, and evaluating ideas and actions. Feeling, in contrast, is spontaneous, unrestrained, and heedless of consequences. Accordingly, if we are guided by our feelings, we are more likely to take unnecessary risks, to reject helpful criticism, and to speak without first considering the impact of our words.

Feelings are oblivious to logic. "The power of reason," American psychologist Harry Overstreet noted, "is the power to see logical relationships of similarity and difference, of cause and effect, of relationships in time and space, of quantity and quality, of the subjective and the objective, of importance and unimportance."[86] Reason thus enables us to assess events and offer a rationale for our assessment. In contrast, emotion permits us to say only "This is how I feel about that."

Following feelings hinders personal growth. Ideally, as we grow older and add to our store of experience, we become more knowledgeable, wiser, more discerning. However, this can happen only if we are able to profit from our experiences, and to do that requires reflecting on our experience, evaluating it, and discerning its meaning.[87] Figure 4.1 diagrams the superiority of thought to emotion in achieving this goal.

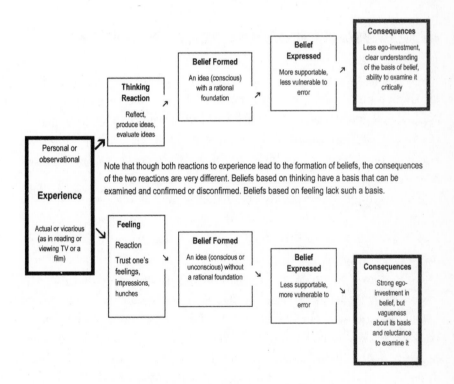

Figure 4.1. Comparison of Intellectual and Emotional Reactions.

Nothing said thus far about feelings should be taken to mean that feelings have no value. Many feelings are noble and therefore should be cherished and cultivated; rejecting them would diminish our humanity. Other feelings, however, are ignoble and should be resisted and overcome. The problem is, we cannot know whether a particular feeling in a specific situation is noble or ignoble until we evaluate it. Simply said, feelings need to be tested before being trusted. And testing is a function of thinking.

Given all the shortcomings of feelings noted above, anyone who chooses to be guided by feelings rather than by reason runs the considerable risk of becoming what one writer termed "the very slave of circumstance and impulse borne by every breath" and another called "a devotee of the great God Whim."[88]

ARE ALL FORMS OF SEXUAL EXPRESSION NATURAL AND WHOLESOME?

In answering this question it will be helpful to recall our chapter 2 discussion of Alfred Kinsey's work. Kinsey's dual studies claimed that homosexuality, adult-child contact, and even bestiality are all as normal as heterosexuality; that incest can be satisfying and enriching; and that the sexual prohibitions that have been accepted for hundreds of years are not only unjustified but harmful.

Kinsey made these claims under the banner of science—that is, he claimed that his research provided indisputable documentation for them— and it took years before the quality of his research and the validity of his findings were subjected to scrutiny. By that time his disciples, notably Hugh Hefner, had succeeded in demonizing traditional sexual morality and embedding Kinsey's views in mass culture. Magazine articles about sexual functioning tripled, and the focus changed from sexual ethics to the "quality" of sexual activity and encouragement of sex outside marriage. Soap opera depictions, too, overwhelmingly emphasized extramarital sex.[89] Today, sexual content is even more pervasive in TV, cinema, and print and includes a "trend toward portraying children and sometimes even babies as sex objects."[90]

Many years after Kinsey's views of sex became an integral part of mass culture, Kinsey was revealed to have been more a zealot and a *pervert*—

no lesser term fits his behavior—than a scientist. A masochist from child-hood, he was fond of inserting foreign objects in his penis. In choosing his research staff, he sought out people with sexual preferences that matched his own and sexually harassed them by "demand[ing] access to them and, occasionally, their wives." As all his coauthors—Paul Gebhard, Wardell Pomeroy, and Clyde Martin—later admitted, he focused his research dis-proportionately on homosexuals, prostitutes, sexual adventurists, and child molesters. He collaborated with active child molesters, including Rex King, who had about eight hundred sexual contacts with children, and Fritz von Balluseck, a Nazi officer who had sexually abused children first in concen-tration camps and then after the war.[91] Moreover, he used his research to find his own, mostly homosexual, partners.[92]

It is noteworthy that while Kinsey was conducting his research, Abraham Maslow (to his great credit) privately warned him that his use of volunteers would inflate the statistics on unconventional sexual behavior and yield untypical and therefore unscientific results. Later, Maslow con-ducted some research of his own and proved that "the whole basis for Kinsey's statistics was . . . shaky." Any reputable scientist, when presented with such fundamental challenges, would give them careful attention, but Kinsey completely ignored them.[93] (Unfortunately Maslow's criticism was not discovered until much later.)

Other analysts of Kinsey's research found "evident throughout [his] books . . . the view that sex is to be enjoyed as early in life as possible, more frequently, with a greater number of partners of the same or opposite gender, and without the guilt of Judeo-Christian cultural restraints." Also, that sex with animals is natural and that those who engage in it feel guilty only when they later learn of the social taboo against it; and that sexual contact between young girls and older men is not likely (in Kinsey's words) "to do the child any appreciable harm if the child's parents do not become disturbed"; and that such activity could even "contribute favorably to [the girls'] later socio-sexual development."[94]

The self-serving bias and intellectual dishonesty of Kinsey's method-ology are sufficient cause to seriously question his views. Nevertheless, by themselves they are insufficient to discredit the idea that all forms of sexual expression are natural and wholesome or its corollary that sexual restraint is harmful. For that determination, a different kind of evidence is necessary.

The terms *natural* and *wholesome*, as applied to human behavior, have come to mean little more than "whatever people do." By this relativistic standard, there is no such thing as right or wrong behavior, and everything people do is beneficial. Traditionally, however, the terms had more restrictive meanings based on the idea that human nature is more than animal nature and includes *intellect*, the ability to discern the consequences of actions, and *will*, the power to resist unworthy instincts and urges and to choose behavior responsibly.

In the traditional view, we should desire for ourselves and for other people what is good for us and for them. In other words, we should honor the principle of respect for persons, which includes the following three requirements: "First, that each and every person should be regarded as worthy of sympathetic consideration, and should be so treated. Second, that no person should be regarded by another as a mere possession, or used as a mere instrument, or treated as a mere obstacle, to another's satisfaction. And third, that persons are not and ought never to be treated in any undertaking as mere expendables."[95]

Some cultures define person narrowly, meaning, for example, only a member of one's own tribe. Yet whether the person is narrowly or broadly defined, respect for persons is nevertheless honored in virtually every human culture. In the traditional view, it is also understood that the appeal of an action or the temptation it poses is not a reliable measure of its rightness—evil can appear to be good and vice versa.

The principle of respect for persons provides a way to judge sexual behavior: a sexual act is "natural" or "wholesome" if it does not harm or degrade the people involved.[96] Thus, regardless of the attraction adultery may hold, we can classify it as wrong because it violates the vow of fidelity; it also carries the risk of destroying a marriage and, where children are involved, a family. Incest is wrong because it violates the parental obligation to protect children from predation. Sex with children or the mentally impaired is wrong because it takes unfair advantage of their incapacity and risks causing them physical and/or emotional harm.[97] Sadism is wrong because it treats another human being as an object for one's own gratification; masochism, because it violates one's own dignity and does violence to oneself. Promiscuity is wrong because it is inimical to the characteristic that differentiates human from animal sexuality—emotional intimacy.

Although it is possible to take issue with one or more of these traditional moral views, it is clear that the traditional perspective is more mature and responsible than the relativistic Kinseyan view because it acknowledges that consequences, vows, and responsibilities *matter* in human relationships.

Renowned historian Arnold Toynbee offered a more pragmatic argument against the Kinseyan view of sexuality, and he presented it during the first wave of that view's impact on mass culture.[98] Rather than focusing on the morality of Kinsey's view of sex, Toynbee addressed its short- and long-term social consequences. In doing so, he drew upon his exceptional knowledge of the rise and fall of civilizations. He began by noting that the achievements of Western civilization are in great measure explained by "postponing the age of sexual awakening," thereby making it possible to extend formal education. He then when on to argue that "premature awareness of sex" fostered in modern times can be so distracting to the education process as to represent "intellectual suicide." Although he praised the provision of college and graduate school opportunities for all, he warned "we shall be plowing the sands if we do not simultaneously revert to our grandparents' practice of prolonging the age of sexual innocence."

Other defenses of sexual restraint as opposed to sexual indulgence include French existentialist philosopher Albert Camus's argument that whereas sexuality tends to be a "kind of opium," chastity "is connected with personal progress."[99] Also, Viktor Frankl's observation, based on his psychiatric clinical experience, that "sexual 'pleasure-seeking'" leads to "sexual neuroses." He explains that "the more a male patient wishes to demonstrate his potency, the more surely he is doomed to failure," and "the more a female patient wishes to demonstrate to herself that she is capable of orgasm, the more likely she is to wind up with frigidity."[100]

But there is another, even more powerful argument for sexual restraint and it goes to the heart of our human nature. Without question, we are sexual creatures and in most of us the sex urge is strong. But equally strong, perhaps more so, is the desire to love and be loved. The two urges are profoundly intertwined. The physical intimacy of the sex act implies metaphysical intimacy: two-in-one flesh suggests two-in-one spirit. This is not just idealistic speculation, and the proof is revealed in the disappointment, traditionally felt by women but increasingly by men as well, when a relationship they regarded as more than sexual is revealed to have been nothing more than that for the other person.

Love quite naturally invites sexual expression.[101] Likewise, sexual expression invites love. Even after half a century of conditioning to believe that sex and love are not strongly linked, sexual relationships still tend to produce emotional bonds and the desire for exclusivity. The reason adulterers typically find it awkward to have sex with their spouses is not so much that they have been unfaithful as that they have *transferred* fidelity and intimacy to their partners in adultery. This transfer is often the principal reason for divorce.[102]

This is not to say one cannot simultaneously have sex and avoid emotional bonding and exclusivity. Promiscuous people, predators, and prostitutes do so all the time, but they do so at the expense of genuine intimacy. By rejecting restraint, they frustrate the fundamental human desire to love and be loved. This is hardly the accomplishment Kinsey and his followers would have us think. It is, rather, a tragic loss.

THE IDEAS IN COMBINATION

So far we have discussed the ideas advanced by Humanistic Psychology separately and exposed their *individual* flaws. But those ideas are often intertwined and, taken together, constitute a more or less comprehensive view of human nature with the idea that human beings are inherently wise and good as the foundation. Here is how the comprehensive view might be expressed:

> *Because human beings are inherently wise and good*, their highest need is to actualize these qualities.[103] Moreover, these inherent qualities entitle them to

high self-esteem; enable them to create their own truth; justify implicit trust in their feelings; and guarantee that their sexual expression, whatever form it may take, is unquestionably natural and wholesome.

Humanistic Psychology's composite view is as deeply ingrained in mass culture as are its component ideas—and every bit as mistaken. It amounts to what G. K. Chesterton called the "most horrible of all the horrible religions—the worship of the god within." He reasoned as follows: "That Jones shall worship the god within him turns out ultimately to mean that Jones shall worship Jones. Let Jones worship the sun or moon, anything rather than the inner light; let Jones worship cats or crocodiles, if he can find any in his street, but not the God within . . . [because by] insisting that God is inside man, man is always inside himself."[104]

Such self-centering brings not freedom but imprisonment, not empowerment but impotence, not fulfillment but frustration and anxiety. Paradoxically, Chesterton argued, one becomes larger only by having the humility to see one's smallness. (This argument recalls Socrates's observation that acknowledging one's ignorance is the first step toward knowledge and wisdom.) Such criticism of the Romantic view embedded in modern psychology is not limited to philosophers. Don Campbell, president of the American Psychological Association in the 1970s, claimed that psychology is largely responsible for producing "underinhibited, overly narcissistic and overly selfish individuals."[105]

We have seen that the central tenet of Hereditarianism and the major tenets of Humanistic Psychology, whether considered individually or in combination, fail the test of everyday experience and the more demanding test of formal analysis. This explains why their embrace by mass culture has created a host of social problems. And it makes more urgent the challenge of rediscovering and reaffirming vital truths about human nature. Before we turn to that challenge, however, we will devote a chapter to the vexing questions that continue to baffle contemporary social analysts.

5

MORE VEXING QUESTIONS

We have seen how Social Darwinism undermined the traditional view of human nature and produced Hereditarianism, the pessimistic perspective on human intelligence that became a central tenet of late nineteenth-century and early twentieth-century psychology. We have measured the profound influence of that perspective on American social institutions, in particular, the debasement of education and the spawning of Progressivism and the Eugenics movement.

We have also noted how Humanistic Psychology, instead of correcting the reigning pessimism, replaced it with an absurd optimism that divinized human nature, rode the wave of technological innovation, became embedded in the emerging mass culture, and produced a wide array of social problems.

Finally, we have exposed the fundamental fallacies of both Hereditarianism and Humanistic Psychology. But some vexing questions remain, including some raised by our analysis. In a number of instances, where the fallacious idea should lead to one behavior, it instead leads to a very different behavior. The most interesting—and vexing—of these instances are the following:

★ Why are many who preach tolerance and civility so intolerant and uncivil?

★ Why do educators who believe that people create their own truth and reality force their personal views on students?

★ Given the dominance of the extravagantly optimistic Humanistic Psychology, why is Hereditarian pessimism about human intelligence still present in education and business?

★ Why do government officials blame the medical, energy, banking, and health-insurance industries for problems that government itself caused?

★ Why do elected officials curtail the individual rights and freedom of choice they claim are fundamental?

★ Why are so many of the decisions and actions of elected officials woefully at odds with common sense and/or elementary fairness?

★ Given the supposed importance of self-actualization, why does the government pursue policies that make success difficult? And why is it intent on "redistributing" the wealth of successful people to the unsuccessful?

★ Why have many *conservatives* set aside their social and fiscal convictions and supported liberal initiatives?

★ How did Progressivism regain its influence in recent decades?

★ Why did the one of the most conservative institutions in history, the Catholic Church, ignore its own intellectual tradition and embrace Progressivism's view of social justice?

Before addressing these inconsistencies individually, let us note one overarching reason for all of them: the lamentable failure of Humanistic Psychology to recognize the most obvious feature of human behavior, ego.

THE EGO FACTOR

The ego factor is the tendency for people to perceive themselves and all things associated with them as better than other people and things. Though the ego factor is sometimes set aside temporarily, especially when we envy others, it is our *default perspective* on ourselves and the world. In less self-absorbed ages, the force of ego was underscored by philosophers and lampooned by wits.[1] A distinguished member of the latter group, Ambrose Bierce, was referring to the ego factor when he offered these tongue-in-cheek definitions in his *Devil's Dictionary*:

Absurdity—a statement of belief manifestly inconsistent with one's own
    opinion

Bigot—one who is obstinately and zealously attached to an opinion that
    you do not entertain

Egotist—a person of low taste, more interested in himself than in me

I—the first letter of the alphabet, the first word of the language, the
    first thought of the mind, the first object of affection

Self-esteem—an erroneous appraisement

Rogers, Maslow, and their associates may have been unfamiliar
with such witticisms. They may also have been ignorant of more serious
philosophical commentary because philosophy lay outside their academic
training. But they certainly should have been aware of the considerable
research and commentary *within their own field* on egocentrism, ethnocentrism,
and narcissism—that is, on the characteristic tendency of many people to
overvalue their own opinions and values and to ignore or undervalue other
people's. Before Humanistic Psychology gained prominence, experimental
psychologists provided an abundance of evidence demonstrating the role
of the ego in human affairs.

The ego factor manifests itself early in life and endures ever after in the
form of "mine is better" thinking. Children believe their moms are prettier,
their dads stronger, their bikes faster than other children's. Adults regard
their religious and political beliefs and their opinions about all manner of
things as better than other people's. Although often subtle in its expression,
the ego factor is powerful enough to convert the best-intentioned egali-
tarian ideas into affirmations of one's own superiority.

Here is how the process works with the six central ideas of Humanistic
Psychology:

Original Ideas	Personalized Version	"Mine Is Better" View
Human nature is inherently wise and good	I am inherently wise and good	I am wiser and better than other people
Self-actualization is the highest human need	Self-actualization is my highest need	My self-actualization is more important than other people's
Self-esteem is prerequisite to achievement	Self-esteem is prerequisite to my achievement	My self-esteem is more important than other people's
People create their own truth and reality	I create my own truth and reality	My truth and reality are more valid than other people's
Feelings are more reliable than reason	My feelings are more reliable than my reason	My feelings are more reliable than other people's
All sexual expression is natural and wholesome	My sexual expression is natural and wholesome	My sexual expression is more natural and wholesome than other people's

Note that with the ego dominant, everything is about *me, my* desires, *my* needs, *my* rights. The ego is difficult to control even in the best of circumstances, but when exalted, even divinized, in this way it is virtually impossible to control. In addition to increasing our infatuation with our own opinions and beliefs, such self-centeredness blinds us to other people's insights. Recall the research findings of Thomas Gilovich presented in chapter 4. He concluded that, "One of the most documented findings in psychology is that the average person purports to believe extremely flattering things about himself/herself—beliefs that do not stand up to objective reality" and "a large majority of the general public thinks that they are more intelligent, more fair-minded, [and] less prejudiced . . . than the average person."[2]

Humanistic Psychology's message to such people has been: "Guess what. You haven't been flattering yourself *enough*. You are even more intelligent, more fair-minded and less prejudiced than you thought!" This is hardly an exaggeration. Consider author Thomas Moore's praise of self-adulation. Narcissism, Moore argues, is "not a personality defect, but the soul trying to find its otherness." He goes on to say that "it is wrong to be negative toward the ego and even egotism. The ego needs to be loved, requires attention, and wants exposure. That is part of its nature. . . . The narcissistic person tries very hard to be loved, but he never succeeds because he doesn't realize yet that he has to love himself as other before he himself can be loved."[3]

No one who follows Moore's advice is likely to have much interest in overcoming weaknesses in her own views or recognizing insights in other people's views.

To put the matter simply, in the traditional view the ego was believed to require a strong leash. Humanistic Psychology ignored that perspective and the evidence supporting it and *not only unleashed the ego but fed it steroids!*[4] That was every bit as irresponsible as prescribing booze for an alcoholic or porn for a pervert. It should come as no surprise that millions of people have developed an exaggerated view of their rights and privileges, an unrealistic expectation of how others should treat them, and a tendency to be hostile toward anyone who does not meet that expectation. The following list provides more specific examples.

When the abstract "human nature is inherently wise and good" becomes the concrete "I am wiser and better than other people," we consider other people's intelligence and virtue inferior to our own and regard their ideas as unworthy of our attention. The more their perspective disagrees with ours, the more we take offense at it and them.

When the abstract "self-actualization is the highest human need" becomes the concrete "My self-actualization is more important than other people's," we value not only our rights over other people's rights, but also our *desires* over their *rights*, and we feel justified in doing whatever is necessary to achieve our goals.

When the abstract "self-esteem is prerequisite to achievement" becomes "my self-esteem is more important than other people's," we expect that others should agree with and praise us (without, of course, any reciprocal obligation on our part). If they do not meet this expectation, we are apt to be outraged.

When the abstract "people create their own truth and reality" becomes "my truth and reality are more valid than other people's," we tend to believe that those who do not share our views lack intelligence, integrity, or both.

When the abstract "feelings are more reliable than reason" becomes "my feelings are more reliable than other people's," we expect other people to respect not only our feelings but also the views that derive from them. We also consider it inappropriate for them to ask us to support our views with evidence.

When the abstract "all sexual expression is natural and wholesome" becomes "my sexual expression is more natural and wholesome than other people's," we are disinclined to discuss or debate sexual ethics or related legal issues and take offense at even mild criticism of our sexual beliefs and behavior.

That uncontrolled ego can work great mischief is not a new discovery. Famous historian Arnold Toynbee made the following observation:

> I am convinced, myself, that man's fundamental problem is his human egocentricity. . . . All the great historic philosophies and religions have been concerned, first and foremost, with the overcoming of egocentricity. At first sight, Buddhism and Christianity and Islam and Judaism may appear to be very different from each other. But, when you look beneath the surface, you will find that all of them are addressing themselves primarily to the individual human psyche or soul; they are trying to persuade it to overcome its own self-centeredness and they are offering it the means for achieving this."[5]

By ignoring the ego factor, Humanistic Psychology increased the likelihood of contradictions between its ideals and goals and actual behavior. With this fact in mind, it is easier to answer the questions posed at the beginning of this chapter.

WHY ARE MANY WHO PREACH TOLERANCE AND CIVILITY SO INTOLERANT AND UNCIVIL?[6]

Examples of this contradiction between principle and practice are plentiful. Turn on the evening news and you will find one or more instances in which an elected official or commentator laments the decline of civility and then, often in the next breath, calls others racists, homophobes, or fascists; or uses vile sexual references to describe them; or wishes that grave illness or assassination be visited upon them.

Other examples of intolerance are found on college campuses that ban speakers of one political or intellectual persuasion or that enact codes broad enough to stifle any speech that campus officials disapprove of. One college banned any speech or action that causes a loss of self-esteem or "a vague sense of danger." Other colleges forbade utterances that show "insensitivity to the experiences of women," "inconsiderate jokes," and stories "experienced by others as harassing."[7]

Because tolerance, respect for diversity, and civility are not only consistent with, but also a necessary corollary to Humanistic Psychology's claim that people are inherently wise and good, it would be reasonable to expect practice to reflect principle: if my neighbor is inherently wise and good, I owe him nothing less than unconditional respect. Why, then, are *in*tolerance and *in*civility so prevalent? Because another of Humanistic Psychology's claims gets in the way—the idea that it is better to follow feelings than reason. This idea justifies withholding the respect I owe my neighbor on the slenderest of bases, *whim*. (Journalist John Stossel has observed that "there is no end to how much speech may be censored, because under sexual-harassment law, *the offended get to decide* which speech is offensive."[8])

Tolerance and civility become issues only where there are differences of race, creed, ethnicity, or opinion. (To be upset with those who share our view would be bizarre.) The greater the difference, the more likely we are to *feel* threatened by others and the more inclined we are to respond intolerantly and uncivilly. If we think critically about that feeling, we can understand its shortcomings and thus increase our chances of achieving tolerance. But Humanistic Psychology cautions *against* reasoned thought, and therefore prevents us from reaching the very goal it recommends.

When we see people who preach tolerance and civility ridiculing others—for example, commentators indiscriminately charging "racism, sexism, and homophobia," or mocking other people's religious beliefs— our first reaction may be to consider them hypocritical. A kinder and often more accurate interpretation is that they are simply confused by the contradictions of Humanistic Psychology. Moreover, that, having received little or no training in forming, framing, and defending their own arguments (thanks to the continuing legacy of Hereditarianism in education), they have no means of engaging those who disagree with them other than demonization.

WHY DO EDUCATORS WHO BELIEVE THAT PEOPLE CREATE THEIR OWN TRUTH AND REALITY FORCE THEIR PERSONAL VIEWS ON STUDENTS?

In such cases, we would expect teachers to go out of their way to *withhold* their personal views and encourage students to develop their own. There are several reasons that many teachers fail in this regard. The most obvious one is that they were probably taught this relativistic view of truth when they were students, accepted what they were told, and never thought further about it. (If they had examined the idea critically, they would have realized, as we saw in the last chapter, that it is false.)

Another reason is the ego factor—in other words, however deeply the educators believe that truth and reality are personally constructed, they believe even more deeply that their ideas are superior to other people's. Chances are that this belief has been reinforced (as if it needed reinforcement) in their own childhood when parents and teachers sought to raise their self-esteem by telling them how wise and wonderful they were. Now that they are teaching others, they continue to believe that *their personal truth trumps other people's truths*. The larger their egos, the more intent they are to impose their opinions on others. Some teachers proselytize in matters far outside their own subject areas—English teachers offering sermons on religion and politics, for example, and science teachers on ethics. And woe to students who dare to question what they say.

A third reason many teachers impose their views on students is that they don't know any way of teaching other than the way they were taught, and most of them were taught by the method known as mind stuffing—that is, telling students what to think. So even if they wanted to use a different approach, they would have to invest the time to learn it and suffer the initial awkwardness of applying it in the classroom. It is much easier to do as they have always done, and as most of their colleagues do, and ignore the contradiction between their relativistic belief and their autocratic behavior.

GIVEN THE DOMINANCE OF THE EXTRAVAGANTLY OPTIMISTIC HUMANISTIC PSYCHOLOGY, WHY IS HEREDITARIAN PESSIMISM ABOUT HUMAN INTELLIGENCE STILL PRESENT IN EDUCATION AND BUSINESS?

In case some readers disbelieve such pessimism is still present, let's begin by demonstrating that it is.

The teaching method employed in most classrooms, which most readers will recall, is the teacher "telling information" and then measuring how much of it students have retained. In this scheme, the teacher is not a fellow learner but the source or fount of knowledge, and the process of education consists in the transfer of that knowledge from his or her head to those of the students. Some of the information that is told comes solely from the teacher and the rest is provided by a textbook. In the most pathetic and painful form of classroom practice, followed not only in the lower schools but in many college classrooms as well, the students first read the text and then listen to the teacher *read it again* in class. (Twice told, alas, does not equal better remembered.) Periodically during the course, and again at the end, students are tested to see how much knowledge they can regurgitate. The "objective" form of most tests tends to be very restrictive: one must choose among a, b, c, or d; or fill in the blank with the phrasing from the book or lecture; or answer true or false.

That is the way education is today and the way it has been for seventy-five or so years. There is little or no effort to follow Francis Bacon's advice—to neither accept nor reject what is presented but instead to "weigh and consider" it. Nor is there any effort or attempt to train students in the activities one scholar described as the essential components of reading: "collating, criticizing, interpreting, questioning, comprehending, comparing."[9] In fact, students are discouraged from pursuing different lines of thought than the "official" ones in the textbook or lecture, and the form of the tests does not allow for challenging the assumptions underlying a question, adding a qualification, or most important of all, presenting a rationale for one's answer.

In short, contemporary education still reflects the pessimistic belief that intelligence is fixed and thinking skill cannot be increased through instruction or practice. The reason is that Humanistic Psychology did nothing to correct the central error of Hereditarianism and bring genuine optimism to education. All it did was introduce lessons designed to inflate students' self-esteem—"you can be anything, accomplish anything you want to," "you are intelligent, talented, admirable," and so on. The method that was employed for these lessons was the same as in all mind stuffing—to *tell* them to students as information to be remembered.

As to why Hereditarian pessimism is still present in business, the answer is that most business leaders still embrace the top-down "scientific management" model, under which management makes the decisions and workers carry them out, more or less mindlessly. In extreme cases, decision making is reserved to executives only; in others, it is delegated to midlevel management and even to supervisory personnel. But decision making is seldom, if ever, the province of workers. Of course, no company has banners proclaiming "Only executives have the ability to think" or directives stipulating "Workers need to be told exactly what to do, down to the last detail, and must never depart from those instructions." There is no need for such communication—the messages are *assumed*.

But what of those companies that finally embraced W. Edwards Deming's idea of quality management, after rejecting it and losing market dominance to the Japanese who (as explained in chapter 1) had accepted it earlier? Didn't those companies recognize the problem-solving potential of all employees and involve them in decision making? More often than not, no! Many responded like the large energy company I was acquainted with some years ago. That company emblazoned Deming's fourteen points on its lobby wall in foot-high letters, issued company-wide memos proclaiming his principles, and then proceeded to do business as usual, excluding workers from problem-solving activities.

In the early 1990s, I did consulting work with a number of companies, offering a quality-control approach derived from my area of specialization, creative and critical thinking. One of my training exercises was to organize small problem-solving groups, each composed of one executive, one mid-level manager, and two hourly wage employees. My goal was not only to introduce them to a specific problem-solving model but, equally important, to cultivate in the executives and managers an awareness that employees closest to the problems often provide the best solutions. This was one of Deming's most valuable insights and my workshops fostered its application.

I especially remember one company, a midsize bank, that I worked with. In a private meeting at the end of my consulting period, the bank president thanked me for providing his employees with the tools for implementing a successful quality program. He then added that, though he hoped they could continue using my approach, he was not certain they could because the bank's directors had just hired a large and expensive consulting firm to install a different, system-wide quality program. I asked him a single question: "Will the program involve midlevel management and hourly employees, and not just top management, in decision making?" Knowing from our prior discussions the import of the question, he answered sheepishly, "No, only upper management will be involved." Such experiences explain why, toward the end of his life, W. Edwards Deming said of American business leaders, "They still don't get it."[10]

WHY DO GOVERNMENT OFFICIALS BLAME THE MEDICAL, ENERGY, BANKING, AND HEALTH-INSURANCE INDUSTRIES FOR PROBLEMS THAT GOVERNMENT ITSELF CAUSED?

The obvious answer is that blaming leaders of industries for social problems is an extension of blaming parents and teachers for their personal problems. Less obvious, but no less relevant, is that the inflation of egos has led government officials to believe that they are more qualified than trained professionals to deal with matters in which they have no experience—for example, managing the banking, auto-making, and healthcare industries. Economist Thomas Sowell terms this self-congratulatory arrogance "the vision of the anointed" and believes that it has been responsible for replacing the insights of centuries and even millennia with "unsubstantiated theories and self-flattering fancies."[11]

WHY DO ELECTED OFFICIALS CURTAIL THE INDIVIDUAL RIGHTS AND FREEDOM OF CHOICE THEY CLAIM ARE FUNDAMENTAL?

The list of examples of such curtailment is long and growing. Here is a brief sampling: laws requiring the use of seatbelts and motorcycle helmets; restrictions on the purchase of firearms; bans on smoking, which in some cases extend beyond public places and into people's own homes; the outlawing of religious displays, notably at Christmas, and references to God at graduations; placing restrictions on salt, "trans fats," and high-caloric content in restaurant food; mandating fuel-efficiency standards for automobiles; and assessing financial penalties for not purchasing healthcare insurance.

This contradiction is rooted in the conflict between America's founding documents and Hereditarianism. The former claim that every individual possesses inalienable rights; the latter asserts the incapacity of the masses to exercise such rights intelligently. Several generations of Americans have grown up believing that the masses are intellectually deficient and therefore cannot be trusted to manage their own affairs. Given the exaltation of ego contributed by Humanistic Psychology and the inflation of ego that generally attends election to public office, it is hardly surprising that increasing numbers of today's elected officials believe they have the right, and even the sacred obligation, to exercise control over other people's lives.

WHY ARE SO MANY OF THE DECISIONS AND ACTIONS OF ELECTED OFFICIALS WOEFULLY AT ODDS WITH COMMON SENSE AND/OR ELEMENTARY FAIRNESS?

Decisions and actions that fit this description include the following: Denying California farmers the water necessary to grow their crops in order to save the endangered "delta smelt." Treating foreign terrorists as common criminals, giving them the rights of US citizens, and trying them in civilian courts. Forcing banks to lend money to people who could not repay the loans and then blaming the banks for the resulting financial disaster. Charging illegal aliens in-state tuition at colleges and universities while legal residents from neighboring states are charged higher out-of-state tuition.

The list could be continued: Legislators passing transformative health-care legislation without first reading it and trying to solve an out-of-control federal deficit by spending trillions more dollars. Government spokespeople flying around the country in fuel-guzzling private jets to browbeat citizens into purchasing fuel-efficient vehicles. The refusal of government officials to reconsider the issue of global warming even though many knowledgeable people believe that it is at best a mistaken notion and at worst a scam. The refusal to accept the fact, documented in both the Kennedy and Reagan administrations, that lowering tax rates generates more tax revenue. The decision to overcome past racial discrimination by legislating new programs of racial discrimination (e.g., "affirmative action").[12] Finally, and most pathetically, elected officials' denouncing as extremists the individuals and groups who object to such absurdities.

Such decisions and actions are based on a potent blend of Hereditarianism and Humanistic Psychology. Elected officials easily fall into the trap of believing that (a) their constituents are intellectually deficient and must be led like sheep; (b) they, the elected officials, are qualified to be shepherds (a notion confirmed by their elected status and magnified by their egos); and (c) logic is no longer applicable, so reality can be manipulated to suit their fancy.

GIVEN THE SUPPOSED IMPORTANCE OF SELF-ACTUALIZATION, WHY DOES THE GOVERNMENT PURSUE POLICIES THAT MAKE SUCCESS DIFFICULT? AND WHY IS IT INTENT ON "REDISTRIBUTING" THE WEALTH OF SUCCESSFUL PEOPLE TO THE UNSUCCESSFUL?

Given the persistence of the notion that self-actualization is the highest human need, we might expect government to pursue policies that provide tax incentives to entrepreneurs and private companies. (Private companies, after all, are noteworthy examples of the activation of human potential.)

Yet instead, elected officials attempt to punish successful people by confiscating a large percentage of their earnings and "redistributing" the money to the less productive, and by placing private industries—including the finance, auto, and healthcare industries—under public control. Why this contradiction?

Early twentieth-century Progressives were not familiar with the concept of self-actualization. However, they were aware of the deprivation of the masses, in many cases caused by exploitation by the wealthy and powerful, and their concern produced many laudable social reforms. Unfortunately, they also embraced the Hereditarian view that most people are intellectually deficient and the associated fear that the common gene pool would be polluted if the most deficient individuals were permitted to reproduce. (This perspective led many to support Eugenics programs.)

When Humanistic Psychology replaced that pessimistic view with one at the opposite extreme, it also introduced the concept of self-actualization. The relationship of that concept to the central theme may be stated as follows: *People are born wise and good and self-actualization is their highest need. Any failure to express their inherent wisdom and goodness or to achieve self-actualization is not their fault but the fault of society.*

Late twentieth-century Progressives not only retained the original opposition to exploitation, they also added the perspective of Humanistic Psychology and expanded the rationale for their political programs: *If people are inherently good and wise, then everyone should enjoy similar prosperity ("equality of outcome"), and where some are poor, the rich must have stolen from them and should be held to account. Moreover, exploitation does not occur in one area or one industry or another; it is in the very nature of society. And it not only prevents people's inherent wisdom and goodness from shining forth, it also blocks their highest and most human need, self-actualization. Such exploitation is not just a problem, it is also a crisis that calls for immediate, drastic, transformative action.*

But there is more. The new Progressives were educated in a school system that still harbored the Hereditarian fallacy that the masses are hopelessly deficient in intellectual capacity, even as it preached the contradictory notion that everyone is wise and good and deserving of boundless self-esteem! Given that background and belief system—mutually contradictory as its components may be—and the power of unleashed egos, it is not surprising that Progressives adopted the following credo:

> Because I and those who share my views are much wiser than others, we should manage their self-actualization. We should also be in charge of the redistribution of wealth, deciding which people and corporations are entitled to government largesse and which corporations should be punished by being taken over or managed. Moreover, we should also be exempt from the rules and regulations we create for others, including our massive healthcare program, because of our meritorious service to others.

The fact that this credo, for many people, may take the form of a feeling or attitude rather than a carefully formulated belief does not diminish its influence over their behavior. In fact, it may be all the more powerful for being unconscious.

WHY HAVE MANY CONSERVATIVES SET ASIDE THEIR SOCIAL AND FISCAL CONVICTIONS AND SUPPORTED LIBERAL INITIATIVES?

The belief systems of liberalism and conservatism have changed a great deal over the past century. For example, classic liberals were opposed to large government and in favor of the free market, positions that today are associated with conservatism. Modern liberals, sometimes called "welfare liberals," favor government involvement and even intervention in social and economic matters. They also differ from classic liberals on issues such as same-sex marriage, abortion, the death penalty, and the place of religion in public life. In a real sense, modern liberalism has *become* Progressivism. Early Progressivism's emphasis on social reform played a role in the change, but the more immediate, efficient cause was Humanistic Psychology's rejection of traditional philosophic and religious values.

This explains how today's liberals came to embrace viewpoints that liberals of the past rejected. However, the question remains, what caused many *conservatives* to abandon their convictions and embrace or at least accommodate Progressive ideals and programs? The answer is, *the very same*

Humanistic Psychology that changed liberals. After all, conservatives have been marinated in the same mass culture as liberals. They have attended the same schools, read the same books, seen the same movies and television shows. They have been taught that reason and logic are suspect, feelings are reliable, truth is relative, values are subjective, and others are responsible for their mistakes. As if those influences were not enough, they have been cajoled, prodded, and shamed into supporting Progressive programs. Little wonder that they have succumbed. The real wonder is, rather, that any conservatives have maintained their convictions.

HOW DID PROGRESSIVISM REGAIN ITS INFLUENCE IN RECENT DECADES?

Progressivism, which derived from Hereditarian pessimism about human nature, was a powerful force in the first half of the twentieth century but had lost much of its influence by midcentury.[13] At that time, Humanistic Psychology was from all indications replacing pessimism about human nature with extravagant optimism. Many thought this development delivered a decisive blow to Progressivism. So how did it survive that blow?

We have noted that Humanistic Psychology's main tenet that people are inherently wise and good had an important corollary—whatever goes wrong in life is not the fault of the individual but instead of society. This scapegoating played a large role in creating the radical movements of the 1960s and was enshrined in the popular slogan, "Never trust anyone over thirty." Moreover, the new psychology's exaltation of feelings led not only to sexual libertinism but also to a more sweeping rejection of traditional moral and intellectual codes. Whatever their parents affirmed, the young radicals rejected; and whatever their parents rejected, they affirmed. This mindless rebellion left them vulnerable to the influence of individuals with more focused agendas.

Two such individuals were Richard Cloward and Frances Piven, who in 1966 introduced the concept of *redistributing wealth* from the haves to the have-nots.[14] This idea eventually became central to the resurgent Progressivism. But its appeal to 1960s radicals lay in its resonance to Humanistic Psychology's claim that evil resided not in individual hearts but in social institutions, particularly those in capitalist systems.

Even more influential was Saul Alinsky, the author of *Rules for Radicals*, which offered guidance for cloaking radicalism in middle-class values. The book began by praising the young radicals' idealism: "If the young were now writing our Declaration of Independence . . . their bill of particulars would range from Vietnam to our black, Chicano, and Puerto Rican neighbors, to the migrant workers, to Appalachia, to the hate, ignorance, disease, and starvation in the world."

Alinsky went on to explain that "*The Prince* was written by Machiavelli for the Haves on how to hold power. *Rules for Radicals* is written for the Have-Nots on how to take it away." Most of the book was devoted to the argument that the ends justify the means—in other words, that whatever one says or does is justified if it achieves one's ends. This idea sharply contrasted with the principle of traditional ethics that a good end *never* justifies the use of evil means. Alinsky also advised young radicals to put aside confrontation and adopt an approach that masked their goal of social havoc. He wrote: "Tactics must begin within the experience of the middle class, accepting their aversion to rudeness, vulgarity, and conflict. Start them easy, don't scare them off." This approach, he explained, would facilitate "the radicalization of the middle class."[15]

In brief, Progressivism regained its influence because Humanistic Psychology made it fashionable to project blame for all that is wrong in the world onto social institutions; people like Cloward, Piven, and Alinsky gave that projection a political focus; and their young radical disciples, Hillary Clinton and Barack Obama notable among them, embraced them as core convictions. They hardly needed convincing. It was a very short step from "Our ignorant, oppressive parents are responsible for all that is wrong with our lives" to "Previous generations corrupted every social institution," and from there to "Let's change the system, rewrite the Constitution, while we're at it, do a little social justice by redistributing all the ill-gotten wealth to the victims."

WHY DID ONE OF THE MOST CONSERVATIVE INSTITUTIONS IN HISTORY, THE CATHOLIC CHURCH, IGNORE ITS OWN INTELLECTUAL TRADITION AND EMBRACE PROGRESSIVISM'S VIEW OF SOCIAL JUSTICE?

Many people, including more than a few Catholics, are not aware that this embrace occurred. They may, of course, know that many Catholic laypeople reject certain of the Church's teachings, notably concerning birth control. They may even be aware that entire religious orders, in particular the Jesuits, have openly rebelled against the authority of the Church hierarchy and challenged moral theology, as explained in chapter 2. However, few know that *many bishops and cardinals* have also rejected the Church's intellectual tradition and adopted a radical perspective on the important subject of social justice. If they knew this, they would certainly wonder how it could have happened in an institution that has historically treasured and maintained its intellectual tradition. Of all the questions addressed in this chapter, this one is arguably the most complicated.

Before considering how the hierarchy abandoned Catholic tradition, let us briefly consider the document that best represents the traditional view of the Catholic Church on social justice: Pope Leo XIII's 1891 encyclical, *Rerum Novarum*.[16] Leo had been a student of the Italian priest Luigi D'Azeglio, who originated the term *social justice* and who believed the solution to poverty lay in the actions of home, church, and community rather than government initiatives. *Rerum Novarum* affirmed the rights of workers, but it also rejected the notion that conflict between employers and workers is necessary and natural, denounced the socialist idea of "community of goods," and argued that "the first and most fundamental principle" in overcoming poverty "must be the inviolability of private property."

The key to overcoming economic disparity, Leo claimed, is not to take away the property of some and give it to others, which "neither justice nor the common good allows," but instead to enable larger numbers of people to become property owners. This approach can work, he added, only if people's income is not "drained and exhausted by excessive taxation." Among the most significant ideas in the encyclical was that the obligation to help those in need is one of *charity* rather than of justice.[17] (This idea is even more important today than it was in Leo's day, for it effectively counters the contemporary, worldwide fixation on "entitlements.")

A little over a century later, the US Conference of Catholic Bishops (USCCB) ignored Pope Leo's balanced view of social justice and adopted a socialist/Progressive perspective. The most important example of this view appeared in a 1986 position paper titled "Economic Justice for All,"[18] which

★ spoke of poverty in minority communities as if it were caused solely by economic factors and never by people's self-defeating behavioral patterns or ill-conceived government policies. (This, despite the fact that numerous scholars, from Daniel Patrick Moynihan to Thomas Sowell, have demonstrated the disastrous effects of those patterns and policies.[19])

★ declared that "the first line of attack against poverty" is to increase jobs in the private sector but made no mention of the government regulations that make it difficult for private companies to expand the workforce.

★ claimed that "the concentration of privilege results far more from institutional relationships [that] distribute power and wealth inequitably than from differences in talent or lack of desire to work." (Translation: the rich are to blame for their wealth, but the poor are never to blame for their poverty.)

★ expanded human rights to include, among other things, "rights to life, food, clothing, shelter, rest, medical care, and basic education . . . [the] right to security in the event of sickness, unemployment, and old age . . . [and] the right to employment." This view ignored the crucial distinction between the right to having an *opportunity to pursue goods* and the right to *possess* goods. (It goes well beyond the idea of a "safety net," which reasonable people of all philosophic and theological perspectives affirm.)

★ asserted that social institutions should guarantee everyone "*the ability* to participate actively in the economic, political, and cultural life of society [emphasis added]." In reality, of course, ability includes such matters as individual aptitude, effort, and interest, over which social institutions have no control.

★ argued that "the government should assume a positive role in *generating employment* and establishing fair labor practices [emphasis added]." This clearly advocates an expansion of government into the realm of private enterprise. (It is also at odds with the bishops' claim that the initial effort should be in the private sector.)

★ urged the United States to support a system of *global* government.

Since "Economic Justice for All," the bishops have been even more forceful in advancing the Progressive agenda.[20] In 1991 they urged that the government not only increase the supply of "affordable housing," but also "help families pay for it." In 2008 they declared their support for Congress's affordable-housing act. (Incidentally, this was the act that most authorities agree contributed significantly to the 2008 financial crisis.) Later that year, the bishops issued two letters that advocated, among other federal actions, an increase in food stamp benefits and unemployment benefits and the passage of "another stimulus plan." One of the letters invoked the principle of subsidiarity in support of the federal government "step[ping] in," a curious invocation given that subsidiarity is, by definition, a preference for *smaller* agencies over larger ones. In 2009 the bishops urged that government allocate "major new resources to address the serious impacts of climate change," a matter about which scientists are increasingly divided, and which is at best on the outer fringes of theological concern.

What could possibly have caused the Catholic hierarchy to change its view of social justice so dramatically? One thing was Liberation Theology, the movement founded by Gustavo Gutiérrez, a Dominican priest, in the 1960s. This theology, which reflected the founder's experiences with the poor in Latin America, had two seemingly incompatible wellsprings: the Gospel command to feed the hungry, clothe the naked, and care for the sick; and the Marxist doctrine of class struggle against capitalist oppression.

As Joseph Cardinal Ratzinger (now pope emeritus) noted in 1984, this unholy marriage of the gospel and Marxism created pressure on Church leaders: to be regarded as friends of the poor and comrades in their struggle against the rich, they would have to embrace the Marxist view; to do otherwise would mark them as indifferent to the poor or, worse, as oppressors of the poor.[21] Those who rejected Liberation Theology would thus risk losing their highly valued, historic standing as defenders of the poor.

Another cause of the bishops' embrace of the Progressive view of social justice was the example offered by the Jesuit order. As we noted in chapter 2, two historians, who were also members of the order—Malachi Martin and Joseph Becker—detailed how it was strongly influenced by Humanistic Psychology. Martin went so far as to suggest that the ideas and values of Carl Rogers and Abraham Maslow *replaced* those of the order's founder, St. Ignatius. To that observation must be added that Jesuits were among the most ardent supporters of Liberation Theology. Jesuit Arthur McGovern, for example, rejected capitalism and portrayed Jesus as a revolutionary. Jesuit Francis Carney urged Christians to be more supportive of "armed revolution, socialism, Marxism, and communism." Jesuit Juan Luis Segundo argued that armed revolution was the *only* way to overcome "capitalism and transnational imperialism from Central America" and declared "to be a Christian is to be a revolutionary."[22]

A third factor in the bishops' embrace of the Progressive view of social justice was the timing and goals of Vatican Council II, in which Catholic hierarchy from around the globe participated. The council lasted from 1962 to 1965 and, at its outset, Pope John XXIII famously declared that it was time to "open the windows" of the Church and let in some fresh air, a perfectly defensible idea that many believed was long overdue. The fresh air that came in was, however, mainly the Liberation Theology that had permeated the Jesuit order (among others) and the Humanistic Psychology that was in the process of permeating mass culture. Though it would be an exaggeration to say that the council *endorsed* the ideas of Gustavo Gutiérrez, or those of Rogers, Maslow, and Kinsey, it is fair to say that it provided the occasion for those ideas to be seriously considered by the hierarchy. The fact that the two movements were in some ways mutually reinforcing—both antiauthoritarian, both focused on the blamelessness of individuals and the oppression of society, and both urging rebellion, though of different kinds—surely increased the impact of each.

In brief, members of the hierarchy of the Catholic Church, most of whom have considerably more experience as *administrators* than as scholars, were persuaded by renegade Catholic intellectuals to abandon the Church's traditional view of social justice and to embrace a view rooted in Progressivism and Marxist liberation theology. The traditional view is based on the long-held belief that social injustices exist because human nature is flawed and individuals, individually or collaboratively, frequently ignore the dignity and rights of others. In contrast, the Progressive/Marxist view rejects the idea of a flawed human nature and individual failings (or sins) and instead blames social injustice on the inherent enmity presumed to exist between social classes.

The bishops embraced the Progressive/Marxist view of social justice not so much in a spirit of rebellion as because it came appealingly wrapped in Christian compassion for the poor and echoed the precepts of Humanistic Psychology that, at least in the beginning, seemed friendly to religion. (Although these facts make the bishops' decision understandable, they in no way lessen its impact.)

The discussion in this chapter completes the critical analysis of Hereditarianism and Humanistic Psychology and their relationship to the social problems that have ruined lives, corrupted society, and endangered America's future. The remaining chapters offer what I believe is a more accurate view of human nature than the views propounded by those movements and suggest ways to restore that view to individual lives and social institutions.

6

A WISER PERSPECTIVE

At roughly the same time that Abraham Maslow was working out his hierarchy of needs, with self-actualization at the peak of popularity, a continent away another scholar was recounting the findings of a very different research project. That scholar was the eminent Austrian psychiatrist Viktor Frankl, and his research was done amid the horrors of the Nazi concentration camps. Frankl himself spent years there, and through his own suffering and that of his fellow prisoners, he gained incomparable insights into the human condition.

Before World War II, Frankl had achieved distinction as a neurologist, psychiatrist, and brain surgeon and was a protégé of the leading psychotherapists of that time, Sigmund Freud and Alfred Adler. He corresponded with Freud, met him, and published an article on his recommendation. Next, Frankl was associated with Alfred Adler, who published Frankl's second article. In time, however, Frankl came to dispute both Freud's notion that the main drive in man is sexual and Adler's notion that it is power. (Adler was so upset by Frankl's disagreement with him that he had him expelled from the Society for Individual Psychology.)[1]

When war broke out, Frankl and his whole family were sent to Nazi concentration camps, where his wife and parents eventually died; only Frankl and his sister survived. Before entering Auschwitz, Frankl had sewed into the lining of his coat a draft of his research, titled *The Doctor and The Soul*. However, when he arrived there, he was forced to throw the coat into a pile of inmate clothing and he never saw it again. He also narrowly escaped death at that time. The infamous Dr. Joseph Mengele was separating prisoners, pointing to the right for labor in the camp and to the left for the gas chambers. He directed Frankl to the left, but when Mengele wasn't looking, Frankl went to the other line, where he saw people whom he knew. Recounting the experience many years later, Frankl commented, "Only God knows where I got that idea or found the courage."[2]

The concentration camps were, as Frankl put it, "the true test of my maturation"; and Auschwitz, in particular, was "the *experimentum crusis*" that provided a uniquely dependable foundation for a theory of human nature and fulfillment.[3] Time and again, the experience of the camps tested the reigning views of human behavior and found them wanting.

Freud had claimed that the drive for pleasure/sex was the fundamental human drive. But Frankl noted that in the camps there was almost no concern about sex, even in dreams, and "little sexual perversion." Yet there was interest in politics and even more in religion—the latter interest "the most sincere imaginable," so much so that "the depth and vigor of religious belief often surprised and moved a new arrival." In addition, there was art of at least a low level. The prisoners devised makeshift cafes where singing, jokes, and laughter helped them survive.[4]

Adler had claimed that the fundamental human drive was the drive for power. Yet Frankl found that in the most trying of circumstances, competition and contention gave way to cooperation and mutual support. For example, he tells the story of how a starving inmate stole some potatoes from the storehouse. When the camp officers learned of the theft, they gave the inmates the choice of either giving up the guilty man or giving up their own food for a day. Though the culprit was known by the inmates, and though they were on the verge of starvation, all 2,500 of them chose to give up their food to protect him.[5]

MEANING AND TRANSCENDENCE

Long after the supposedly fundamental drives had ceased to be evident, another drive remained strong in the camp inmates—the drive to find meaning in the horrible circumstances of their lives. Frankl concluded from the camp experience that the *will to meaning* is the central feature of human nature.[6]Also, that the search for meaning is thwarted by self-absorption and self-indulgence and enhanced by "self-transcendence and self-distancing . . . the reaching out beyond ourselves for something other than ourselves."

It was precisely this movement beyond self that enabled inmates to survive the horrors of the concentration camps, Frankl explained:[7]

> In a word, existence [in the camps] was dependent on "self-transcendence," a concept that I introduced into logotherapy as early as 1949. I thereby understand the primordial anthropological fact that being human is being always directed, and pointing, to something other than oneself: to a meaning to fulfill or another human being to encounter, a cause to serve or a person to love. Only to the extent that someone is living out this self-transcendence of human existence, is he truly human or does he become his true self.[8]

Frankl was emphatic in claiming that the essential task in life is not our search for *ourselves*, as modern psychology claims, but our search for meaning. Further, that meaning is not found in ourselves or in our psyches but in the world.[9] He was equally emphatic in arguing that the more we stop focusing on ourselves, the more human we become. As he put it, "the humanness of man is most tangible when he forgets himself—and overlooks himself,"[10] and "human existence is not authentic unless it is lived in terms of self-transcendence."[11]

The search for meaning, in Frankl's view, is not a matter of asking abstract questions but, instead, of "answer[ing] the questions that life asks of us, and to these questions we can respond only by being responsible for our existence."[12] The concept of responsibility, which he regarded as a crucial balance to the modern overemphasis on rights, appears often in Frankl's works. Indeed, for Frankl, being human is ultimately a matter of being responsible.[13]

How is meaning achieved? Long before his experience in the concentration camps, Frankl had identified three broad ways: through deeds or creative works; through experiences, human encounters, or love; and through changing our attitude toward suffering, such as that associated with incurable illness, and turning it from a defeat into "a human triumph." Specific meanings, he acknowledged, will vary among individuals and can be achieved at any time of life, even on one's deathbed.[14] Incidentally, no fewer than twenty empirical studies support this claim.[15] Rejecting the notion that there is a single universal meaning for all of us, Frankl argued that there are "only the unique meanings of the individual situations," but because situations can be similar, "there are also meanings which are shared by human beings across society and, even more, throughout history."[16]

Sometimes deep meaning can be found in small events. Frankl recounts an experience of his own. Shortly after the United States entered WWII, he obtained a visa to emigrate to America, but he was troubled at the prospect of leaving his parents in Austria at such a perilous time. One day, while visiting them, he noticed a piece of marble on the table and inquired about it. His father explained that he had found it in the rubble of a synagogue destroyed by the Nazis, adding that it had been part of the commandment to "honor thy father and thy mother." Frankl was moved by that detail to remain in Austria and was eventually sent to a concentration camp.[17] A similarly small event provided the "deepest experience" Frankl had in the camps. As noted earlier, he had lost the manuscript of his first book when his coat was taken away. Later, in the pocket of a ragged coat he had acquired, he found a single page of "the most important Jewish prayer, *Shema Yisrael*." This experience he interpreted as "a challenge to *live* [his] thoughts instead of merely putting them on paper."[18]

The conclusions validated in the concentration camps challenged not only the Freudian and Adlerian views that dominated the first half of the twentieth century, but also the views of Humanistic Psychology that would dominate the last half of the century and continue on to the present. Let us look more closely at how Frankl's views challenged the newer psychology.

FRANKL ON SELF

The differences between Frankl and Humanistic Psychologists on the matter of self could not be more profound. Frankl argued that a person does not *have* a self; rather, he *is* a self.[19] Moreover, that the focus of one's attention should not be on self, but on something *outside* the self.[20] In a television interview, he was even more insistent: "Normally, fundamentally, originally, primarily, basically, any human being is concerned with something out there in the world . . . a work to do, a job to complete, a task, a meaning, a mission in life waiting . . . to be actualized by him and by no other person." This reaching beyond oneself, he explained, should always be for "the sake of a cause to serve or another person to love, and never for himself."[21]

Focusing beyond oneself is central to Frankl's perspective; indeed, he regarded it as the essential quality of human existence and source of one's personal identity.[22] No researcher was more aware than Frankl that the circumstances of life can be unfortunate, even tragic. Yet there is no hint in any of his writings of the scapegoating promoted by Humanistic Psychology—that is, no reference to "dysfunctional" families or abusive parents or incompetent teachers or genetic shortcomings or socioeconomic deprivation as an excuse for people's attitudes and behavior. On the contrary, he maintains that "a faulty upbringing exonerates no one," and "facts are not fate. What matters is the stand we take toward them."[23] People have the power to decide whether to succumb to circumstances or to rise above them.

As an illustration of the power to choose how one responds to circumstances, Frankl cites the case of identical twin brothers, one of whom became a criminal and the other, a criminologist. These individuals shared the same genetic makeup and, we can presume, essentially the same cultural influences. The difference between their very different outcomes, Frankl points out, can be traced to a difference in attitude and choice of action.[24] We all have the capacity to make such choices, he reminds us, and how we use that capacity ultimately determines who we are: "After all, man is that being who invented the gas chambers of Auschwitz; however, he is also that being who entered those gas chambers upright, with the Lord's Prayer or the *Shema Yisrael* on his lips."[25]

Frankl also took a very different position from Humanistic Psychologists on the subject of guilt. Most of them classify it as a harmful emotion, mainly because they regard humans as victims. That view takes away our human dignity and ignores the reality and force of conscience, Frankl argues. By inspiring feelings of guilt, conscience reminds us when we are not doing what we ought to do or being what we ought to be, and motivates us to improve. From this perspective, "it is a prerogative of man to become guilty. To be sure, it is also his responsibility to overcome guilt."[26]

Even though Humanistic Psychology has rejected individual guilt, it has generally embraced the concept of *collective* guilt. Given that psychology's propensity for blaming an individual's faults and failings on other people, notably parents, this embrace is not surprising. Frankl, however, rejected the concept of collective guilt, citing examples of individuals who resist the pressure to behave ignobly. For example, he knew of a Nazi who had spent large sums of his own money on medical supplies for concentration camp inmates. In appreciation, after the camp was liberated, Jewish inmates hid the man and then delivered him to the American troops only on condition that he not be prosecuted or harmed. Frankl himself hid another Nazi after the war because he didn't deserve prosecution.[27]

FRANKL ON SELF-ACTUALIZATION

Frankl challenged Maslow's notion that self-actualization is the highest and most important human need. According to Frankl, self-transcendence is more important; it is, in fact, the essence of human existence.[28] As he explains:

> Self-actualization is not man's ultimate destination. It is not even his primary intention. Self-actualization, if made an end in itself, contradicts the self-transcendent quality of human nature. Like happiness, self-actualization is an effect, the effect of meaning fulfillment. Only to the extent to which man fulfills a meaning out there in the world, does he fulfill himself. If he sets out to actualize himself rather than fulfill a meaning, self-actualization immediately loses its justification.[29]

More devastatingly, Frankl goes on to show that his assessment of self-actualization is a more reasonable interpretation of *Maslow's own research*, offering several citations from Maslow's work to document this fact.

Among the achievements of Frankl's system of psychotherapy, which he calls *logotherapy*, has been to reveal that the direct pursuit of self-actualization blocks its realization. The same paradox exists with certain other pursuits. For example, *try* to fall asleep and you will have difficulty doing so; try harder and you will become anxious, which will heighten your insomnia. (A similar effect occurs when men become anxious about getting an erection or women worry about achieving orgasm.)[30]

Incidentally, Frankl also exposes the error in another of Maslow's key premises, the idea that lower needs must be met before higher ones can be pursued. In situations such as those in concentration camps, Frankl points out, though the inmates were sick and starving, "the thirst for meaning, even ultimate meaning, [broke] through irresistibly."[31]

FRANKL ON SELF-ESTEEM

Humanistic Psychology places great importance on self and especially on feeling good about oneself. In fact, Maslow went so far as to claim that without self-esteem, achievement in life (educational, professional, or personal) is virtually impossible. In contrast, Frankl was convinced that the proper focus is not *on* ourselves—or on our feelings about ourselves or esteem for ourselves—but *beyond* ourselves. As he put it, the very essence of our humanity is "relating, and being directed, to something other than oneself"—in a word, "self-transcendence." And because of this, humankind is "basically concerned with reaching out beyond [itself], be it toward a meaning to fulfill, or toward another human being to encounter."[32]

The proper approach to living, in Frankl's view, is not to focus on ourselves, as Humanistic Psychology teaches, but to become, as far as possible, *detached from ourselves*.[33] Man, he believed, "functions best when he is overlooking and forgetting himself." Looking inward, he claims, is not only foolish but futile! To explain this, he uses the example of the human eye.

When it is healthy, the eye does not see itself—it sees what lies outside itself. Only when it is diseased does it see clouds or halos of light.[34]

What matters in our lives, from Frankl's perspective, is not how we think or feel about ourselves, but how well we meet the challenges life poses for us.

FRANKL ON REALITY AND TRUTH

Whereas Humanistic Psychology held that reality is personal and subjective, Frankl argued that it is impersonal and objective: "The only thing that is subjective is the perspective through which we approach reality, and this subjectiveness does not in the least detract from the objectiveness of reality itself."[35] In addition, Frankl's theory of human psychology is rooted in the traditional idea of truth as being discovered rather than created according to one's preferences. He spoke of the search for meaning as a matter of detection rather than invention[36] and of every question having a "*right* answer," every situation "a true meaning."[37]

Frankl's entire career was devoted to determining the truth about human nature and the human psyche, which entailed detecting the errors in the various competing views of his day. As a result of his belief that truth is objective, he was sensitive to the power of true ideas to elevate us and false ideas to debase us. This sensitivity is nowhere more evident than in his indictment of intellectuals in the case of the concentration camps. He wrote: "If we present a man with a concept of man which is not true, we may well corrupt him. . . . I am absolutely convinced that the gas chambers of Auschwitz, Treblinka, and Maidanek were ultimately prepared not in some Ministry or other in Berlin, but rather at the desks and in the lecture halls of nihilistic scientists and philosophers."[38]

FRANKL ON REASON AND FEELINGS

It is impossible to read any of Frankl's books without noting his appreciation of the role of feelings in human life. Nevertheless, he does not overstate the importance of feelings nor in any way make them a substitute for reason. On the contrary, the central feature of his theory of human psychology, the search for meaning in life, concerns rational activities—observing, interpreting, evaluating, and understanding—rather than emotional ones.

It is no coincidence that Frankl spoke of the "search" rather than the drive for meaning. He stressed that meaning is not something that pushes us, but instead something that pulls or attracts us and requires a conscious choice on our part. As he put it, "meaning fulfillment always implies decision-making."[39] Moreover, what he calls "the two uniquely human capacities," self-detachment and self-transcendence, are matters of intellect and will, rather than emotion.

FRANKL ON SEX

Frankl believed that the contemporary view of sex—the view promoted by Kinsey and endorsed by Humanistic Psychology—depersonalizes and thereby dehumanizes sex by divorcing it from love. This tendency consists of seeing the other person as an interchangeable object to be used for sexual pleasure rather than as a human person. Not only is this depersonalizing immature—it precludes love—but it also frustrates our search for meaning.[40]

Such ideas appear frequently in Frankl's writings. "The really mature person," he writes, will "consider a sexual relationship only where sex is the expression of love," because to be healthy and meaningful, eroticism must be "consonant with human dignity" and sexuality must be "the expression and crown of a love relationship."[41] Furthermore, "grasping the uniqueness of a loved one understandably results in a monogamous partnership," and conversely, denying that uniqueness leads to promiscuity and unhappiness.[42] In light of this, Frankl concludes that anyone who advises young people "must oppose sexual relations, must veto them if he can, whenever young people want sexual intercourse without real love."[43]

These observations on sex are profoundly connected with Frankl's view of self-transcendence. In other words, he sees sexual expression as being not an end in itself, but a means of manifesting love and thereby achieving self-transcendence.[44]

Frankl's insights into the human condition became the foundation of his logotherapy. Frankl's associate Joseph Fabry enumerates the "fundamental formulations" of that therapy as follows:

> That all reality has meaning (*logos*) and that life never ceases to have meaning for anyone; that meaning is very specific and changes from person to person and, for each person, from moment to moment; that each person is unique and each life contains a series of unique assignments which have to be discovered and responded to; that it is the search for one's specific assignments, and the response to them, that provide meaning; and that happiness, contentment, peace of mind are mere side effects in that search.[45]

Even a brief review of Frankl's singular contributions to psychology, such as those provided in this chapter, leaves one wondering why his ideas did not achieve dominance in the second half of the twentieth century and why they continue to receive less attention, particularly among psychologists, the clergy, and other counselors, than do the ideas of Rogers, Maslow, and Kinsey.[46] To begin with, Frankl was better educated than they, having both an earned medical degree and an earned doctorate in philosophy, and therefore understood not only the various theories of psychology and psychiatry but also the rich tradition of Western philosophy.[47] Moreover, his research was not limited to armchair speculation about clients or the reported experience of selected people, but instead encompassed closely observed experiences of people in the most extreme conditions ever devised, conditions he himself experienced. Most importantly, his conclusions pass the test of common sense and everyday experience, which, as we demonstrated earlier, those of Rogers, Maslow, and Kinsey do not.

One reason Frankl received less attention was the language barrier.

Although much of Frankl's work was available in German editions in the late 1940s, little was available in English until the 1960s. *Man's Search for Meaning* was well received when it was published in 1963 and was used as supplementary reading, primarily in humanities and philosophy courses,[48] but by then the ideas of Rogers and Maslow had won the approval of the psychological establishment and many religious leaders. Another reason Frankl received less attention was that the rapidly expanding and increasingly influential entertainment and communications media had already embraced Rogers, Maslow, and Kinsey and offered the general public an unremitting barrage of books, articles, and dramatic presentations promoting their ideas.

Ironically, when Abraham Maslow became aware of Frankl's work, particularly his challenges to self-actualization and self-esteem, he revised those views and acknowledged the greater importance of self-transcendence.[49] But by then, his famous pyramid was so well established in academe and in mass culture that he was powerless to diminish its influence.

Frankl's insights not only repudiate the errors of Humanistic Psychology (and the shallow pessimism of Hereditarianism); they also provide the impetus to rediscover forgotten truths about our human nature and to solve the social problems that have resulted from our forgetting. To that task we now turn.

7

HUMAN NATURE REVISITED

T hroughout the analysis in previous chapters, we have seen that both Hereditarianism and Humanistic Psychology have been mistaken about every major human attribute and need. Mistaken about human intelligence; about humankind's supposed wisdom and goodness; about the importance of self-actualization and the value of self-esteem; about the way in which human beings apprehend truth and reality, the comparative reliability of emotion and reason, and sexual morality. Moreover, these mistakes have infected our culture for almost a century. As a result, the great majority of people in the United States and in countries that share our mass culture are confused about what it means to be human. The most pressing challenge of our age is therefore to clarify the meaning and characteristics of human nature.

A good place to start our analysis of human nature is with the concept about which Rogers, Maslow, and other Humanistic Psychologists were most profoundly confused—the concept of "self."

The fundamental confusion concerns whether the self is actual or only apparent, whether it is an inner core or an entire entity, and whether that entity is singular or plural. The answers are found in the analysis set forth in previous chapters. They are as follows: The self is *actual* rather than apparent. (To save a lot of technical discussion, perform this simple test— touch a hot stove.) The self is not merely an inner core but an entire entity, also known as a *person*.[1] Or as Frankl put it, a self is not something one *has* but something one *is*. Finally, each self is a singular entity with several dimensions,[2] as shown below:

Dimensions of Self

Let us examine more closely each of the parts of the diagram and their interrelationships. The *physical* dimension of self consists of our anatomy and physiology and includes our potential for health and susceptibility to illness. The *metaphysical* dimension consists of intellect, emotion, conscience, and will—in a word, the *mind*—and includes our potential for wisdom and goodness and our susceptibility to foolishness and evil.[3] The key words here are *potential* and *susceptibility*. They reflect one of the most prominent characteristics of human beings—a characteristic that Humanistic Psychology denies (and Hereditarianism exaggerates)— our imperfection. We are no more inherently wise and good than we are inherently healthy. We are, instead, *capable* of good health, wisdom, and goodness but *vulnerable* to illness, foolishness, and evil. G. K. Chesterton noted that one fact stands out about the origins of humans: "Original sin is really original. Not merely in theology but in history it is a thing rooted in the origins. Whatever else men have believed, they have all believed that there is something the matter with mankind."[4] That "something" is best understood as imperfection.

The physical and metaphysical dimensions are overlapped in the diagram to illustrate their interdependence: the metaphysical dimension depends on the physical for the electrical/chemical reactions and the sensory data that enable it to operate; the physical dimension depends on the metaphysical for the cognitive and emotional responses characterized as specifically human. As traditional philosophy rightly claimed, the brain and the mind are complementary but distinct. Thought takes place in the mind, not in the brain, but requires the cooperation of the brain. The brain is *necessary* for the mind's activity but not *sufficient*. One effect of ignoring the mind/brain distinction is the mistake of conceptualizing mental illness as a physical affliction. Thomas Szasz, a psychiatrist and an outspoken critic of this tendency, argues that "the mind (whatever it is) is not an organ or part of the body. Hence, it cannot be diseased in the same sense as the body can. When we speak of mental illness, then, we speak metaphorically. To say that a person's mind is sick is like saying that the economy is suffering or that a joke is sick."[5]

The *behavioral* dimension is surrounded with a broken (rather than solid) line in the diagram because it is technically not a separate dimension at all but a manifestation of the metaphysical dimension—specifically, our words and deeds. It is appropriate to present this manifestation as a quasi-dimension because, unlike the act of choosing that produces it, it is entirely discernible by others and, accordingly, defines the quality of our human-ness, especially in the eyes of other people.[6] (Socrates was more restrictive, claiming that we are not what we do but what we *repeatedly* do.)

More precisely stated then, the self is *a single entity with two dimensions*—a visible physical dimension and an invisible metaphysical dimension, the latter manifested in words and actions.[7]

Two factors influence the degree to which we realize our physical and metaphysical potential. One is *culture*, the people and agencies that touch our lives and the values and beliefs associated with them. All things being equal, we are more likely to be healthy if our culture minimizes impediments to health and provides treatment for illness, and we are more likely to be wise and good if our culture encourages and rewards wisdom and goodness. The second factor is *choice*—that is, our application of will in deciding what to think, say, and do.[8] Sometimes choice is conscious, at other times it is the result of habit. (An act performed out of habit, of course, is always the product of a *prior* choice.) Ironically, *surrendering* our power of choice and imitating others is also a form of choosing.

The power of culture to shape lives is most obvious in coercive dictatorial regimes, but is also evident in less extreme cases in which cultural agencies merely promote the same values or endorse the same programs. In either case, however, individuals always retain the essential freedom to choose their responses to culture. As noted in chapter 6, Viktor Frankl offered the example of identical twin brothers, one of whom chose to become a criminologist and the other became a criminal, as well as the innumerable cases of chosen behavior in the concentration camps.

Not everyone believes that choice plays a role in human affairs. Twentieth- century Behaviorists denied the existence of free will (and intellect), preferring to explain all behavior as conditioned responses to stimuli. Some twenty-first-century neurologists hold the same viewpoint but speak of neurons, chemical transmitters, and synapses instead of conditioned responses. Both groups take the extreme position that what billions of people over several millennia have perceived to be their conscious choices were actually illusions. Consider, for a moment, the implications of that claim. If people really don't choose their behavior, then they cannot reasonably be held responsible for their actions. Accordingly, police forces should be disbanded and courts shut down. Furthermore, the entire prison population—including hundreds of thousands of convicted thieves, rapists, child molesters, and murderers—should be set free. And at the simplest and most practical level, as Chesterton pointed out, it will no longer make sense "to curse, to thank, to justify, to urge, to punish, to resist temptations, to incite mobs, to make New Year resolutions, to pardon sinners, to rebuke tyrants, or even to say 'thank you' for the mustard."[9]

Throughout history, most informed people have affirmed our power to choose our responses to the circumstances and challenges of our lives.

Irving Babbitt noted that the classical spirit in general and the great Greek philosophers in particular believed that man possesses "a power of control over impulse and desire."[10] Arnold Toynbee argued that "as human beings, we are endowed with freedom of choice, and we cannot shuffle off our responsibility upon the shoulders of God or nature. We must shoulder it ourselves."[11] In doing so, we must understand that choice is intimately related to self-transcendence. Our proper concern, as Frankl noted, is not what we expect from life but what life expects from us: life is questioning us, challenging us, and the choices we make in response define our character. Every choice represents an opportunity to transcend our preoccupation with self and reach for something larger. Moreover, self-transcendence is not at all like Maslow's self-actualization that, once achieved, is possessed forever. Self-transcendence must be achieved again and again, many times each day.[12] In other words, achieving self-transcendence is very much like acquiring a virtue. (Indeed, in an important sense, self-transcendence is a virtue.) Consider, for example, the virtue of humility. The moment we achieve a measure of humility, we are tempted to feel *proud* of ourselves and thereby forfeit our gain.

THE REALITY OF CHANGE

We have demonstrated Carl Rogers's mistake in urging people to "become what they are." That is a contradiction in terms and therefore an impossibility. We *are* what we are; we can *become* only what we are *not*. And this process of changing, though subtle and incremental, is constant and inexorable throughout our lives. Sometimes the changes are for the better, sometimes not. Just as our physical health improves or worsens over time, so does our metaphysical "health." In the latter case, our intellect becomes more or less understanding and discerning, our emotions more or less balanced, our conscience more or less sensitive to right and wrong, our will more or less faithful to our intentions.[13]

Because human nature is imperfect, we may make little or no effort to direct the changes that occur in us but instead leave them to chance. But even if we are diligent, we are still susceptible to error, so our efforts at self-improvement are often inconsistent and our progress erratic; for every two steps forward, we often slip one (or two, or three) backward. Good mental habits are as difficult to maintain as balanced nutrition. Even the wisest among us act foolishly from time to time and the most virtuous can all too easily fall from grace. Nor do the quality of our intentions and the degree of our resolve guarantee success. We can resolve to speak and act in a certain way, rehearse our responses, but then at the crucial moment violate our resolution.

In short, change happens whether we exercise control or simply drift in the cultural current. To control the process of change in ourselves and ensure that we advance in wisdom and goodness, we need to aim for good choices and, if we fail in that attempt, to acknowledge and correct our mistakes and redouble our efforts.

THE VALUE OF GUILT AND SHAME

One of our human imperfections, as we have seen, is the tendency to justify or explain away our mistakes, thus prompting us to repeat them and make them habitual, in which case we become even more inclined to justify them. To break this harmful cycle, we need to replace pride with humility and defensiveness with honest self-appraisal. This is why guilt and shame are relevant and necessary aspects of personal growth and self-improvement.[14]

The English word *guilt* has had various meanings over time—"offense or crime," "responsibility or fault," and "the fact of having committed an offense." Its present meaning—"the state of having committed an offense"—dates from the 1500s. The word *shame* is older than *guilt* and is derived from the Teutonic word for "disgrace" or "infamy." Over the centuries, *shame* has meant both the fact of having behaved dishonorably and the awareness of such behavior. The related adjective *ashamed* refers to "a recognition that one's actions or circumstances are [in some way] not to one's credit."[15]

As these definitions make clear, the words *guilt* and *shame* traditionally reflected the common understanding that people who do wrong are, by that very fact, guilty of wrongdoing and that the appropriate response to being guilty is to feel ashamed. Despite being unpleasant and even painful, feelings of shame traditionally were considered positive and constructive because they motivate us to make reparation, seek forgiveness, and behave better in the future. Nor was this common understanding unique to English-speaking peoples. In ancient China, for example, the philosopher Mencius taught that:

> The feeling of compassion is the beginning of benevolence; the feeling of shame and self-reproach, the beginning of righteousness; the feeling of courtesy and modesty, the beginning of propriety; the feeling of right and wrong, the beginning of wisdom. These four beginnings are like the four limbs of man and to deny oneself any of these potentialities is to cripple oneself.[16]

Humanistic Psychology, particularly in its popularized form, rejects that common understanding, arguing that guilt and shame serve no useful purpose but instead pose a danger to our intellectual and emotional health. Extremists like psychologist Wayne Dyer argue that guilt is "not a natural behavior" at all but "the most useless of all erroneous zone behaviors."[17] Psychiatrist David Burns ignores guilt's basis in fact and classifies it as a harmful emotion that always involves a total condemnation of self. (His chapter on guilt is titled "Ways of Defeating Guilt.") Remorse, which Burns somehow manages to separate from guilt, is "normal and healthy," whereas guilt is always "self-defeating and distorted."[18]

While not all authors of such books match Dyer's or Burns's rhetorical excesses, virtually all regard guilt and/or shame with suspicion, if not scorn. Abraham Twersky, for example, writes, "The guilty person says, 'I feel guilty about something I have done.' The shame-filled person says, 'I feel shame for what I am.'"[19] This view allows that guilt might be harmless but rejects the possibility that shame can ever be anything but total self-loathing. A leading psychology text takes a similar view in its statement that "guilt arises from the perception that you did something bad; shame arises from the perception that you are bad."[20]

Note, however, that all the authors cited ignore guilt-as-fact and acknowledge only guilt-as-perception. This is traceable to psychology's poverty of aspect: historically, practitioners of the discipline have been so fixated on perception that they have ignored the insights of other disciplines, notably law and ethics.[21] In criminal legal proceedings, *perceived* guilt is virtually meaningless; what matters is *actual* guilt, so the question before the judge and jury is always "Did the person in fact commit the crime he or she is charged with?" In ethics the challenge is somewhat different, but the focus on reality is the same. Ethicists are concerned with to what extent, if any, an act is dishonorable and therefore worthy of condemnation—in other words, to what extent it is *shameworthy*. Whether the person perceives the act's moral quality is, in most cases, irrelevant.[22]

American philosopher and classicist Allan Bloom was hardly exaggerating when he called psychologists "the sworn enemies of guilt."[23] Nor was he alone in protesting the unreasonableness of their assault on guilt and shame. Psychiatrist Willard Gaylin lamented that "there is so much nonsense [in Humanistic Psychology] about feelings. All the pop psychologists are misleading people about guilt and conscience. Guilt is a noble emotion; the person without it is a monster."[24]

COMMON SENSE ABOUT HUMAN NATURE

The description of human nature presented thus far in this chapter is little more than a common-sense view readily confirmable in everyday experience. Nevertheless, it differs dramatically from the view advanced by Hereditarianism and Humanistic Psychology and embedded in virtually every social agency and in mass culture.[25] The following contrast illustrates the differences:

★ Instead of "human intelligence is genetically determined and unalterable," common sense says "**Human intelligence is the sum of capacity and performance; the former inherited, the latter achieved by acquiring knowledge and mental skills**."

★ Instead of "human nature is inherently wise and good," common sense says "**Human nature is inherently imperfect**."

★ Instead of "self-actualization is the highest human need," common sense says "**Self-transcendence is the greatest human challenge**."[26]

★ Instead of "self-esteem is prerequisite to achievement," common sense says "**Achievement leads to justified self-esteem**."[27]

★ Instead of "people create their own truth and reality," common sense says "**Truth and reality are objective rather than subjective and discovered rather than created**."[28]

★ Instead of "feelings are more reliable than reason," common sense says "**Reason is more reliable than feelings**."[29]

★ Instead of "all sexual expression is natural and wholesome," common sense says "**Only sexual expression that neither harms nor degrades is natural and wholesome**."

When the proposed ideas are seen in expanded form—that is, with all the other ideas that follow logically or are implied, encouraged, or invited, as well as with the likely consequences of their acceptance—the differences from the dominant view are even more evident.

IDEA

Human intelligence is the sum of capacity and performance (intelligent behavior); the former inherited, the latter achieved by acquiring knowledge and mental skills.

EXPANDED MEANING

Capacity for intelligence may be unalterable, but performance can be improved. Capacity cannot be measured, so there is no way to determine its limits.[30] It is irresponsible to make any *assumption* about any individual's capacity for intelligence or lack thereof.[31] Performance can be measured, but because performance can vary from one occasion to another, it is inappropriate to take performance on any single occasion as the definitive measure of a person's intelligence.[32] Given that intelligent performance is desirable in all human activities and fields of endeavor, the principal goal of a teacher should be to increase students' intelligence by expanding their knowledge and mental skills.

PROBABLE CONSEQUENCES

Curriculums and courses would be changed, as necessary, to make the increase of students' intelligence their central aim. The methodology of mind stuffing—simply telling students information to be remembered for the exam—would be discouraged (if not forbidden). The methodology of mind building—providing students with approaches and strategies for solving problems and analyzing issues and frequent guided applications—would become standard. Teachers who were not familiar with the new methodology—in some cases, that would be entire faculties—would be provided sufficient training to become proficient in its use. Textbooks would be redesigned to fit the new goals and methods, wherever possible inviting students to compare, interpret, and evaluate points of view, rather than simply memorize information. Tests would be revised to require more than choosing a prefabricated answer—specifically, for students to apply their thought processes and compose their answers.

Leaders in business and the professions would, in time, realize employees' abilities to solve problems and make decisions, and these leaders would provide opportunities for their employees to use that ability in the workplace. Every business and profession would benefit from its members' improved creative and critical thinking.

Elected officials would not only be better prepared for the intellectual challenges of their jobs, they would also be more respectful of and attentive to their constituents.

IDEA

Human nature is inherently imperfect.

EXPANDED MEANING

We can behave foolishly or in an evil way on our own, without outside influence. When something goes wrong for us, someone else may *or may not* be at fault. Before blaming others, we should be sure that the fault is theirs rather than our own. Most of what we know comes from outside ourselves (through our senses), so education and other forms of self-improvement are essential.[33] Because we can err, we need to consult external sources of insight and wisdom. Individuality is neither automatic nor constant but must be achieved and maintained by effort. We need rescuing—not once for all time but regularly—from our own tendencies to foolishness and malevolence.[34] External standards, expectations, and norms are relevant and valuable. Whenever we commit an offense, intentionally or not, we should feel guilt and shame and should offer an apology, both because those feelings are appropriate and because they remind us of the need for self-improvement.

PROBABLE CONSEQUENCES[35]

Social scientists would assume, in the absence of concrete evidence to the contrary, that individuals are responsible for their behavior. Schools would abandon "values clarification," return to moral education, and emphasize evaluation of behavior, including one's own. Awareness of their own imperfections would enable students to accept the guidance of parents and teachers, to be less judgmental of others, and to be more open to learning.

Members of religious communities would be motivated to practice humility where appropriate and therefore less likely to rebel cavalierly against their leaders and their churches' doctrines. As scapegoating of parents and teachers and country declined, "liberation theology" would lose adherents.[36]

As acceptance for one's own behavior became the norm, the blaming of others and "society" for one's failures would decline, politicians would be less inclined to create entitlements and "redistribute" wealth, and jurists would return to judging criminal cases on facts rather than sociological agendas. As people became more aware of their tendency to cause their own problems, litigiousness (the legal expression of felt grievances) would diminish.

IDEA

Self-transcendence is the greatest human challenge.

EXPANDED MEANING

Self-transcendence is incompatible with self-absorption and self-indulgence.[37] To become self-transcendent, we must overcome self-absorption and self-indulgence (and because we are imperfect, this overcoming is an ongoing process). Overcoming self-absorption entails increasing our concern for other people's rights, needs, and desires and acknowledging our obligations to others. The way to curb self-indulgence is to practice self-control and self-restraint.

PROBABLE CONSEQUENCES

Incivility would decrease and civility would increase. As consideration for others increased, more and more people would give a higher priority to others' rights and needs than to their own desires. Marital discord and infidelity would decrease, marriages would become more stable, and the divorce rate would decline. The quality of parenting and care for the elderly would improve.

Elected officials would be motivated to show greater concern for their constituents' interests than for their own advancement. Employers and employees would be more observant of codes of ethics and workplace obligations, notably customer service. Corporate executives would be less focused on personal gain and more dedicated to the welfare of the company, its employees, and its stockholders.

IDEA

Achievement leads to justified self-esteem.

EXPANDED MEANING

Achievement does not depend on self-esteem. The more difficult the achievement, the more self-esteem one is justified in feeling.[38] Some self-esteem is unjustified: it is possible to feel more (or less) self-esteem than one deserves. Undeserved self-esteem creates false confidence and thus contributes to failure. Undeserved praise, including self-praise, leads to inflated self-esteem (and thus contributes to failure), whereas warranted criticism, including self-criticism, aids improvement and therefore promotes achievement.

PROBABLE CONSEQUENCES

Scholars and authors would change their perspectives on both achievement and self-esteem, presenting achievement as the goal and self-esteem as a by-product. Schools would stop trying to build self-esteem and return to the traditional emphasis on effort and excellence. Accordingly, they would also raise performance standards, tighten grading practices, and impose stricter discipline. Parents would stop worrying about their children's emotional fragility and demand appropriate, responsible behavior from them at home, in school, and in the community.

Courts would ban "low self-esteem" criminal defenses. Print and broadcast media would stop extolling self-indulgence and return to honoring self-discipline, self-control, and self-sacrifice.

All the above consequences would produce others. Ignorance, innumeracy, illiteracy, and semi-literacy would decline; the learning gap between the United States and other countries would disappear. Children would stay in school longer and reach adulthood better educated and ready to meet the challenges of work and relationships. The need and political support for entitlement programs would decrease.

IDEA

Truth and reality are objective rather than subjective and discovered rather than created.

EXPANDED MEANING

Believing something does not make it true, and changing one's mind has no effect on reality. Opinions that accurately represent reality are true; those that distort reality are false. Moral opinions, like other opinions, may be true or false. Encyclopedias and other knowledge sources, including philosophical works and the moral teachings of religious works, help in the discovery of truth. The rules of logic help us avoid false opinions, and contradictions of thought or expression offer signals of error.

PROBABLE CONSEQUENCES

Educators would pay more attention to the evaluation, judgment, and expression of ideas. Students would be more motivated to learn and, as a result, would grow in knowledge and skill. In education, business, and the professions, cheating, including plagiarism, and résumé fraud would carry a stigma and thereby be reduced.

Lexicographers would return to a prescriptive philosophy and distinguish between accepted and unaccepted usage. Authors and filmmakers would stop blurring the distinction between good and evil, heroes and antiheroes. Government officials would act more rationally—for example, barring tax cheats from leadership in the Internal Revenue Service and recognizing the distinction between legal and illegal aliens. Jurists would honor their oath to uphold the Constitution by restraining their urge to change it.

Journalists would strive to be objective, distinguish between fact and opinion, and separate reporting and advocacy. Authors of history books would be faithful to the facts, even those that are unflattering to their personal viewpoint. Hosts of TV talk shows and their guests would behave more courteously and focus their debates on the pursuit of truth rather than gamesmanship.

IDEA

Reason is more reliable than emotion.

EXPANDED MEANING

Feelings, impressions, intuitions, and hunches should be tested before being trusted. Before acting, it is wise to entertain alternative views and to consider consequences. Emotional restraint is desirable.

PROBABLE CONSEQUENCES

Social scientists would be more careful about classifying behavior as "compulsive." Teachers would emphasize sound thinking and the support of assertions with evidence.[39] The traditional moral code, rather than being dismissed as irrelevant, would once again receive thoughtful consideration. People would be more inclined to consider the rights, needs, and feelings of others,[40] and thus more inclined to honor their marital and parental obligations.

With fewer excuses for their failings, people would be better able to resist temptations to undesirable behavior, including irresponsible gambling, substance abuse, promiscuity, and gluttony. Irrational offenses, such as sexual harassment, discrimination, and hate crimes would decrease,[41] as would impulsive behaviors such as shoplifting, rape, assault, and road rage.[42] People would be more motivated to respect traditional taboos against incest and sexual molestation. With people more inclined to control their reactions, public discourse would become more civil.

IDEA

Only sexual expression that neither harms nor degrades is natural and wholesome.

EXPANDED MEANING

Sexual expression that harms and/or degrades is unnatural and unwholesome. The traditional distinction between love and lust is meaningful.[43] There are general standards governing sexual behavior, notably ones arising from the distinction between love and lust. Traditional rules about sexual behavior, notably religious rules, deserve thoughtful consideration, as does the issue of teenage sexual activity.[44] Sex education in the schools should avoid assumptions and oversimplifications and encourage students to think critically about the issues surrounding sexuality. People should feel guilt or shame over sexual behavior that is harmful or degrading.[45]

PROBABLE CONSEQUENCES

If they knew that sexual expression can be harmful and degrading, people would be more discerning about it. Accordingly, the incidence of promiscuity, infidelity, adult-child liaisons, sexual assault, abortion, and sexually transmitted disease would likely decrease.

Authors and filmmakers would reduce the level of gratuitous sex in their works. Questions about whether pornography, prostitution, and sadomasochism should be considered natural and wholesome would be more seriously addressed, as would the issues of gay marriage and polygamy.

Schools would reconsider the focus and content of sex education and sex counseling. Young people would feel less pressure to become sexually active; as a result, more would choose to delay sexual experience and thereby remain longer in school. The courts would treat sexual criminals with increased severity.

In each case, the common-sense idea leads to positive, wholesome consequences that benefit and strengthen society and enrich culture. The stated meanings and consequences, it should be noted, are not based on idle speculation but rather on the logical relationships among the ideas. To appreciate this more fully, it may be helpful to recall what was explained in chapter 3. Causation in the realm of ideas is different from causation in the material world but is no less real for that fact. In the realm of ideas, effects are not forced to occur; they are, instead, *invited*, *encouraged*, or *inspired*. This means that, though people's power to resist the influence of an idea prevents predicting its effects with certainty, it is possible to speak of its *probable* effects, especially when the idea is deeply embedded and/or widely accepted, and thus more influential.

For readers who suspect that I am being overly optimistic or, less innocently, that I am employing verbal sleight of hand to bolster the case against the reigning view of human nature, a simple test will overcome that suspicion. Just examine the meanings shown for each idea to see if they really do flow from it or are implied by it; similarly, examine the consequences and decide whether they are likely to follow. A single example will illustrate how easily this can be done:

To examine the *meaning* of the idea that human nature is inherently imperfect, ask: If this is so, does it follow that "we can behave foolishly or evilly on our own without outside influence," that "when something goes wrong for us, someone else may *or may not* be at fault," and that "before blaming others, we should be sure that the fault is theirs rather than our own"? (And so on through the other expanded meanings.) Concerning the *probable consequences*, ask: Would the idea that human nature is imperfect invite the belief that individuals are generally responsible for what goes wrong in their lives? And would that idea encourage schools to return to traditional moral education and emphasize critical analysis of beliefs and behavior? (And so on through the other consequences.)

Such an examination, I submit, will confirm the logical connections of the idea, its expanded meaning, and its probable consequences. In addition, testing the idea that *achievement leads to justified self-esteem* will reveal that it leads logically to "achievement does not depend on self-esteem" and "it is possible to feel more (or less) self-esteem than one deserves"; also, that as a consequence of accepting these ideas, scholars and authors would likely change their perspectives and present achievement as the goal and self-esteem as a by-product.

Similarly, testing the idea that *truth and reality are objective rather than subjective and discovered rather than created*, will reveal that it leads logically to "believing something does not make it true," "changing one's mind has no effect on reality," and "opinions that distort reality are false"; also, that if these ideas were accepted, educators would pay more attention to the evaluation, judgment, and expression of ideas and students would be more motivated to learn and therefore grow in knowledge and skill.

For the favorable consequences described above to occur, of course, the common-sense view about human nature must be restored, and the opposing views of Hereditarianism and Humanistic Psychology are too deeply rooted for that restoration to occur easily. The only hope for change is if millions of Americans embrace the more reasonable view of human nature, allow it to inform their lives, and work together to transform the various social institutions and the general culture.

8

REORIENTING OURSELVES

An accurate understanding of human nature is essential to meaningful living. But understanding alone is not enough. We also need to develop habits and attitudes consistent with that understanding. Historian Arnold Toynbee refers to this development as the "conquest" of our "innate human egocentricity." He adds that this can be accomplished only individually, never collectively, precisely because "human emotions, consciousness, and will are not collective; they are faculties of an individual human being."[1] To appreciate the difficulty of that challenge, we need only to reflect on the fact that false views of human nature have been influential for a century and have *dominated* our culture for a half century. Several generations have accepted those views and, with the best of intentions, passed them on to their children as truths to guide their thoughts, words, and actions.[2] And mass culture has reinforced the lessons.

As a result of these influences, all of us have been partly or entirely misled about what it means to be human, and our behavior understandably reflects the errors. Our challenge now as individuals is to realign our views and behavior with the realities of human nature. The fact that we have a significant investment of ego in the way we are may make us reluctant to change. However, the reality that our behavior *defines* our identity, for good or for ill, is a compelling reason to change it for the better. The specific strategies that follow are arranged according to the seven insights about human nature detailed in chapter 7.[3]

INCREASING OUR INTELLIGENCE

Human intelligence is the sum of capacity and performance. The former, we are born with; the latter improves or declines depending on our effort to acquire and apply knowledge and mental skills. There is no certain way to tell how much capacity (potential) we have. Measuring our heads won't do it, though in the early days of psychology, many experts staked their reputations on that claim. Taking an IQ test is a less silly approach but not much more reliable, the claims of test makers notwithstanding. The results of an IQ test are, in fact, not a measure of capacity at all but only of a particular performance on a specific occasion, and a rather narrow kind of performance at that.

Over the years, many theorists of intelligence have mistakenly equated performance with capacity. To understand the seriousness of that mistake, consider how it would work in other situations. Imagine, for example, that an analyst examined some correspondence a person had written by hand and noted that in all of it the slant of her writing went up, down, and back up again and that individual letters in her words were inconsistent in size and poorly shaped. The analyst could legitimately conclude that, assuming the samples were typical of the woman's handwriting, she had poor penmanship. But he could make no judgment at all about her *capacity* for penmanship because the cause of her poor performance could as easily be that she paid no attention in school or made no effort to write well, rather than that she was lacking in capacity.

The only way to gauge the woman's capacity for penmanship would be for her to begin exercising care in writing and see if her handwriting improved. The answer would not be final, of course, because there would always be room for improvement. It is the same with intelligence. The greater our effort to improve, the more we realize that our capacity is greater than we had imagined. Here are some ways to make that effort successful.

IDENTIFYING OUTSIDE INFLUENCES

This should not be a onetime effort but an ongoing practice because all of us *continue* to be influenced by what we see and hear. The fact that the world impacts us is not something to lament; through this process we are able to learn and grow. Problems arise only when we react to the influences unthinkingly, as we all do on occasion—it is virtually impossible to be on our intellectual guard every moment of every day.

The first step is to consider ideas that we hold strongly, asking which of them we formed after careful analysis and which we merely absorbed from others. It should come as no surprise that some, or even many, of our ideas fall into the latter category. The realization that we have embraced, and perhaps passionately defended, ideas we have never really examined is certainly not pleasant, but it is the essential first step in increasing our independence of mind.

EVALUATING BORROWED IDEAS

When we find ideas that have taken up residence in our minds without our full and informed consent, we shouldn't dismiss them—after all, they could prove to be sound. Instead, we should investigate further, compare them with competing ideas, and decide whether the borrowed ideas *deserve* our acceptance. If they don't, we should replace them with better ones. This process can seem like a betrayal of the older ideas, but it is not. Rather, it is an exercise of freedom of choice and a demonstration that *we own our ideas*, and not the other way around.

APPROACHING INTELLECTUAL CHALLENGES SYSTEMATICALLY

It is tacitly accepted that people with a lot of education and many degrees are necessarily better thinkers than those with a more modest education. However, that is not necessarily the case. As we have seen, for over a century education has focused more on stuffing minds with facts than on developing skill in thinking. As a result, when it comes to skill in thinking, highly educated people do not necessarily have an advantage over less educated people.

The key to effective thinking is something that is not taught well or consistently, if it is taught at all, in most schools and colleges—employing a systematic approach to problems and issues. The simplest and easiest approach is the W.I.S.E.[4] approach:

> The first step, WONDER, applies *reflective* thinking to examine experiences and identify interesting problems and issues and promising lines of inquiry.
>
> The second step, INVESTIGATE, answers the questions raised by reflection and provides the information necessary to address the problem or issue responsibly.
>
> The third step, SPECULATE, applies *creative* thinking to produce possible solutions to problems or ideas for resolving issues.
>
> The final step, EVALUATE, applies *critical* thinking to compare the possible solutions and decide which is most practical, or ideas for resolving issues to decide which is most reasonable.

For best results, the first step—wondering—should be employed *constantly* to help us recognize problems and issues when they arise. When we find a challenge that deserves immediate attention, we can proceed with the other three steps.

BEING ALERT FOR ERRORS IN OUR OWN THINKING, AS WELL AS IN THE THINKING OF OTHERS

Errors in thinking can occur despite our best efforts, so it is always helpful to check for them, especially before stating our ideas. This approach can spare us the embarrassment of having others detect our errors. Here are the most common errors, with tips for avoiding or correcting them.

> *Making unwarranted assumptions* means taking too much for granted. Solution: take nothing for granted that is not supported by the facts or experience.

Oversimplifying means offering easier answers than the situation warrants. Solution: where complexity exists—for example, where the evidence is conflicting or where no one viewpoint is completely satisfactory—we should construct a viewpoint that reflects that reality.

Forming hasty conclusions means making a judgment about something before we have sufficient evidence. Solution: we should consider all possible conclusions and decide which one the evidence best supports.

Overgeneralizing means ascribing to all members of a group characteristics or behaviors that apply to only some members. Solution: we should resist the urge to judge the many by what we observe in the few.

Contradiction means saying or doing something that is in direct opposition to something we said or did previously, without a reasonable explanation. Solution: we should be consistent in our thoughts and actions unless we have a sound reason for being inconsistent (for example, having changed our minds in light of new evidence).

Shifting the burden of proof means demanding that others disprove our assertions. Solution: we should remember that the one who *makes* an assertion has the burden of proof.

Creating a "straw man" means attributing to someone a statement or argument that he or she did not make and then disproving the statement or argument. Solution: we should be accurate in quoting and paraphrasing others and never attribute statements falsely.

Attacking the person means attempting to refute an argument by disparaging the person who expresses it. Solution: remember that an argument can be disproved only by exposing *its* weaknesses, not the personal weaknesses of the person who presents it.

In looking for errors in our own thinking, we should be especially alert for ones to which experience has shown us to be particularly vulnerable.

OVERCOMING OUR IMPERFECTIONS

In portraying human beings as inherently wise and good, Humanistic Psychologists claimed to be overcoming what they saw as the depressingly negative views of Freudianism, Behaviorism, and the Jewish and Christian religious traditions. Their view was not entirely without merit. Freudianism was focused on aberrant behavior rooted in unconscious sexual drives. Behaviorism compared human beings to Pavlov's famous dog whose responses were governed by cued salivation rather than conscious mental activity. And Calvinism taught that original sin reduces human beings to total depravity.

Where Humanistic Psychology went wrong, however, was in ignoring the fact that the older and more mainstream Jewish and Christian traditions asserted humankind's essential *deprivation* (not depravity), which we have been referring to as *inherent imperfection*.

There is no need to repeat the evidence documenting that humans are imperfect. But what should be underscored is that this view is not in the least negative or depressing. Without human imperfection, life would not be very interesting. Take sports, for example. The excitement of any contest is generated by the knowledge that because neither team is perfect, each will make mistakes. As the contest progresses, particularly between well-matched teams, tension mounts and the fans wonder, "Which team will perform better [that is overcome its imperfections] in the crucial moments? Will the outcome be decided by a brilliant play or an untimely blunder?" It is no different in other, more serious areas of life, including marriage and parenting, business and the professions, government, and even the arts. Our inherent human imperfection adds the drama of uncertainty to life. More importantly, it challenges us to make our lives meaningful. The following section details some strategies for meeting that challenge.

ACKNOWLEDGING OUR IMPERFECTIONS AND FAULTS

Popular culture has brainwashed us into thinking that our mental and emotional health depend on thinking only complimentary thoughts about ourselves, rejecting all criticism (including self-criticism), and filling ourselves will pride and self-esteem. That is exactly the opposite of the advice offered by wise men and women for millennia. They understood that, though admitting our weaknesses and faults is unpleasant, doing so is the only way to grow in wisdom and goodness.

FOCUSING ON IMPROVEMENT

When we begin to recognize our imperfections and faults, we naturally feel embarrassed and ashamed. Such feelings can lead in a positive or negative direction depending on our attitude. A morbid, defeatist attitude—"I am a wretched person and there is no hope for me"—is not helpful and may even cause emotional harm. That attitude, it should be noted, usually reflects an *inflated* view of self. In other words, what it really means is, "I am so special and so important that the basic rule of life—that I should keep trying—doesn't apply to me." A more wholesome and beneficial attitude is, "OK, I've behaved foolishly (or immorally), but I can and *will* do better in the future." That attitude is appropriate no matter how many times we fall short of our goal because it is always a spur to positive effort.

EXPECTING LESS OF OTHERS AND MORE OF OURSELVES

One consequence of Humanistic Psychology's exaltation of self has been to expect much more of others than we do of ourselves. This has led, in turn, to increased disappointment and resentment. The founders of that psychological movement did not expect these effects, but they should have. When we are taught to think of ourselves as wise and wonderful and *entitled* to the praise, esteem, and deference of others, we naturally expect them to respond accordingly. And when they don't, we feel insulted and take offense. Of course, the whole dynamic is silly on its face. We know that others have also been taught to regard themselves as highly as we regard ourselves, so it should be obvious that they are too absorbed in their own expectations to think much about meeting ours.

The best way to lessen our disappointment and resentment is to lower our expectations of other people. There are several ways to do this. One is to remember that other people, like us, are imperfect and sometimes behave badly, even when they want to behave well. Another is to reflect on the difficulty we have in correcting *our own* unacceptable behavior and, accordingly, to be patient with others. (If they give no outward sign of trying to change, we can still be gracious and give them the benefit of the doubt.) A third way is to practice *noblesse oblige*—that is, to acknowledge that knowledge carries responsibility, so those of us who understand how culture influences people's behavior should meet a higher standard than those who do not understand.

ACHIEVING SELF-TRANSCENDENCE

As we have seen throughout this book, misunderstanding of the concept of self has done considerable mischief. Many people are unaware of the penetrating insights provided by such scholars as Viktor Frankl (see chapter 6) mainly because the perspective of Humanistic Psychology is so deeply embedded in mass culture. From that perspective, self is something to indulge, exalt, and celebrate rather than restrain and control. Frankl's research, which was based not only on extensive clinical experience but also on the unique opportunities for observation in his years in Nazi concentration camps, reaffirmed the wisdom of the ancient view that the greatest human challenge is to *transcend* self. The following strategies are helpful in meeting that challenge.

UNDERSTANDING THE PARADOX OF SELF

"If you would save yourself, you must lose yourself" is best known as a biblical injunction, but it has philosophical import, as well—if we would become the better selves we ought to be, we must transform (and in that sense, *lose*) our present selves. As long as we cling to our present selves, the necessary transformation cannot occur. The difficulty is that in our human imperfection, we have conflicting desires. We aspire to be better than we are, yet at the same time enjoy being as we are; part of us wants to change, and part doesn't. Which part wins the contest depends on how we exercise our power of choice.

ENDING OUR PURSUIT OF SELF-ACTUALIZATION

Humanistic Psychology's notion that the highest human goal is to "actualize" ourselves has been a main theme of education, psychological and spiritual counseling, literature and entertainment, and self-help literature for half a century. We have been conditioned to believe that our fulfillment as human beings depends on our pursuit of self-actualization. But as we have seen, that idea is false. Fulfillment comes from finding *meaning* in our lives, and meaning can be found only outside the self, never within it.

Accordingly, the less we focus attention on ourselves, the better our chance of reaching fulfillment. This task is far from easy. We have been encouraged to be absorbed and even obsessed with ourselves. One simple way to overcome this habit is to monitor the occurrence of *I*, *me*, *my*, and *mine* in our thoughts and words. Some concern for self is unavoidable, of course, but when it seems excessive, we should shift our attention to the problem or issue before us, or to the people involved. Another approach is to make a conscious effort to forget about *getting* things from others— including attention, recognition, and praise—and to focus instead on *giving*. A third is to remain alert for and take advantage of opportunities to rise above mere self-interest.

ACCEPTING RESPONSIBILITY FOR OUR BEHAVIOR

Mistakes are best acknowledged as soon as possible. The longer we wait, the more inclined we will be to save face by blaming other people or circumstances or bad luck. Does blame *ever* lie elsewhere than with us? Of course, but if we focus on that explanation, we are likely to ignore any responsibility for our behavior. The fact is, though we may have little or no control over the circumstances and situations life presents, or over other people's behavior, we have free will and can always choose *our responses* to them. Moreover, it is our responses, and not our good intentions, that define us.

As important as it is to admit our mistakes, it is unwise to *dwell* on past events and choices. Doing so can cause us to miss opportunities to make wise choices in the present. After all, the present moment is the only one in which choice is possible. The most positive and constructive way to take responsibility for our behavior is to stay mentally awake, consider our options for responding to present situations, and choose wisely.

BEING ALERT FOR MEANING IN LIFE

As Viktor Frankl explained, meaning can take many forms; most notably, *a cause to serve, a role to play, a person to love,* or *a suffering to endure.* It is unrealistic to expect meaning to announce itself with the sound of trumpets. It comes quietly, unexpectedly, fleetingly, and often beneath the surface of events. If we are not looking for it, we may easily miss it, as the following actual case illustrates.

A man I know was depressed that his mother was suffering from advanced Alzheimer's disease. Whenever he visited her, his heart went out to her. Yet he also felt angry and resentful: "Why," he wondered, "must this wonderful, caring woman suffer such a wretched disease?" Then one day while visiting her with his stepfather, he detected meaning that he had not perceived before. Here is how he later explained it to his stepfather, who shared the story with me:[5]

> I carried my negative feeling with me during our visits with Mom. Then one time, I recall just sitting and watching you with her. How you gently stroked her head. How you fed and cared for her. How you held her hand and looked lovingly into her eyes. How you kissed her and gently whispered, "I love you." How you prayed with her. Then it hit me: I was looking at the wrong person. What I was supposed to learn was not from Mom but from you. I want to thank you, not just for your tireless efforts in caring for Mom, but for showing me the true measure of devotion and love. When my children ask me what true love is, I'll know how to respond.

The habit of reflection is an invaluable aid in the search for meaning. A helpful approach is to set aside a time, for example fifteen or so minutes before bedtime, and review the events of the day, and then consider what hints or clues those events contain that can make our lives more meaningful.

REVISITING OUR RELIGIOUS OR ETHICAL HERITAGE

Historically, the search for meaning in life has been associated with religion. This association is understandable because, generally speaking, religion and many nonreligious ethical traditions hold the view that the locus of authority is outside the human person.[6] Unfortunately, Humanistic Psychology challenged this view, claiming—erroneously, as we have seen—that authority lies within the individual. As this notion became fashionable, many people drifted from their religious beliefs and ethical traditions or recast them in a narcissistic mold. Reacquainting ourselves with our families' religious or ethical traditions offers several benefits. It helps to free us from self-absorption. It increases understanding of our parents' and grandparents' values and convictions and diminishes our sense of alienation. And it focuses our attention on the profound questions that have been prominent in people's search for meaning for millennia: "Does God exist?" and "If so, what effect should this have on my life?" and "If no God exists, what ethical tradition should I embrace?"

RESPECTING OTHER PEOPLE

Respect for persons is arguably the most fundamental principle of ethics. It not only requires us to regard human beings as worthy of respect, but it also prohibits us from treating any human being as "a mere possession" or "a mere instrument" or "a mere obstacle" to our ends.[7] The three criteria of ethical judgment—obligations, moral ideals, and consequences—are derived from this principle. In other words, because people are deserving of respect, we should honor whatever obligations arise from our relationships with them; treat them in accord with the ideals of fairness, honesty, gratitude, compassion, and loving kindness (among others); and avoid behaving in ways that have negative consequences for them. By practicing respect for persons and putting their rights and needs above our wants, we not only honor them but also advance toward self-transcendence.

AVOIDING ENVY

At best, envy is a distraction. At worst, it mires us in self-pity, which is but another form of the self-absorption that hinders transcendence. In either case, envy is based entirely on speculation because we can never rule out the possibility that the person we envy has greater problems than we have. Edwin Arlington Robinson dramatized this fact in his 1897 poem titled "Richard Cory." (The poem has been widely anthologized and is also easy to find online.)

> Whenever Richard Cory went down town,
> We people on the pavement looked at him:
> He was a gentleman from sole to crown,
> Clean favored, and imperially slim.
>
> And he was always quietly arrayed,
> And he was always human when he talked;
> But still he fluttered pulses when he said,
> "Good-morning," and he glittered when he walked.
>
> And he was rich—yes, richer than a king—
> And admirably schooled in every grace:
> In fine, we thought that he was everything
> To make us wish that we were in his place.
>
> So on we worked, and waited for the light,
> And went without the meat, and cursed the bread;
> And Richard Cory, one calm summer night,
> Went home and put a bullet through his head.

ACHIEVING JUSTIFIED SELF-ESTEEM

Humanistic Psychology is responsible for the widespread notion that we must have high self-esteem before we can achieve anything. As we have seen, the voluminous research that has been done on the subject lends no support to this idea—in fact, it gives ample reason to reject the idea. The basic mistake of self-esteem theory is that it puts the proverbial cart before the horse—that is, it claims that self-esteem leads to achievement when in fact it is achievement that leads to genuine, justified self-esteem. Following this flawed model, educators, self-help authors, and counselors have been advising people to esteem themselves outside the context of effort and for no good reason—in effect, to esteem themselves for the sake of esteeming themselves. The result has been an increase in underachieving and, therefore, in the number of disappointed people, a condition perplexed advisors try to solve by more excited exhortations to self-esteem. Helpful ways to achieve genuine, justified self-esteem include the following.

REMEMBERING THAT GENUINE SELF-ESTEEM IS EARNED

We can begin by recalling the accomplishments in our lives. First some small ones, like learning to jump rope, dribble a basketball, or ride a bike; then bigger ones, like learning to play a musical instrument, drive a car, or grasp the content of a difficult academic subject. We should also try to reconstruct our feelings at various stages of the experiences: when we took up the challenge, while we were struggling with it, and when we succeeded. In most cases, we began with some degree of trepidation, unsure of whether we would succeed. As we proceeded and encountered difficulty, we no doubt felt inadequate and may have even entertained the thought of quitting. If we managed to persevere and proceeded to overcome each difficulty, however, we gained confidence and were encouraged to keep trying. Eventually, when we achieved success, we felt satisfaction and pride. The common lesson in all these experiences is that success depends mainly on courage and perseverance. If these are present, it doesn't matter how good we feel about ourselves at the start—we can be reasonably sure we'll have that feeling when we finish. And that is what matters.

ENDING OUR CONCERN ABOUT SELF-ESTEEM

For decades we've heard that we should take care that our self-esteem is sufficiently high. The only way to do that, of course, is to keep asking ourselves "How do I feel about myself now? Better than I did an hour ago? Is my self-esteem rising or falling?" That's much like taking our pulse a hundred times a day to be sure it stays in the normal range. If we aren't neurotic when we begin either regimen, we will likely become so in the process. Among the simplest and most obvious facts of life is that the way we feel about ourselves will vary throughout the day, generally in relation to the quality of our behavior at various moments. If we are engaged in worthy thoughts, words, and deeds, we are likely to feel good about ourselves—and rightly so. If we are otherwise engaged, we are likely to feel bad about ourselves, also rightly. In short, if we strive to behave wisely and well, we needn't worry about our self-esteem—it will take care of itself.

BEING LESS CONCERNED ABOUT RECOGNITION AND PRAISE

It is perfectly natural to enjoy receiving recognition and praise because they make us feel good about ourselves. That is precisely why the gurus of self-esteem have assigned them such importance and prominence. As a result, many people feel deprived, even cheated, when they are not constantly complimented and held up for adulation. But that attitude leads inevitably to disappointment and even despair. Far better to accept these basic realities: First, most people are too involved addressing their own challenges or, given the influence of self-esteem theory, with maintaining their own self-image, to devote much time to recognizing and praising others. Second, there is little correlation between deserving recognition and receiving it. Many of the most deserving people among us are seldom noticed, let alone celebrated. The poet Thomas Gray said it best: "Full many a flower is born to blush unseen, and waste its sweetness on the desert air." Of course, the flower is no less sweet for that fact. Nor will we be any less worthy if our accomplishments and good deeds go unrecognized.

The best way to reduce the desire for recognition and praise is to focus all our attention on being estimable—that is, *deserving* of esteem. In other words, being diligent in meeting responsibilities, conscientious and enthusiastic in responding to life's challenges, and faithful to our beliefs, principles, and ideals. If recognition for those accomplishments comes, we will be pleasantly surprised. If it does not, we will have achieved something more precious—the knowledge that we are worthy of it.

VIEWING CRITICISM POSITIVELY

The idea that all criticism, including self-criticism, is harmful has been popularized by the gurus of self-esteem theory, but it is a foolish notion. Given the right perspective, *all* criticism works to our advantage. Valid criticism provides us with insights for improving ourselves. Invalid, unfair criticism alerts us to others' misperceptions and to the challenge of changing their minds. Self-criticism is especially helpful because it allows us to identify and correct our mistakes before others see them, thus sparing us embarrassment.

VALUING TRUTH

The reigning view, often subtle and unstated, is that everyone creates his or her own truth. As we have seen, the idea is not a new one. Humanistic Psychology borrowed it from the Romantic movement of the late eighteenth and the nineteenth centuries, particularly from the work of Jean Jacques Rousseau. Though this idea is often considered enlightened, it is utterly foolish. If truth were created, then there would be no such thing as error and no point in seeking facts or consulting evidence. Accordingly, we would have no need of doctors, scientists, engineers, jurists, teachers, or any other professionals. Yet the briefest reflection will reveal that error does exist, facts are important, and the skills of professionals are essential, particularly in dealing with complex questions. The following strategies help us maintain and apply a sensible view of truth.

FOCUSING ON DISCOVERING (RATHER THAN CREATING) TRUTH

Because truth is discovered rather than created, seeking truth always involves looking outside ourselves—that is, beyond our beliefs and preferences, desires and expectations.[8] Wishing that something were true will not make it true, nor will refusing to acknowledge a truth make it any less true. The way to search will depend on the situation. For mathematical truth, we gather numbers and perform calculations; for historical truth, we compare and evaluate different interpretations; for political truth, we examine conflicting claims, check facts, and evaluate opinions. In some cases, truth is easy to find; in others, it is complex and elusive, notably in philosophical and religious matters. What is most important to remember is that the truth about anything does not differ from person to person; it is objective, the same for all people.

BASING OPINIONS ON EVIDENCE

When people are asked why they believe something to be true, the typical answer is "It's my opinion." The unspoken meaning of this feeble response is, "I don't need a basis for my opinion; it's something I have a right to," the implication being that having a right to an opinion *makes that opinion correct*. Such thinking derives from the belief that truth is created and it is no less false than that belief. We do have a right to form and hold our opinion, but that does not guarantee that our opinion will be correct. It is correct when it accurately reflects reality and wrong when it does not.

Forming opinions is a natural function of the human mind, and it can be done more or less conscientiously. We show intellectual maturity and respect for the truth by identifying the possible opinions on the subject, considering the facts and arguments that support each of those opinions, and choosing the opinion that proves to be most reasonable. This approach increases the chances that our opinions will be defensible. It also enables us to give a meaningful answer when asked why we hold an opinion.

BEING WILLING TO REVISE OUR OPINIONS

As important as it is to form opinions with care, that alone is not enough. We must also be willing to revise our opinions when there is good reason to do so. Knowledge is constantly expanding, and the evidence available at the time we formed an opinion might have been challenged by later research. Revising opinions doesn't come easy, especially if we have wrapped our ego around them. American logician Rowland Jepson explains why:

> When we have once adopted an opinion, our pride makes us [reluctant] to admit that we are wrong. When objections are made to our views, we are more concerned with discovering how to combat them than how much truth and sound sense there may be in them. . . . We all know how easy it is to become annoyed at the suggestion that we have made a mistake; that our first feeling is that we would rather do anything than admit it, and our first thought is "How can I explain it away?"[9]

To overcome the tendency to cling irrationally to our opinions, we need to remind ourselves that there is no shame in changing a viewpoint in light of new evidence and that it is not only foolish, irresponsible, and potentially embarrassing to hold to a viewpoint after it has been disproved, it is also a violation of our commitment to truth.

AVOIDING DISHONEST TERMINOLOGY

In his famous 1946 essay titled "Politics and the English Language," George Orwell observed that "if thought corrupts language, language can also corrupt thought." Among his examples of corrupting terminology were these terms: *pacification* to describe killing innocent people and destroying their property (the modern equivalent is *collateral damage*); *transfer of population* for forcing people out of their homes and localities; and *elimination of unreliable elements* for imprisoning people without cause. His point was that when we use such terms, we reduce unpleasant realities to abstractions and hide or deny the truth about them.

Two contemporary examples of dishonest terminology are *redistribution of wealth* and *potential human being.* The former term hides the fact that the process in question is a form of governmental theft, taking what one person has earned and therefore has a right to and giving it to another person who has no legitimate claim to it. The latter term is used in discussions of abortion and is considered a scientific synonym for *fetus.*[10] In reality, *potential human being* is neither scientific nor synonymous with *fetus.* The scientific definition of *fetus* is "an unborn human being"; in other words, something that (a) has existence or is alive, and (b) is a member of the species *homo sapiens.* When the word *potential* is added, the designation changes radically, and falsely, from "already human" to "not-yet-human." This inaccurate and therefore dishonest formulation makes opposition to abortion seem unscientific when, in reality, it is firmly rooted in science.

If our viewpoint is valid, we should be able to defend it with honest terminology. If we cannot do so, we should consider the possibility that it is mistaken.

ELEVATING REASON OVER FEELINGS

In discussing reason and feelings, the issue is not which is good and which is bad. Both have an important role to play in our lives. The issue is, instead, which is more reliable and therefore should take precedence. As we have seen, reason is more reliable. The error of Humanistic Psychology lay not in valuing feelings but in *over*valuing them and, in the process, deprecating reason. Mass culture has promoted this view and conditioned people to behave impulsively. The following are strategies for overcoming this conditioning and restoring a healthy balance between feelings and reason in our lives.

ACKNOWLEDGING THE BENEFITS AND LIMITATIONS OF FEELINGS

This acknowledgment will be more helpful if it is based on actual personal experiences rather than abstract, hypothetical ones. We should, for example, think of occasions when feelings of gratitude and appreciation motivated us to express thanks, feelings of sympathy or compassion inspired us to perform acts of consideration and kindness, and love for others led us to sacrifice our interests to theirs. We should also recall when feelings led us to harm ourselves or others. For example, occasions when feelings of anger or resentment caused us to do harm, feelings of envy or covetousness led us to lie or steal, and acting impulsively caused us to violate our own moral code. Such recollections help us appreciate that, though feelings can encourage good behavior, they also can encourage bad, and thus should never be followed blindly or taken as the measure of their own worth.

BEING MORE AWARE OF OUR FEELINGS

The essential first step in dealing with our feelings is to realize that we have them. This is easier to say than to do because feelings arise without prior announcement. They also have a variety of triggers—not just the obvious one of present events, but also the more subtle ones of memories, associations, assumptions, and expectations. The story is told of a man who had a flat tire late at night on a lonely road. Looking in his trunk and finding no jack, he decided to walk back to a farmhouse he had passed a half mile before. As he walked, he wondered about the reception he would receive: "There are no lights on so the farmer is surely sleeping. He'll no doubt be annoyed at my waking him. I wouldn't be surprised if he thought me a fool for not carrying a jack in my car. He might even laugh aloud at me. Worse, he may refuse to lend me a jack." By the time he reached the house and knocked on the door, his imagination had made him so angry that, before the farmer could say a word, the man shouted, "Keep your damn jack" and stomped away.

One way to become more aware of our feelings is to think back over significant events that created strong emotional reactions in us and identify our "emotional triggers." This awareness will help us to anticipate potential reactions before they occur and to decide whether they are appropriate.

TESTING FEELINGS BEFORE TRUSTING THEM

It is fashionable to believe that feelings represent a direct, even infallible, path to insight. We are told "trust your gut," "first impressions are truest," and "trust your hunches . . . hunches are usually based on facts."[11] These views may be explained by the tendency to remember good experiences and forget bad ones, the same tendency that causes gamblers to remember their wins and forget their losses, even though the latter may be many times greater; or the tendency that makes us recall our high school days as joyous when they actually may have been a time of anxiety and disappointment.

In the case of feelings, we tend to remember the times when later events proved them accurate and forget all the other times—for example, times when we felt someone was trustworthy and later found he was not. As noted in chapter 4, feelings can be capricious and contradictory, and they can distort our perception. In addition, they often reflect what we *wish* to be true rather than what *is* true and therefore invite self-deception. The only way to be sure that a feeling, an impression, a hunch, or an intuition is correct is to determine whether more objective evidence confirms it. Trusting feelings before testing them is dangerous.

THINKING CAREFULLY BEFORE EXPRESSING NEGATIVE FEELINGS

Humanistic Psychology encourages us to express our negative feelings on the grounds that suppression is harmful. Expressing anger, for example, is said to "get it out of our systems," whereas holding it in allows psychic pressure to build up and eventually explode, much as steam does when suddenly released from a pressure cooker. However reasonable this may sound, it is false.

In *Anger: The Misunderstood Emotion*, Carol Tavris did an in-depth study of the research on anger. She found that "the psychological rationales for ventilating anger do not stand up under experimental scrutiny." In fact, many studies documented that the more people talk about their anger, *the angrier they become.* Studies also reveal that when people ignore their anger, it often dissolves; even if it does not, the passing of time at least gives people a chance to choose a suitable way to deal with it.[12] The same insight applies to other negative emotions, including feeling annoyed, frustrated, offended, disrespected, unappreciated, cheated, and betrayed. Many a relationship has been destroyed, and many a job lost, by ill-considered expressions of negative emotions.

Before expressing a negative feeling, we should take some time, at least a day but preferably longer, and during that time ponder these questions:

What do I hope to achieve besides the satisfaction of speaking my mind? To make the person feel guilty, have him or her apologize, and, as a result, cause him or her to behave differently in the future? If so, is it reasonable to expect this reaction to occur at once, or is it likely to take longer? How long would it take *me* to give such a reaction to someone else?

Is it possible that the person will respond differently than I expect? For example, to deny my allegation and even to argue that I am responsible for my own negative feelings? Might that argument be, at least in part, true? If so, what changes should I make in myself?

Finally, we should decide whether it will be better to remain silent than to express the feelings, or at least to modify what we originally felt like saying.

BEING RESPONSIBLE ABOUT SEX

That sex is the most pleasurable of human activities is a truism that modern media never tire of accentuating in living color. But media enchantment with this theme has tended to obscure a vital fact: human sexuality is much more complex than animal coupling. It is not just physical and physiological but metaphysical as well, involving emotion, intellect, and will. Being responsible about sex means appreciating this complexity, understanding the ways in which sexual behavior impacts our lives and those of other people, and behaving accordingly. The following are some ways to do so.

UNDERSTANDING THE ROLE OF LOVE IN SEX

"Let's not talk of love at a time like this" was the caption accompanying an old *Playboy* cartoon of a couple in an excited, amorous embrace. It nicely summed up the modern notion that love and sex are only tangentially related, if indeed they are related at all. Rogers, Maslow, Kinsey, Hefner, and their many disciples have been remarkably successful in embedding this message in mass culture. Accordingly, millions of people have grown up believing—mistakenly—that sexual activity should be enjoyed with little or no regard for love.

The English language, though rich in many respects, is unfortunately limited in its terminology for love. Whereas we have a single word, *love*, to cover our sentiments toward our parents, spouses, children, pets, and even our sports teams, the ancient Greeks had four words: *eros* for physical passion, *storge* for affection toward family, *philia* for affection toward friends, and *agape* for respect, charity, and empathy toward all people, including strangers and people of other races, cultures, and religions.

Agape differs from the other terms in that it applies to everyone in all circumstances. This kind of love is the foundation of the Golden Rule, "Do unto others as you would have them do unto you," which is found in virtually every religion from African tribal religion to Zoroastrianism, as well as in secular philosophies.[13] *Agape* can therefore be said to be an essential element in each of the other three forms of love.

DISTINGUISHING BETWEEN EROS AND LUST

Someone once suggested that the difference is that erotic love is about *giving* and lust is about *getting*. That is the essential difference, to be sure. But there are others. Erotic love, like other kinds of love, cares for the other person, wants the best for him or her, even to the point of being willing to forego personal satisfaction and happiness in the other person's interest. Lust, on the other hand, aims exclusively for pleasure and regards the other person not as a person at all, with complex emotions and a mind, ideals, and aspirations, but merely as an object to be used for personal gratification.

An even more important distinction between erotic love and lust is in the matter of intimacy. Erotic love desires intimacy, not only in the physical sense, but also in the emotional or spiritual sense; it seeks a mutual sharing of hopes, fears, dreams, and the most secret matters of the individual psyche. In contrast, lust has no interest in intimacy—that is why it is indiscriminate and profligate.

AFFIRMING THE RELEVANCE OF MORALITY TO SEXUAL BEHAVIOR

We have noted that the fundamental principle of morality is respect for persons. The form of love that the ancient Greeks called *agape* is virtually synonymous with this view. That principle is applicable in all social interactions, including sexual ones. One could argue that it is even applicable in autoerotic sex, when there is only one person involved, because as persons we are obligated to respect ourselves as we do others. Incidentally, the same moral argument underlies the traditional view of suicide as immoral.

The founders of Humanistic Psychology did not acknowledge the relevance of the principle of respect for persons in moral matters, either because they knowingly ignored it or because, more likely, they were ignorant of the subject of ethics. In any case, they were mistaken in regarding sexual behavior as outside the domain of ethics. *Sexual behavior that is consistent with respect for persons (agape) is moral. Sexual behavior that is inconsistent with respect for persons is an offense against the other person's humanity and is therefore immoral.* What conclusions can be reached about various forms of sexual behavior when this criterion of respect for persons is applied? A full, nuanced answer would require considerably more space than is available here. Nevertheless, the following lines of thought deserve consideration.

> *Sexual activity outside marriage* (fornication), particularly in the teenage years, aside from presenting the risk of sexually transmitted disease or pregnancy, poses several dangers. If the motivation of either party is lust rather than love, the other person is thereby disrespected ("used," in the vernacular) and demeaned, even if that

person acquiesces in the demeaning. For example, a man who has casual sex with a woman whom he knows is acting out of a desperate craving for attention is no less guilty of disrespecting her, and perhaps even more so. But what of cases in which the motivation of both parties is *love*? Is respect for persons present then? It can be, but is not automatically present. If either party realizes that harmful consequences are likely to occur and cause the other person pain, then he or she should forego sexual involvement out of respect for the other person's welfare. For example, when it is clear that the relationship has little chance of lasting, the intimacy will then be in vain, and the other person will likely be emotionally scarred as a result.

Promiscuity is self-demeaning and creates an obstacle to achieving genuine intimacy in the future, not least because it makes one likely to withhold the truth about past behavior. Also, in many cases, promiscuity (like lust) disrespects sexual partners by considering them instruments of one's own fulfillment rather than persons.

Adultery disrespects one's spouse in two ways: (1) by violating the obligation to exclusivity that is stated or implied in the marriage contract and (2) by betraying intimacy.

Autoeroticism (masturbation) is quite literally a form of self-indulgence and, as such, can be an obstacle to self-transcendence. Moreover, the viewing of pornography that often accompanies autoeroticism entails a disregard for other people's humanity by using their *images* for sexual arousal, without regard to their personhood.

It should be noted that this discussion of the relevance of morality to sexual behavior is entirely philosophical, without any reference to theological doctrine. In addition to addressing the issue, the fact that such discussion is meaningful demonstrates that moral reasoning is not confined to religion and not relevant only to "religious people."

REVIVING CONSCIENCE

Conscience may be defined as the ability to tell right from wrong.[14] This ability varies among people. In some it is highly developed; in others, less so. In rare cases such as serial killers and assassins who show no remorse, conscience is virtually nonexistent. A number of factors are involved in the development of conscience. One is upbringing: parents and teachers who offer guidance in distinguishing right from wrong aid in that development, as do friends who value the distinction. Another factor is the view of morality enshrined in the culture; the view that there are objective standards of right and wrong encourages the development of conscience; opposing views retard it. A third factor is habit; the practice of basing behavior on considerations of right and wrong, as opposed to acting on impulse, enhances the development of conscience.

Over the last century, unfortunately, Humanistic Psychology has persuaded many people that morality is subjective, feelings are infallible, and conscience need not be developed or nurtured. As a result, many people have been deprived of moral guidance at home and in school, conditioned by the communications and entertainment media to deny objective moral standards, and discouraged from thinking very much about moral questions. As a result, their consciences have been compromised in a way Samuel Johnson described as follows:

> Not only [do] our speculations influence our practice, but our practice reciprocally influences our speculations. We not only do what we approve, but there is danger lest in time we come to approve what we do . . . for no other reason than that we do it. A man is always desirous of being at peace with himself; and when he cannot reconcile his passions to [his] conscience, he will attempt to reconcile his conscience to his passions.[15]

Those of us who have allowed conscience to be suppressed will need to revive it in all moral matters, but especially in sexual morality, for that is the area that relativism has permeated most dramatically. One way to do so is to be mindful of our obligations—not only the obligation of fidelity to a fiancé or spouse, but also the more general obligation of respect for others.

Another way is to set high moral ideals, especially the ideals of fairness, empathy, compassion, and kindness. A third is to regard discussions of sex in books and magazines and sexual themes in movies and television more thoughtfully, deciding whether they reflect or oppose our view of right and wrong.

CONTROLLING SEXUAL IMPULSES

Sexual desires and the inclination to act on them are part of the human condition. The degree to which the desires and urges are stimulated, however, differs from one cultural era to another; and it is fair to say that the stimulation has never been greater than it is today. The reasons are that the prevailing attitude toward sexual expression is permissive and indulgent and that technological sophistication has created an unprecedented number of ways to transmit that stimulation. Simply said, sexual temptation is pervasive and inescapable.

The dilemma for those who realize that morality applies to sexual expression is how to exercise sexual self-control in an age that scoffs at the very idea. The time-honored approach of exercising willpower and resisting temptation is still valid, but it is more difficult than ever to accomplish. Another way is to develop the habit of reflection: whenever we experience a sexual urge, we can consider the possible consequences of acting upon it, focusing not just on the positive, pleasurable ones, but also on the negative ones and, in light of those possible consequences, deciding what behavior is morally responsible. Yet another approach is to imagine how those closest to us would feel if they learned that we had acted on the urge, and how we would feel if they knew. Finally, in situations in which the urge persists even after we realize it should be resisted, we can use the approach our mothers employed when, as children, we couldn't take our eyes off the grocery store candy rack—that is, distraction. In other words, we can turn our thoughts to something both wholesome and engaging or take up an activity in which we can easily become engrossed.

PONDERING GUILT FEELINGS ABOUT SEX

We have seen that Humanistic Psychology was mistaken in claiming that feelings of guilt are always unhealthy. The more accurate view is that, though feelings of guilt are unhealthy when they are without foundation, they are *healthy* when we have done something wrong. In the latter case, feelings of guilt are the sign of a sound conscience. Whenever we experience a feeling of guilt about sexual behavior (or, for that matter, about any other behavior), we should not dismiss the feeling—doing so could suppress the "voice" of conscience. Instead, we should consider whether the feeling is appropriate; that is, whether it is a response to something we did that was morally wrong. If the answer is yes, we should accept the feeling of guilt as a motivation to behave differently in the future.

GUIDING CHILDREN

As important as it is to overcome misconceptions about human nature in our own lives, for those of us who have children it is equally important to provide them with the guidance they need in such matters. Parents have a responsibility to help children understand their human nature and live meaningful lives, both for their own sake and for the sake of society. Following are suggestions for meeting this responsibility.

ACCEPTING THE CHALLENGE

False ideas about parenting are as common as false ideas about human nature. One of the most insidious of these ideas is the notion that parents have neither the right nor the expertise to guide their children. Many parents have been persuaded that sharing their beliefs with their children somehow violates their children's individuality. Adding to the problem, many children have been persuaded that parental guidance is an imposition that they are justified in resisting.

Such ideas rest on the foolish notion that if parents refrain from sharing their beliefs and values with their children, the children will develop on their own, free from outside influences. In reality, there are plenty of influences at work in children's lives in addition to parental influences—the influences of teachers, peers, filmmakers, actors, musicians, journalists, and advertisers, among others. The notion that such people will provide wiser, more helpful guidance than the parents who gave the children life and who love them is absurd. Parents need to reject such nonsense and commit themselves to the challenge of communicating to their children their understanding of human nature, in particular the ideas discussed earlier in this chapter and in preceding chapters, and the beliefs and values that flow from that understanding.

RECOGNIZING TEACHING OPPORTUNITIES

Teaching opportunities are difficult to schedule and impossible to force. They arise naturally and often unexpectedly, so we need to be alert for them. The most obvious example of a teaching opportunity is when our children ask us a direct question. Another example is when, while driving somewhere or eating dinner together, we are discussing their experiences at school or ours at work. Yet another is after watching reporters and commentators present information and opinions on issues or after watching a dramatic program. We can, for example, ask children to react to the news stories, to explain whether they agree or disagree with the commentators, or, in the case of a drama, to evaluate the plot, characters, and theme. In addition, we can have them explain their reactions to the various commercials that punctuate the programs. All these approaches are excellent discussion starters. Of course, as children grow older, the times when they and their parents are together become fewer and more hurried. In such cases, families will need to make a special effort to seize whatever opportunities are available.

KEEPING THE ATMOSPHERE POSITIVE

Note that in all the examples of teaching opportunities, the children give their views first. Parents who are inclined to equate teaching with *lecturing* will find this strange. Such parents should understand that lecturing is the worst approach to take. (Contrary to popular belief, it doesn't work very well in the classroom either.) When children are young, they tend to be intimidated by lectures; when they are older, they feel insulted. When parents stifle the urge to dominate and make a conscientious effort to listen more than they speak, several good things happen. First, they learn what their children think—that is, where they deserve praise and where they need to broaden or correct their perspective. In addition, they get a better sense of how best to respond—for example, on one occasion, the parent might ask a question that encourages the child to expand upon or examine his or her idea; on another, the parent might introduce some facts the child is not aware of; on still another, the parent might state her own view. The aim should always be to make conversations a mutual exploration of ideas so that children look forward to them.

ANTICIPATING DISAGREEMENT

Nothing can destroy a positive atmosphere more quickly than parents' expectation that their children either already share their views or will be quick to adopt them once they are expressed. This expectation is more common than might be expected, given the chasm between what many parents believe and what mass culture promotes. The best way to maintain a positive atmosphere is for parents to anticipate disagreement—indeed, to *expect* that their children, especially older ones, hold views that differ from theirs. Moreover, that the reason they hold such views is not necessarily disrespect for their parents or a spirit of rebellion (though it may be either or both). A more likely possibility is that the influence of mass culture has been more effective than parental influence.

We cannot in fairness blame our children for influences outside their awareness and control. Nor should we be surprised when they stubbornly cling to views that they have *absorbed* from the culture—to them such ideas are indistinguishable from ones they have carefully thought out. Therefore, when disagreements grow heated and emotions threaten to undermine civility, parents should take the initiative and reduce the volatility. The surest way to do this is to resist the urge to make assertions, particularly ones proclaiming parental authority, and instead to *ask questions* that invite the child to explain his rationale for thinking as he does. In the course of answering such unthreatening questions, there is a good chance he will discover whatever weakness may exist in the viewpoint.

MAINTAINING RESPECT

The most important attitude we as parents can bring to the task of guiding our children is respect for them as persons. In practical terms, that means acknowledging their inherent dignity and the reality that they alone have the responsibility of meeting the challenges in their lives. We can guide, sympathize, encourage, and provide good examples, but we cannot live our children's lives for them. Although we have the right to set and enforce rules in our homes, that right does not extend to demanding that our children's beliefs and values mirror our own. We should be grateful when they agree with us, tolerant and patient when they disagree, and mindful that the goal of having them become responsible, thinking adults necessarily involves achieving intellectual independence from others, including us.

9

REFORMING THE CULTURE

As difficult as it is to change ourselves, given the ideas, habits, and attitudes we have acquired over the years, it is even more difficult to reform our culture. The goal of this broader cultural reform can be stated simply—to replace false conceptions of human nature that have infected the various social institutions with the common-sense view described in chapter 8. Accomplishing this goal will require the cooperation of many people and an effective strategy for dealing with entrenched bureaucracies and determined resistance to change. We will begin by considering the specific changes that are needed in the various social institutions and then consider the ways for the average citizen to contribute to the effort.

REFORMING EDUCATION

For the past century, American education has been controlled by Hereditarianism and Humanistic Psychology. The former implanted the notion that most people are irremediably unintelligent and thus profoundly altered the aims, methods, and materials of education. As a result, course syllabi present long lists of topics to be "covered," leaving little or no time for the kinds of challenges that develop students' powers of mind. Teachers tell students what to think rather than teaching them how to think. Textbooks typically do most of the thinking for students, thus discouraging them from wondering, inquiring, discovering ideas, and reaching their own conclusions.[1] Examinations typically restrict choices to preformed answers, thus preventing students from exercising judgment, expressing their thoughts in their own words, and providing nuance and qualification to their answers.

Humanistic Psychology persuaded educators to be less demanding of students and less critical of their academic performance, all in the name of heightening their self-esteem, but strangely offered no challenge to the entrenched aims, methods, and materials introduced by Hereditarianism. Contemporary education is therefore twice cursed.[2] The following reforms will solve both problems.

EMPHASIZE INTELLECT RATHER THAN MEMORY

The first change needed in education is to affirm that the human mind is humanity's greatest natural resource and its cultivation should be the primary focus in every classroom, from kindergarten through university. This cultivation should center on improving students' proficiency in reflective, creative, and critical thinking. It is not enough for schools and colleges to make general statements of purpose filled with fashionable catchwords and slogans. Most schools have had such statements for years, but they have had little bearing on what is done in the classroom.

What are needed instead are substantive changes in every curriculum and in each component course. The emphasis should be on students learning the thought processes used in the subject area—examining appropriate data sources, asking probing questions, evaluating possible answers, and deciding which is best. Simply said, students should learn to think like historians in history courses, scientists in science courses, literary analysts and critics in literature courses, and so on.

This is a very different perspective on teaching and learning than the one in which most teachers themselves were taught. They were taught, at least implicitly, that their subjects are collections of names, dates, and events to be remembered. And they teach accordingly. They need to adopt a different perspective and see their subjects as the challenging problems and issues that led to the strategies, protocols, and insights that define the subjects. In short, they need first to see their fields *dynamically* instead of statically and then to teach them that way. The difference between the two ways of seeing can make an enormous difference in the quality, excitement, and success of teaching and learning.

A personal story offered by a participant in a seminar on the teaching of thinking illustrates this difference. The man explained that he took physics in high school and hated every moment of it because the teacher presented the subject as a body of dry facts. As a result, the man was led to believe that there are no longer any challenges remaining in the subject—everything that could be known was already known. He vowed never to take another physics course. But as luck would have it, when he registered for his freshman classes in college, all the science courses except introductory physics were closed. So he enrolled in the physics class, met a professor who challenged students to wrestle with real physics problems, and came to realize that the subject is vibrantly alive. The man ended his story by explaining that he went on to earn a doctorate in physics and to make it his life's work.[3]

A number of authors have offered detailed plans for dynamic teaching and learning centered on mind building. Two that deserve special mention are the Paideia program and problem-based learning.[4] The Paideia Program was created by Mortimer Adler, a noted American philosopher and cofounder of the Great Books Program. There are three separate Paideia volumes, the first detailing the program, the second discussing the "problems and possibilities" in implementing it, and the third offering a program syllabus and essays by experts in the various fields of study.[5]

The Paideia Program rests on two principles: (1) That all students "have the same inherent tendencies, the same inherent powers, the same inherent capacities. . . . Individual differences are always and only differences in degree, never differences in kind." (2) That "all genuine learning is active, not passive" and is "a process of discovery in which the student [rather than the teacher] is the main agent. The role of the teacher, in Adler's view, is not to stuff minds with information but to guide students in discovering "by inviting and entertaining questions, by encouraging and sustaining inquiry, by supervising . . . exercises and drills, by leading discussions," and by giving examinations that elicit thoughtful as opposed to rote replies.[6]

Three distinct modes of learning are represented in the Paideia

Program. The first is "the acquisition of organized knowledge" in the academic areas of language, literature, and fine arts; mathematics and the natural sciences—physics, chemistry, and biology; and history, geography, and social studies. The second mode is "the development of intellectual skills," including language, math, science, and critical thinking skills. The third is the "enlargement of understanding" achieved by reading and discussing books other than textbooks, including historical, scientific, literary, and philosophical works.[7]

The first mode, acquiring organized knowledge, may include a degree of didactic learning (teacher telling) but the other two modes do not. The second uses coaching—having students perform the skills, correcting their mistakes, and having them try again. The third mode focuses on Socratic discussion. Adler notes that the learning that results from coaching and discussion is longer lasting than the learning from telling information. When there is only telling information, "the student's mind at the end of the process is no better than it was at the beginning."[8] But he acknowledges that each mode has its place and that education is most effective when the three modes are integrated. The Paideia Program is a practical expression of what Viktor Frankl described as the purpose and procedure of education: "Education must equip man with the means to find meanings," and the role of the teacher is to give to students not their own meaning, but "the personal example of his own dedication and devotion to the cause of research, truth, and science."[9]

Problem-based learning (PBL) was created by Howard Barrows, MD, and Robyn Tamblyn, BScN, after studies of medical school learning revealed significant problems with the traditional lecture method. That method presented massive amounts of factual information, which students succeeded in memorizing for examinations but soon forgot when the course ended. Tests of medical school graduates revealed unexpected ignorance, even of basic information about anatomy and physiology. The solution to the problem, developed by Barrows and Tamblyn and successfully implemented at McMaster University Medical School in Toronto (and adopted by other medical schools), was to replace the lecture system with a tutorial system in which small groups of students, under the guidance of a tutor, acquire medical knowledge by solving a series of medical cases. The cases, largely simulations of actual case histories, are carefully designed and sequenced to reflect the specific course matter and level of complexity. Throughout the PBL program, the emphasis (like that of the Paideia Program) is on dynamic learning through students' discovery. Barrows subsequently developed an application of PBL for the public school system.[10]

Paideia, PBL, and other meaningful educational reforms are built on the common-sense precepts that people have the capacity to increase their intellectual proficiency, that knowledge and wisdom are not inborn but must be acquired, that truth is objective and must be discovered, that reason (rather than emotion) is the path to learning, and that self-esteem follows rather than precedes achievement.

RESTORE THE TRADITIONAL CURRICULUM

It is important to note that both Paideia and problem-based learning are perfectly compatible with the traditional academic curriculum. The former, in fact, makes that curriculum central to its program by specifying its component subjects—language, mathematics, science, history, and so on. As noted in chapter 1, some reformers—notably E. D. Hirsch Jr.—have erroneously claimed that teaching students how to think is somehow the enemy of subject-matter learning. In fact, such teaching *enhances* subject-matter learning, as Howard Barrows's research in medical education dramatically demonstrated.

PROVIDE GUIDELINES FOR THINKING

It is one thing to extol thinking, another to practice it oneself, and quite another to teach others to practice it. In teaching, the most important questions to anticipate from students are the ones they are embarrassed to ask: "What exactly does thinking entail?" and "How can I be sure my conclusions are sound?" Unfortunately, few teachers are prepared to answer these questions adequately. (The failure is due to the fact that their own education has been mainly, if not exclusively, of the mind-stuffing variety.)

So most teachers will need to learn more about the thinking process in order to be effective in teaching it.

The first question may be answered as follows: Thinking entails carefully examining a problem or issue and finding the best solution or resolution. This is best accomplished with a systematic approach to ensure that no important step is omitted. Among the most comprehensive yet easy-to-use approaches is the W.I.S.E. approach—wonder, investigate, speculate, and evaluate.[11]

The answer to the second question is that conclusions are sound when they fit the evidence more completely and reasonably than do other possible conclusions. The way to be sure our conclusions meet this criterion is to (a) take care to consult all available evidence, (b) give a fair hearing to all possible interpretations and conclusions (including those that disagree with the ones we prefer), and (c) check our reasoning for errors. Among the most common errors are hasty conclusion, oversimplification, and unwarranted assumption.[12]

To be clear, these guidelines should not dominate the teaching process, except in courses specifically devoted to logic and critical thinking. But teachers of every subject should be well versed in them and refer students to them, as necessary, whenever problems and issues are being discussed.

REPLACE TEXTBOOKS THAT MERELY STUFF MINDS WITH ONES THAT STIMULATE THEM

This change is among the most difficult to implement. In many cases, all existing textbooks are designed to provide information to remember, so publishers must be persuaded to create new ones. (In situations where citywide or statewide textbook adoptions are the rule, a prior step is needed: to persuade the individuals who sit on the selection committees that the change is necessary and worthwhile.)

Once the publishers are persuaded, they face a serious problem—finding authors to create the books. The authors of existing books generally possess the greatest familiarity with the information base of their subjects and the greatest skill in organizing that material clearly and interestingly. But those authors are likely to have little familiarity with cognitive strategies and even less skill in transforming factual material into cognitive challenges—that is, problems and issues for students to grapple with (and in doing so, learn the subjects).

At first thought, the solution would appear to be having the textbook authors consult the scholars in the appropriate subject areas for help in identifying cognitive strategies and relevant problems and issues to incorporate in the new textbooks. (Seldom are textbook authors *themselves* scholars in the disciplines they write about.) The problem is that most scholars have had little, if any, formal training in cognitive strategies, nor did their mentors. This is not to say that they employ no such strategies in their own work, only that they developed their own strategies informally and privately, by trial and error, and employ them more or less unconsciously. In other words, they may never have conceptualized their strategies, at least not in a way they would feel comfortable explaining to others. Nor, in many cases, are they comfortable discussing their subject matter as a set of problems and issues because they do not see it that way; instead, they see their subjects in essentially the same way they learned them, as a series of historical periods filled with individuals and their accomplishments.[13]

Who, then, would be the best people for textbook authors to consult and learn from? Individuals who either use critical-thinking supplemental texts or develop their own materials and exercises to stimulate student thinking. Such individuals have learned how to turn factual material into thinking challenges and how to make those challenges central to learning. Although these individuals are not in the majority in any academic discipline, diligent textbook authors can find them without much difficulty.

DESIGN EXAMINATIONS THAT TEST THINKING SKILLS AS WELL AS KNOWLEDGE OF FACTS

There was a time when the essay exam was the preferred way to test students' learning, but that was many decades ago. It was never a perfect instrument because clever students, realizing that a long answer appears more substantive than a short one, would multiply words in a way that disguised their ignorance. If the students also had impeccable penmanship, they were almost assured excellent grades, no matter how empty of meaning their answers were. Of course, an alert, discerning teacher could easily detect and punish emptiness; but the more papers one has to correct, the more alertness and discernment fade.

There are ways to offset these disadvantages, as I will explain, and if they are employed, the essay test is the best way to measure students' thinking. Why, then, was it displaced by the "objective" test? Because the latter is much easier to grade—it is so easy, in fact, that a machine can do the job. Moreover, it can be standardized, permitting test results from around the country or around the world to be compared and analyzed and expressed in visually impressive graphs and charts.[14]

To begin with, the "objective" exam is not really objective. The scoring, to be sure, is more objective than the evaluation of the essay exam, but the selection and wording of both the questions and answer choices are *subjective*. In addition, "objective" exams frustrate and discourage thoughtful students by providing no way to explain the thought processes that produced their answers. At the same time, these exams encourage the lazy and unprepared to guess at answers. Teachers are often encouraged to "make examinations *learning* experiences," by discussing the exam questions when the papers are returned. Unfortunately, the very nature of the "objective" exam precludes meaningful discussion. The reality is, certain answers are right and others are wrong because the teacher and the textbook say so. End of story. Thus there can be no consideration of the kinds of things that genuine discussion entails—that is, comparing different points of view, offering evidence, identifying fallacies, finding common ground, and so on. After all, how can one offer a spirited defense of a *guess*? Accordingly, what passes as "making examinations *learning* experiences" is seldom more than a series of protests: "I think question number one is unfair," "I think question number eight is unfair," "I think all the questions are unfair."

The way to make examinations reflect thinking skills as well as knowledge of facts is to modify both the essay and the "objective" exams and use them in combination. First, where important concepts and principles are involved, teachers can use essay questions with word limits. Consider this sample question: "List three factors that led to the economic recession of 2008. Then decide which factor was most significant and explain why in no more than fifty words." (The word limit specified will, of course, vary depending on the complexity of the matter.) This approach requires students to think and express their thoughts with care, and it enables the teacher to evaluate answers quickly. Second, where true-or-false and multiple-choice questions are used, students can be required not just to choose their answers but also to explain the reasoning that led to their choices. To make multiple-choice questions even more challenging, students can also be asked to explain why they ruled out alternative choices.

ABOLISH SELF-ESTEEM PROGRAMS

We earlier exposed the fallacy of the notion that self-esteem is essential to achievement. Abundant research has made clear that many criminals' self-esteem is not too low (as self-esteem advocates claim) but too high, so high that they think the laws don't apply to them. Research has also shown that American students have higher self-esteem and *lower academic performance* than students in other countries, notably Asian countries. If anything, self-esteem programs undermine students' interest in learning and should therefore be abolished.

REVISE SEX EDUCATION

Sex education entered school curriculums in the early twentieth century as a means of dealing with the rise of sexually transmitted disease and the false notion that male health depends on fulfilling sexual urges. The courses, often *named* "Hygiene," were typically circumspect in their approach and reflected the view that sex is legitimate only in marriage.[15] Today's sex education is very different. It is offered to students at younger and younger ages; is more expansive in its treatment, covering forms and even techniques of sexual expression; and generally supports, in some cases even encourages, youthful sexual activity, as evidenced by the dispensing of condoms.

The argument supporting the expansion of sex education has been that it will reduce sexual experimentation, teen pregnancy, and the transmission of sexual diseases. The most obvious and undeniable criticism of such education is that it hasn't achieved its goal and should be reconsidered; many critics would go further and say that it has at best aggravated (if not caused) the very situation it purports to correct and should be abolished.

The most compelling argument for revising sex education is historian Arnold Toynbee's observation that "premature awareness of sex" creates a formidable distraction to the process of education. As noted in chapter 4, he recommended "prolonging the age of sexual innocence." Given the extent of the sexualization of modern culture, Toynbee's recommendation is no doubt impossible to achieve, but we can at least keep sex education from compounding the problems. The way to do that is to change the focus of sex education from providing graphic knowledge of sex to deeper psychological and philosophical matters. What role does sex play in our lives and how does it interact with other roles? When and how does it harm people? In what ways does it represent *using* people? What can we expect it to do, and not do, for us? How does adultery affect family life, and how does promiscuity affect intimacy and love? How does sexual involvement affect academic learning? Exploring these and similar questions would not only provide students with a mature understanding of sexuality; it would also help them enhance their critical thinking skills.

REPLACE VALUES CLARIFICATION WITH ETHICS

Values clarification is based on Humanistic Psychology's false idea that everyone decides his or her own truth, reality, and morality. No learning takes place in this regime, only a serial recitation of self-justifying views. The essential goal of discovery is thwarted by the attitude that there is nothing outside each student's own narrow and largely uninformed opinion.

Teaching ethics does not mean learning names and dates and events, though that will inevitably occur. Rather, it means having students examine questions involving right and wrong, discovering the approaches that have guided thoughtful people in finding answers, employing those approaches to find answers themselves, and then comparing answers and determining the most insightful ones. Neither does teaching ethics involve studying religion, though it will, out of necessity, examine the values and ideals discovered by the great religions of the world.

Ethics has historically been a subdivision of philosophy, but some psychologists such as Martin Seligman, the founder of the Positive Psychology group, have affirmed the importance of good character, free will, and personal responsibility in the *scientific* evaluation of human behavior. Seligman argues that "to be a virtuous person is to display, by acts of will, all or at least most of the six ubiquitous virtues: wisdom, courage, humanity, justice, temperance, and transcendence." These six virtues Seligman and his associates found in almost two hundred sources ranging over three thousand years, from Aristotle and Aquinas to Confucius and Buddha, from the Talmud to the Koran.[16] By probing the relevance of these six virtues and others—notably honesty, prudence, fortitude, and loving kindness—to a variety of situations, students will deepen their understanding of morality as they expand their thinking skills.

BAN PERSONAL AGENDAS AND SELF-AGGRANDIZEMENT FROM THE CLASSROOM

Hereditarianism created the notion that students cannot be taught how to think and must be stuffed with information. Humanistic Psychology made the situation worse by claiming that people create their own truth. So it is hardly surprising that many teachers tend to elevate their personal opinions to the status of truth and to impose them on their students. In the kind of educational reform recommended here, mind stuffing is abolished and students are taught to develop their own minds and engage in the discovery of truth themselves. The role of teachers is to aid and guide them, not to tell them what to think. To overstep this boundary is a serious violation of trust.

REFORMING RELIGION

The belief that human beings are created by God provided religion with significant insulation from the influence of Hereditarianism and the Eugenics movement.[17] On the other hand, the companion belief in responsibility for one's neighbor inclined religion, quite appropriately, to support many of Progressivism's initiatives, such as curtailing child labor and improving safety and sanitation in the workplace. However, religion was much more susceptible to the influence of Humanistic Psychology, precisely because that psychology *seemed* perfectly compatible with religious principles and values. That is why thousands of ministers, priests, and rabbis were sent for counseling training to programs run by Humanistic Psychologists. As a result, the false precepts of Humanistic Psychology are deeply embedded in modern religion, particularly the more liberal denominations. The five most urgent religious reforms are described below.

REAFFIRM HUMAN IMPERFECTION

The traditional religious view of human imperfection does not denigrate humanity: its creation story simply offers what it perceives as a balanced view, as the well-known phrase "created in the image and likeness of God" makes clear. "Created" is a reminder that our very existence is dependent on something other than ourselves. "Image and likeness of God" denotes the perceived special status humans enjoy in all of creation.

Jewish and Christian scriptures, specifically the book of Genesis, add another element to this view of humanity by telling the story of the "fall" of man through the "original sin" of Adam and Eve. Other religions have their own scenarios to explain the origin of human imperfection, but they still acknowledge the reality of it. For example, Islam claims that all human works reflect imperfection, and Buddhism, Hinduism, and Confucianism offer ways to overcome it. In fact, most atheists and agnostics, though they reject the "sacred books" and theological doctrines of the various religions, nevertheless affirm the idea of human imperfection and accept the central role it plays in philosophy.

Traditionally, philosophers described the effects of original sin as a clouding of the intellect and a weakening of the will—in other words, vulnerability to ignorance, misunderstanding, and temptations to act in ways that harm others and/or ourselves. No reasonable person, religious or not, would deny that these vulnerabilities are part of the human condition. After all, we are reminded of them hundreds of times a day in our own behavior and that of the people we encounter. But Humanistic Psychology denies them by claiming that people are born wise and good and therefore should trust their feelings and consult only their "internal locus of authority." The fact that many members of the clergy have fallen victim to this nonsense and, in the process, have betrayed both their common sense and the most fundamental teaching of their religions largely explains why their congregations have dwindled. Every time they recite the theology of the exalted self, they are saying, in effect, "You don't need me or my church because you are fine just as you are." The first step to restoring religion's valuable place in society is for church leaders to reaffirm human imperfection.

PURGE CLERICAL TRAINING OF THE INFLUENCE OF HUMANISTIC PSYCHOLOGY

That clergy have come under the direct influence of Humanistic Psychology is perfectly understandable. They need to understand psychological concepts and approaches in order to provide spiritual counseling to their parishioners. And for fifty or so years, Humanistic Psychology has dominated the field of counseling. But as shown in previous chapters, the precepts and practices of that psychology are based on a false view of human nature and, as a result, do great mischief.

The first step for the churches is to change the way their young clergy are educated in counseling. In cases where that education is provided in secular institutions, the solution is to choose different institutions or programs, ones that are compatible with their theology and philosophy—a notable example would be programs that are based on Viktor Frankl's logotherapy. The situation is more difficult when the education is provided in the denomination's own seminary. Unfortunately, many seminaries are no less influenced by Humanistic Psychology than are secular institutions. In such situations, the church hierarchy must find a way to change the perspective and content of the counseling courses offered in the seminary.

Older clergy, who have already completed their formal training in counseling, pose a different challenge. They must be persuaded of the errors of Humanistic Psychology and the extent to which those errors have undermined their efforts to help parishioners lead more spiritually fulfilling lives. The key to such persuasion is to help them renew their understanding of the church's theological heritage and prayerfully consider how that heritage can best be conveyed in the counseling of congregants.

RESTORE THE CONCEPT OF SIN AND PERSONAL RESPONSIBILITY FOR BEHAVIOR

As the noted psychiatrist Karl Menninger has observed, our culture has discarded the notion of sin and now speaks only of crime and disease. The first designation, crime, focuses on only the breaking of rules; the second denies people's responsibility for their actions. He argues for restoring the concept of sin because it better describes the nature of moral offenses—the fact that they arise from personal weaknesses, notably self-centeredness, and that they do harm to other people.[18] It is worthy of note that Menninger was not offering a brief for religion but writing as a psychiatrist. At the time he offered this observation, the only place there was much talk about sin was in the church pulpit. Today it is difficult to find it mentioned there, at least in the sense of personal offenses against God and neighbor. Many clergy treat the concept of sin with benign neglect. Others, like televangelist Robert Schuller, redefine it in terms borrowed from Humanistic Psychology, as when he argues that "the core of original sin . . . could be considered an innate inability to adequately value ourselves."[19]

The change is even noticeable in the traditional bastion of conservative theology, Catholicism. At the beginning of the Mass, the congregation used to recite in unison this acknowledgment of personal sin: "I confess to Almighty God, and to you my brothers and sisters, that I have sinned through my own fault, in my thoughts and in my words, in what I have done, and in what I have failed to do." Today that recitation is optional and, in many parishes, is seldom used.[20] The sacrament of confession, now known as the sacrament of reconciliation, no longer receives much emphasis from the pulpit and no longer draws long lines of penitents. When homilists speak of sin at all, they tend to do so in the singular— "the sin of the world"—which connotes a vague shortcoming of people in general rather than particular offenses of individuals.

Of the many reasons that could be cited for churches to reject the false precepts of Humanistic Psychology, none is more obvious than the prompting of many members of the clergy to ignore their vows and commitments. Believing that the locus of authority lies within themselves leads to rejecting the authority of the church and of God. Believing that they create their own truth leads to whatever interpretations of scripture serve their predilections. Believing that every personal feeling or urge should be followed leads to adultery among married clergy and unchaste behavior among the unmarried. Even worse, acting on urges leads to clerical pedophilia, which, the selective reporting of journalists aside, has been a serious problem not only in Roman Catholicism but in other religions, too.

FOCUS HOMILIES ON SPIRITUAL MATTERS RATHER THAN ON POLITICS OR PSYCHOLOGY

There is nothing wrong with mentioning contemporary social and political issues to give context to a spiritual point, but in some churches the issues are offered *instead of* the spiritual point. Some years ago, a friend underscored how self-defeating this approach is when he remarked, "I don't need to go to church to have the *New York Times* read to me. I can read it myself at home."[21] Little wonder that churches whose clergy sound like news analysts or Carl Rogers impersonators have lost the most parishioners. Their craving for social and political relevance has, in effect, undermined their spiritual relevance.

It shouldn't need saying (but obviously does for many church leaders) that the only sound reasons for going to church are to praise God and to learn how to live in accordance with his will. Accordingly, the primary emphasis in sermons should be on presenting passages from scripture—for example, the Ten Commandments and the Sermon on the Mount—and the explications offered by scripture scholars, as well as on concrete applications to everyday life. The purpose of any sermon should be to inspire spiritual enlightenment and self-transcendence in the congregation, not to achieve political persuasion. And the underlying theological principles should always be that it is individual people (not social classes, political parties, or governments) who do good and evil and, in the best of outcomes, achieve salvation; that repentance must precede forgiveness; and that the way to assuage guilt is to put an end to the behavior that caused it.[22] In brief, every sermon should be a challenge to choose spiritual nobility over unspiritual self-indulgence. Clergy (and churches) that offer anything less than this abdicate their responsibility.

REJECT LIBERATION THEOLOGY

Liberation theology originated in the frustration of the clergy, notably Catholic missionaries in Latin America, who witnessed the exploitation of the poor by drug lords and corrupt politicians. When their appeals to morality failed, these clergy turned to more confrontational approaches; when those failed, they gave their support to guerrillas, in some cases becoming comrades in arms. In one sense, this progression is a testimony to their devotion to justice and their compassion for their fellow human beings. In another, deeper sense, it demonstrates a misunderstanding of human nature, social reality, and good and evil. Their fellow clergy in the United States and elsewhere, who admired and emulated them, perceived their idealism but failed to realize their error.

Unlike traditional theology, liberation theology aims at political rather than spiritual reform. It is based on a number of false assumptions drawn from Humanistic Psychology and/or Marxism: that human beings are inherently wise and good and all their problems are caused by outside agencies or economic systems (such as capitalism); that the individuals championing the liberation are themselves incorruptible; that the end of liberating the oppressed justifies the means of torture, murder, and terror; and that the liberation will eliminate oppression, rather than merely install a new group of oppressors. In brief, liberation theology denies each individual's potential for evil and the historical reality that "liberators" often turn out to be as exploitive and tyrannical as the people they replaced.

Does inequality, injustice, even oppression exist in our own country as well as in the rest of the world? Undeniably. Do individuals, groups, and countries have a moral obligation to reject these evils and give aid to the victims? Certainly. Should the church be involved in the quest for justice?

Of course. But the deeper question is, what is the church's proper role? The answer is to challenge its followers to change the world by changing themselves—more specifically, to demonstrate love of God and neighbor through virtuous living.[23] That is very different from liberation theology's aim of *coercing* economic and social equality, and it is much more wholesome.

REFORMING GOVERNMENT

Humanistic Psychology's doctrine that people are born wise and good but victimized by society led to the notion that the government owes people a wide range of entitlement programs. (The very idea that people are *entitled* to benefits betrays the belief that it is not only opportunities that are deserved but also *outcomes*.) Believing they could shape reality to their vision, legislators ignored warnings about the negative impact some programs were shown to have. Two such warnings were delivered by senator and sociologist Daniel Patrick Moynihan. The first, in 1965, was titled "The Negro Family: The Case for National Action" and presented evidence that welfare programs were having the unintended consequence of destroying black families and increasing poverty. The second, in 1993, was titled "Defining Deviancy Down" and warned that government and the culture in general had created a climate in which deviant and criminal behavior were being explained away and even accepted as normal.[24] Not only did many of his colleagues in government reject his conclusions, some also branded him an alarmist or a racist.

In recent years, elected officials have grown more extreme in their efforts to redress presumed historical grievances and more reckless in replacing logic and common sense with their own personal "truths." The most notable examples of such efforts include the pressure put by Congress on the banking system to give loans to people who lacked the means to repay them, which led to the banking crisis of 2008, and the profligate spending (and taxation) inaugurated under the banner of "redistribution of wealth," the implication being that the means possessed by those who can afford property must have been ill-gotten.[25] In the judiciary the notion that society has deprived individuals of their natural rights took the form of denigrating the founding fathers and regarding the Constitution as deeply flawed, and therefore requiring ongoing reexamination and correction.

When the public objected to these ideas and actions, the old Hereditarian belief that the masses are stupid resurfaced and politicians began openly disparaging those who objected. Their blatant arrogance and condescension provided the impetus for what has come to be known as the "Tea Party movement" and the call for smaller government that is more responsive to common sense and the will of the people. Although the reforms suggested below in some cases may resonate with the goals of that movement, they are offered to correct a more fundamental problem, the influence of Hereditarianism and Humanistic Psychology.

RESTORE THE IDEA OF GOVERNMENT SERVING THE PEOPLE

Not only are people more intelligent than Hereditarians believed, they are more educated than their forebears in the early 1900s and, in many cases, more educated than the people they elect to office. For this reason, elected officials should conduct their duties humbly and deferentially, never forgetting that in a democratic republic the very purpose of government is to serve the interests of the people, not to be their masters.

Many governmental problems derive from the ego-inflation of elected officials that has occurred since the advent of Humanistic Psychology. To many politicians, election and appointment confers entitlements such as special retirement and healthcare plans unavailable to other citizens, "cozy" relationships with lobbyists, and license to ignore the principles of economics and tax people to the point of personal and national ruin. In times past, politicians took pains to hide their sense of entitlement; more and more, they have been inclined to celebrate it openly.

The changes that will need to be made to restore the ideal of public service are too numerous to detail. However, the following deserve special consideration: Have government business, at every level, conducted openly.[26] Require all elected officials to make time available, on a regular basis and in a public forum such as a town hall, for questioning by constituents. Eliminate special healthcare, retirement, and other benefits for elected officials. As a means of restricting graft and wasteful spending on "pork" projects, eliminate all unrelated riders to proposed legislation. (Legislation eliminating "earmarks" was signed into law in 2010, but both parties have managed to find ways around it.) Restrict the activities of lobbyists and forbid former members of legislative committees from working for firms with business interests in matters of concern to their former committees. (In some cases, weaker and seldom-enforced forms of the latter stipulation exist. They should be strengthened.)

END THE POLITICAL DENIGRATION OF ACHIEVEMENT

This reform will be especially difficult to accomplish. The notion of equal entitlement for all is deeply embedded in political thought and entangled with a false sense of social justice. Many fervently believe not only that poverty is a social problem that needs to be addressed (a time-honored, responsible view), but also that anyone who has more than his neighbor must have gotten it dishonestly and government should therefore take it away and "redistribute" it.

To think this way is not only to ignore common sense and elementary fairness, but also to display astounding arrogance. Not everyone is equally deserving: some work hard, others don't; some are thrifty, others are not; some spend time and money wisely, others don't; some seize opportunities, others squander them. Moreover, to punish achievement doesn't help the have-nots become achievers; all it does is discourage achievers from continuing their efforts—after all, they are human too and affected by discouraging influences. But more important than these profound and complex differences among people is the fact that they are not easily identified in individual cases. Being elected to political office does not bestow the ability to determine who "deserves" success or failure and who does not. Any pretense in that regard undermines freedom and compounds injustice.

TREAT LAWBREAKERS AS OFFENDERS AND NOT AS VICTIMS OF SOCIETY

The criminal-justice system should return to the perspective that guided it before Humanistic Psychology gave virtually everyone a claim to victimhood. In that earlier view, people were presumed to be in control of their behavior absent convincing evidence that some internal or external force had compromised their free will. This should once again be the basis for prosecuting and deciding cases.

Similarly, the courts should end the practice of excluding from trial any evidence that police obtained improperly. That practice treats accused law-breakers as victims and is tantamount to rewarding them by hiding facts bearing on the determination of their guilt or innocence. The only question the courts should be interested in is whether the evidence is genuine. Any impropriety or illegality on the part of the police should be treated separately; where punishment of the police is in order, it should be meted out as impartially as it is to any other class of offenders. The threat of such punishment will in most cases be sufficient to ensure that the police refrain from improper behavior.

ELECT OR APPOINT JUDGES WHO MAKE DECISIONS ACCORDING TO THE CONSTITUTION RATHER THAN POLITICAL AGENDAS

Humanistic Psychology has made it fashionable to blame all our problems on society and to be guided by our personal "truth" in addressing those problems. Progressivism, especially in its current incarnation, has fostered an urgent activist spirit. The combined impact of these ideas and tendencies has shaped many jurists' views of the Constitution and of their responsibility toward it. To begin, many judges view the founding fathers with the same disdain they show their own parents and other contemporary authority figures. (After all, the founding fathers are simply prior representatives of the same offending society.) Given this disdain, it is easy to understand their suspicion toward the document framed by those individuals (the Constitution) and their active efforts to replace it with—or, more euphemistically, to *reinterpret* it in accordance with—the superior insights they claim to possess.

There are several problems with these jurists' perspective. First, it derives from the faulty view of human nature that infected Humanistic Psychology and Progressivism. People are inherently imperfect, and that fact applies to all generations. Some problems are caused by parents and society, others are caused by the individuals themselves, and it is virtually impossible to be certain of who is responsible for what. Moreover, blaming past generations for our problems is as foolish as blaming others in our generation; doing so does little more than hinder our overcoming the problems. Second, the Constitution has passed every test of time. No other comparable document comes close to it in quality. The question is not whether it is perfect—nothing of human invention is—but instead whether it reflects deeper insights into human nature and provides better safeguards from tyranny than any competing document. By any fair analysis, the answer is yes, resoundingly.

Whenever a judge is to be appointed to a high court, the question always arises over whether there should be a "litmus test." Few, if any, of the tests that are sometimes proposed, or that some accuse others of harboring, are acceptable. But I would argue that there is a litmus test that politicians would be well advised to use: Does the candidate acknowledge the excellence of the Constitution and vow to preserve it?

REFORMING JOURNALISM

As explained in chapter 2, the core ideas of Humanistic Psychology have had a profoundly negative impact on journalism. The belief that the locus of authority is within oneself has led many journalists to reject the traditional standards of the profession, in particular the ideals of objectivity and freedom from bias. The belief that wisdom and truth are created rather than discovered has led to a disregard for facts and the investigative process. The belief that self-actualization is the highest human need has led many journalists to put their own causes and agendas above their professional role, and sometimes above honesty and integrity. (The lingering Hereditarian notion that the masses are unintelligent has lent support to this belief by persuading journalists that the masses cannot form opinions without their help.) Prominent among the consequences are a poorly informed public and increasing suspicion of the entire journalistic profession. A number of reforms are urgently needed if journalism is to regain its former stature and credibility.

REAFFIRM THE PRIMARY PURPOSE OF JOURNALISM

Traditionally, the main purpose of journalism has been seen as providing information so that people can have a sound basis for forming opinions and carrying out their civic responsibilities. Over the last century, Hereditarianism and Humanistic Psychology have changed that perspective and, in the process, made journalism paternalistic and manipulative.

The traditional purpose of journalism needs to be reaffirmed because it is based on a sound view of human nature. People are neither inherently wise nor clairvoyant. They need reliable information in order to make sound judgments, and they don't always have the time to conduct the necessary investigation to get it. The job of journalists is to provide that information, which includes not only factual data but also the range of interpretations knowledgeable people place on that data. But it does not include slanting the information to favor their own biases. Such slanting violates the ideals of fairness and objectivity; it not only demeans the profession of journalism but also undermines meaningful discourse and hinders the solution of problems.

ACKNOWLEDGE PERSONAL LIMITATIONS

This is easy enough to do in the abstract, but it is very difficult in concrete situations.

We all tend to think that the two sides to an issue are our side and the wrong side, so we often deceive ourselves into thinking that we need only pay attention to those who agree with us. Reality challenges us to move beyond this self-flattering perspective and realize that, like others, we are capable of error and that the views we hold most strongly can be partly or wholly mistaken. This challenge is especially significant for journalists because their obligation is not only to themselves but also to their audience. Any lack of humility and pretense of omniscience on their part can harm hundreds, thousands, even millions of other people.

RESTORE THE TRADITIONAL RULES OF JOURNALISM

Among the most fundamental rules of journalism is to separate news and opinion. Strictly speaking, news comprises more or less important events and is reported by making *statements of fact*—what happened, and when, where, how, and to whom it happened. Comments made about the event by officials, eyewitnesses, and certain others are also considered statements of fact. (*Statements* of fact should be distinguished from facts: the former purport to be factual; the latter are factual.) *Opinions* are judgments made about statements of fact; for example, judgments about who was responsible for the event's occurrence and what action should be taken as a result.

Traditionally, opinions were gathered in a separate section of the newspaper, the "editorial pages," and took various forms: editorials written by the staff, commentaries by columnists, and letters to the editor. (Essentially the same separation was carried over into early broadcast journalism.) This separation had the practical advantage of allowing the audience to make the fact-or-opinion distinction more easily; it also kept journalists mindful of their responsibilities to their audience and more able to resist the temptation to mix in their opinions with the news and thereby pass them off as facts.

In addition to the rule of separating fact and opinion, the following traditions of journalism should be restored:

In reporting news, all relevant facts should be presented, and not just those that flatter the reporter's view. This rule is often violated by selective presentation of statistics and/or viewpoints.

A serious claim or charge—for example, an assertion of criminal behavior—should never be reported on the basis of a single source. Other corroborating sources should be found and used.

People should be categorized fairly, without loaded language or derogatory labels.

Descriptions of people should be consistent. For example, journalists shouldn't mention the achievements of people they admire or ignore those of people they dislike.

Headlines and lead paragraphs should be honest. An honest headline or lead paragraph highlights the essential facts of the story. A dishonest headline or lead undercuts the main storyline by highlighting minor details. (This device is often used when the story does not support the journalist's viewpoint.)

Opinion pieces and commentaries should not present just the author's judgments; they should explain the reasoning that underlies the judgments and, where appropriate, provide evidence to support them.

Complex issues should not be oversimplified. This is difficult because sound bites and brief written blurbs have become standard in modern journalism. By their very nature, such devices tend to oversimplify. For that reason, journalists should use them only as prefatory material and take care that the full story or commentary reflects the complexity of the issue.

REFORMING PUBLISHING

Humanistic Psychology affected the publishing industry in several ways: It gave new impetus to the old self-help genre, even as it transformed it from self-improvement to self-absorption and self-indulgence. It provided a host of popularizers who offered a steady stream of nonfiction books and articles advising readers about replacing traditional views and values with new, self-friendly ones. It encouraged fiction writers to put aside the restraints on theme and treatment that had guided them, particularly in matters of sex and violence. And for a time it made publishing more profitable than ever.

At the same time all this was happening, however, communications technology was creating problems for publishers. More and more people were devoting less and less time to reading, looking instead for enlightenment and entertainment from television and the Internet. Before long, this development brought about significant changes in publishing. Smaller publishers, who for decades had prided themselves on being more concerned with the quality of their offerings than with their financial balance sheets, were forced to sell to larger houses or close their doors. As conglomerates took over, business types replaced lovers of ideas and profit became the only consideration. This change had the effect of consolidating the influence of Humanistic Psychology, whose celebration of self-indulgence guaranteed a significant income stream. The needed reforms in publishing reflect these historical developments.

RESTORE LOVERS OF IDEAS AND LITERATURE TO POSITIONS OF INFLUENCE

Traditional booksellers viewed their trade not just as a business but more importantly as a vocation to help people grow intellectually and emotionally. Their perspective was idealistic, to be sure, but it was also practical in that it reflected the realization that the quality of ideas in a culture govern the health and longevity of the culture. Given the false ideas that have dominated American culture for many decades, it may be difficult to find many people who hold those old values today and even more difficult to persuade the publishing conglomerates to place them at the highest executive levels. But even a modest number of such individuals working in middle management—notably as editors—will help to bring back the old perspective and values.

HIRE CONSULTANTS WHO ARE WELL-ENOUGH VERSED IN ACADEMIC SUBJECTS TO ENSURE SOUND CHOICES IN BOOK PROJECTS

This is a helpful approach even aside from the goal of reforming the publishing industry because the insights offered by such consultants will be helpful in pruning booklists and improving marketing efficiency. But its main value will be in ending the profligate dissemination of the erroneous ideas of Humanistic Psychology. There is, of course, no guarantee that the academics chosen to be consultants will have freed themselves from the errors, but they are more likely to be aware of the case against Humanistic Psychology than are the popularizers who currently guide the market.

EMPHASIZE GENUINE SELF-IMPROVEMENT, PARTICULARLY IN MATTERS OF CHARACTER

The self-help genre needn't be eliminated, but it should be purged of the nonsense that currently dominates it. Publishers should seek out books that offer an accurate view of human nature and the need for self-improvement, as well as a common-sense perspective on truth, reason, self-esteem, self-transcendence, and sexuality—in other words, books that not only inspire genuine self-improvement but also offer practical strategies for pursuing it.

IN AWARDING BOOK CONTRACTS, PREFER PEOPLE WITH FIRSTHAND EXPERTISE

In recent decades, there has been a growing tendency to base publishing decisions on a prospective author's name recognition or the size of his or her platform than on the person's level of knowledge. As a result, celebrities with nothing meaningful to say and no linguistic skills are given book contracts or featured magazine interviews while scholars who have devoted years to their subjects are rejected. Publishers who behave this way demean their profession and abdicate their responsibility to their readers. The public deserves the insights of informed people. If such people are more difficult to market, then publishers have an obligation to use their ingenuity and find ways to do so. Some publishers may regard this suggestion as too idealistic; they would point to the fact that scholars can always publish their work with university presses and other noncommercial publishers. But that is tantamount to denying the value of providing the general public with the widest possible access to the most informed thought. From the perspective of earlier generations of publishers, it is also a dereliction of professional responsibility.

What about offering book contracts to journalists? This practice has actually been occurring over the last few decades, partly because today's communications conglomerates typically have both publishing and print and/or broadcast (and often film) divisions. When authors are drawn from other divisions of the same company, marketing is made easier and exposure to the public is guaranteed. In one way, journalist authors help to correct the problem—after all, there is a big difference between an ignorant celebrity and a competent investigative journalist. But turning to journalists does not entirely solve the problem for two reasons. First, in any subject outside journalism itself, journalists have only secondhand expertise, which, even when gained through in-depth investigation, is always by definition second-rate. Moreover, they have been trained to write for the lowest common denominator—the reader with a very short attention span—and this fact can lead them to oversimplify. In short, there is no adequate substitute for firsthand expertise.

REFORMING THE ENTERTAINMENT MEDIA

The entertainment media have been even more instrumental in popularizing the ideas of Humanistic Psychology than have the psychologists themselves because the media are the purveyors of mass culture. Reforming them will be especially difficult, not only because they are true believers, but more importantly because they are laboring under a delusion. To be more specific, they have classified their assaults on tradition as "reality"[27] and persuaded themselves that they are providing "what the public wants." This is disingenuous, naïve, or a combination of the two. They would have us believe that when Clark Gable's Rhett Butler said, "Frankly, my dear, I don't give a damn!" in 1939, the public thought, "Wow. This is wonderful. Let's have more swearing, and while you're at it, have the actors remove their clothes and copulate." Actually, the public reaction to Gable's comparatively mild vulgarity was shock and condemnation. The subsequent devolution to contemporary foulmouthed dramatic dialogue and other media representations of "reality" were not requested by but rather *forced on* the public, one crude expression and lewd act at a time. Media spokespeople themselves acknowledge this fact in those unguarded moments when they boast about "pushing the envelope."

STOP THE SELF-DECEPTION

People in the entertainment media should have the courage to admit why they are contemptuous of traditional ideas and values. The answer is not because the public wanted or requested their contempt, but because they have uncritically embraced the tenets of Humanistic Psychology and the Hereditarian notion that the masses are too stupid to have valid insights and therefore require their guidance. More importantly, instead of congratulating themselves on how superior their adopted ideas are, these entertainment types should examine their ideas probingly. If they do, in the manner done in the earlier chapters of this book, they will find they are mistaken.

END THE ERA OF THE ANTIHERO AND GET RID OF SYMPATHY FOR THE VILLAINS

The tendency to see the victim as villain and vice versa can be traced to the Romantic notion of Humanistic Psychology that everyone is born good and anything bad that happens is the fault of some social agency, such as the family, or society in general. There is nothing wrong with presenting human beings in their complexity—in other words, as having some good and some bad traits and behavior—and even, in some conditions, assigning those who do immoral or criminal deeds a measure of sympathy. But it is unrealistic and misleading to absolve wrongdoers of all responsibility or, worse, to celebrate them as heroes because, among other reasons, such portrayals trivialize, glamorize, and therefore encourage evil.

MAKE DRAMA MORE FAITHFUL TO REALITY

Many people in the arts classify filling films and dramatic shows with sex and violence and filling comedy shows with a constant stream of smutty talk as realism. That is a strange designation because in the real lives of the vast majority of people, sex and smutty talk have a much smaller place, and violence has little or no place. Jackie Mason once wittily observed that many people eat soup every day and yet filmmakers feel no compulsion to fill their works with scenes of soup eating (with or without slurping), so their claim of realism is oddly limited in scope.

Even if we allow for the fact that drama necessarily involves compression of events, the sex and violence are excessive. Clearly, the steady increase of these elements on both the large and small screen are a reflection of Humanistic Psychology's urging of unrestrained expression of emotion and their endorsement, with Kinsey, of libertinism.[28] As we have seen, Humanistic Psychology and Kinsey were wrong in these matters. The entertainment industry needs to realize that.

Another erroneous argument that is offered in support of unrestrained sensationalism in art is that creativity demands it. If anything, creativity functions better within boundaries—as G. K. Chesterton observed, "the essence of the picture is the frame." Alfred Hitchcock is but one example of the many accomplished artists who achieved more with simple suggestion than others did with blatant display.

Any effort to make dramatic presentations genuinely realistic should also include fair depictions of parents. The tendency in today's dramas, including comedies, as well as in advertising, is to deride parents as being so out of touch with the world that they need the guidance of their children to cope with everyday affairs. This should be seen for what it is, a kinder variation of Humanistic Psychology's claim that parents ruin children's lives. (In TV depictions, parents are less malicious than clueless, but that is still not much of a compliment.) Even so, it hardly qualifies as realistic. Parents come in many variations of intelligence and character but, worst cases aside, the great majority have much more insight into living than their children do, if only for having lived longer and made more mistakes. For dramatists to pretend otherwise not only insults parents, but it also alienates children from their best and most caring sources of practical wisdom and guidance.

WHAT THE AVERAGE INDIVIDUAL CAN DO

Those who work in the areas discussed above will have no difficulty finding ways to promote the recommended reforms within them. For example, teachers can recommend reform ideas in their schools, elected officials can introduce bills that reform government, and journalists can write articles advocating the reform of their industry. But what can those of us who do not work in any of the specified fields do to support the reforms? Here are some suggestions.

EDUCATION

We can learn what is being taught in our area schools. The administrators will be able to provide copies of the curriculum. We are entitled to such information as taxpayers, even if we do not have children. If we have children in school, they are an additional source of information. We can ask them to describe a typical class in each of their subjects. Better yet, we can arrange to visit selected classes. This will reveal whether the teachers are still practicing mind stuffing or are developing thinking skills. In addition, we can examine our children's textbooks, focusing on the subjects that are likely to have been influenced by Hereditarianism and/or Humanistic Psychology—that is, social studies, history, and English textbooks.

We can also start attending school board meetings on a regular basis. As we become informed on the matters that are discussed, we can speak in support of worthy initiatives and offer constructive criticism of questionable ones. We can even run for the school board. As a member rather than an observer, we will be better able to enlighten the board about the matters discussed in this book, such as the advantages of mind building over mind stuffing and to propose reform ideas such as the Paideia Program and problem-based learning.

If we are alumni of colleges, we can check their current college catalogs and examine their course offerings. We can also read alumni bulletins and, if possible, campus newspapers. The news items—for example, a report on the people being awarded honorary degrees—will often reveal whether the philosophy and values of the institution have changed since we graduated. We can then write to the president of the college, offering praise or criticism as warranted, and making clear our thoughts on the need to restore the traditional commonsense view of human nature to education. Most college presidents pay close attention to the views of alumni because every alumnus is a potential donor to the college fund.

RELIGION

We can become better informed about our religion, if we have one, and not just our local church but also the faith tradition on which it is based. A good starting point is finding out what changes, if any, have occurred since the religion's founding, particularly changes prompted by the spread of the ideas and values of Humanistic Psychology. Next, we can become involved in our church's discussions and dialogues and, where appropriate, point out the errors of Humanistic Psychology and offer ideas for restoring the faith tradition. Keep in mind that false ideas and values have become so embedded in our culture that many religious people (including the clergy) now regard them as matters of revealed truth. We must therefore be patient with them.

Before trying to change anyone's mind about religious (or nonreligious) positions, of course, we must first be sure that our own position is defensible, and that process is not as easy as it might seem. It cannot be based on the mere assumption that our view is right because it is our view. (That notion is as fallacious in religious thought as it is in secular thought.) Rather, it must involve objective consideration of competing viewpoints on the issue(s) and sensitivity to their complexity.

Those who have stopped going to church because they are disgusted with Humanistic Psychology's influence on religion might consider returning so that they can play a role in restoring genuine spirituality to the culture and to their own lives.

GOVERNMENT

A good way to begin is to learn more about America's founding by visiting a bookstore or going online and obtaining copies of the Declaration of Independence and the Constitution. After becoming reacquainted with those documents, we can spend some time reading the writings of the founding fathers, and reflecting on the ways in which modern government has upheld or undermined the original views.

We can also become more active and informed citizens by researching candidates, looking beyond advertisements and formal speeches to actual leadership experience and, where possible, past voting records. When we identify candidates who share our intellectual, moral, and governmental values and have a record of integrity, we can support and vote for them.

Our interest need not and should not end with elections. We can monitor elected officials to determine whether they are honoring their campaign promises and then correspond with them, offering support or constructive criticism, and supporting our views with references to expert opinion and research. When criticizing ideas and programs rooted in the errors of Hereditarianism and/or Humanistic Psychology, it is important to remember that our representatives may lack our understanding and will therefore need to be informed about the nature of the errors and the reasonableness of alternative views before changing their minds.

Communicating with elected officials can be frustrating, particularly when they offer ambiguous, patronizing responses or don't reply at all. Maintaining enthusiasm can be difficult in such cases. One way to do so is to develop a network of like-minded individuals and coordinate communication with them. Elected officials always pay more attention to a deluge of mail on a topic than they do to an individual letter.

JOURNALISM

The only way to know which news and commentary sources are fairest and least biased is to compare them. Given the electronic tools available today, notably the digital video recorder (DVR), this task is easy to accomplish. Some equipment allows us to record more than one newscast at once. Those of us who have a second television set can watch yet another newscast while the others are being recorded. Those who also get a daily newspaper can add that to the comparison. Here is a brief list of questions worth asking:

> Do the news programs differ in what they present? Does any news organization ignore important issues that others cover?
>
> Do news programs "stick to the facts" or do reporters include their personal opinions?
>
> Are news analysts *fair* in the criticisms of groups they disagree with (for

example, liberals or conservatives, those who support abortion and those who oppose it, global-warming advocates and critics)? Do they use slanted language? Do they use pejoratives for one group but not the other?

When panels of analysts are used, does each side of the issue receive proportionate representation? Does the panel moderator speak in favor of one side?

Such a comparison, particularly if done on several occasions, will provide a clear idea of which journalists and which programs are most fair and balanced. (Don't be surprised if none is perfect.) Once we learn this, we can write to the journalists and/or the networks involved and compliment or criticize them accordingly. In the case of criticism, we should realize that young journalists may not be acquainted with the traditional standards of their profession and will need to be informed about them.

PUBLISHING

One helpful approach is to be alert to the authors who are featured on news and commentary programs, particularly those with books on self-understanding and/or self-improvement. We can then go to a bookstore, find the books, and spend a little time skimming them, starting with the table of contents and the publisher's description, often found on the back cover, then reading the introduction and the last chapter. Where appropriate, we can also look up key words in the index and check out the relevant pages. If we work efficiently, this whole process can often be done in ten or fifteen minutes.

Whenever we find a book that is still offering the false views of Humanistic Psychology, we can check the publisher's website for the names and addresses of top executives of the firm, select one, and write a letter pointing out the falsity of the book's views with references to relevant research and analysis. The endnotes of this book contain many such references. We should, of course, make clear that we are not asking for censorship or suppression of any point of view, but merely urging that the publisher achieve balance by publishing authors with opposing views.

ENTERTAINMENT MEDIA

Whenever we see a film or watch a television program, we can consider the ideas about life conveyed in the plot and the dialogue and take note of any that reflect the erroneous ideas of Humanistic Psychology. For example, a comedy show may be based on the idea that children are wiser than their parents, a dramatic show may represent the idea that violence is justified when driven by strong feelings, and a movie may include gratuitous sex, creating the impression that casual coupling is healthy and fulfilling.

Whenever we encounter such ideas, we can take note of the company that produced the film or program, the network that bought it, and the companies that sponsored its presentation. Then we can do a computer search for the appropriate names and addresses and explain our objection. The focus, of course, should be on the research that exposes the false ideas and values and not just on our personal opinion.

These suggestions for what can be done by average people not professionally involved in the areas mentioned are certainly modest and may therefore seem inconsequential. But taken together, they can raise the consciousness of more influential people and motivate them to join the effort to overcome the false ideas that have ruined lives, undermined institutions, and endangered America's future. I believe that, at this crucial moment in our history, there is no more important task.

NOTES

1. THE LEGACY OF SOCIAL DARWINISM

1. Two other schools of psychological thought were prominent at the same time as Hereditarianism: Freudianism, which emphasized the sex drive and the role of the unconscious, and Behaviorism, which emphasized the process of conditioning. But neither challenged Hereditarianism because they had a similarly pessimistic view of human nature. However, both set the stage for the reaction known as Humanistic Psychology, as we will note in chapter 2.

2. The first psychological laboratory was established in 1879 at the University of Leipzig, and the first American counterpart was established in 1881 at Johns Hopkins University. The *American Journal of Psychology* was founded in 1887, and the American Psychological Association in 1892.

3. Cited in Stephen Jay Gould, *The Mismeasure of Man* (New York: W. W. Norton, 1981), pp. 82–107. Given the temptation, even among scholars, to reach conclusions that reinforce one's prejudices, it was not surprising that Broca found white men to be intellectually superior to women and black men.

4. Long after Lombroso established a reputation as the premier criminal anthropologist, it was discovered that many college professors and students had the same skull shape as the convicts Lombroso had studied.

5. Intelligence quotient (IQ) is determined by dividing a person's mental-age score by the person's chronological age. This approach was devised in 1912 by Wilhelm Stern.

6. Cited in Gould, *Mismeasure of Man*, pp. 146–54.

7. Ibid., pp. 160–61.

8. Ibid., pp. 183, 190–91.

9. Edward L. Thorndike, "The Contribution of Psychology to Education," *Journal of Educational Psychology* 1, no. 1 (1910): 5–12, http://psychclassics.yorku.ca/Thorndike/education.htm (accessed August 5, 2004).

10. Edward L. Thorndike, "Animal Intelligence," *Popular Science Monthly* (November 1901), http://psychclassics.yorku.ca/Thorndike/Animal/chap6.htm (accessed August 3, 2004).

11. Cited in Gould, *Mismeasure of Man*, pp. 196–98.

12. Quoted in Margaret Sanger and H. G. Wells, *The Pivot of Civilization in Historical Perspective* (Seattle, WA: Inkling Books, 2003), p. 33.

13. Gould, *Mismeasure of Man*, pp. 218–19.

14. Ibid., pp. 200–21.

15. Ronald J. Pestritto and William J. Atto, eds., *American Progressivism* (Lanham, MD: Lexington Books, 2008).

16. See, for example, *History Matters, The U.S. Survey Course on the Web*, at http://historymatters.gmu.edu/d/5078/ (accessed March 6, 2013).

17. Jews have been hated for being both unintelligent and too intelligent. (The latter attribution has been characterized as "cleverness" and "cunning.")

18. See *Holocaust Encyclopedia*, "Voyage of the St. Louis," at http://www.ushmm.org/wlc/article.php?lang=en&ModuleId=10005267 (accessed March 6, 2013).

19. Mary Moss in the Clackamas Community College *Banyan Quarterly*, http://depts.clackamas.cc.or.us/banyan/1.1/moss.htm (accessed March 7, 2013).

20. Quoted in Michael D'Antonio, *The State Boys Rebellion* (New York: Simon and Schuster, 2004), p. 12.

21. Quoted in Chip Berlet and Matthew N. Lyons, *Right-Wing Populism in America: Too Close for Comfort* (New York: Guilford Press, 2000), p. 93.

22. See full quotation, which begins with "Organized charity itself is the symptom of a malignant social disease," at http://thinkexist.com/quotes/margaret_sanger/ (accessed, March 6, 2013).

23. For Wilson, see Dennis L. Cuddy, "The Dark Roots of Eugenics," http://www.crossroad.to/articles2/009/cuddy/eugenics.htm; for Russell, Shaw, and Wells, see http://www.worldfuturefund.org/wffmaster/Reading/Biology/Eugenics.htm (both accessed March 6, 2013).

24. D'Antonio, *State Boys Rebellion*, pp. 8, 16.

25. See H. H. Laughlin, "The Socially Inadequate . . . ," in Albion W. Small, ed., *American Journal of Sociology*, vol. 27, July 21–May 1922 (Chicago: University of Chicago Press), pp. 55–56, at http://www.jstar.org/stable/2764509?seq-3 (accessed March 19, 2013).

26. D'Antonio, *State Boys Rebellion*, p. 14.

27. Ibid., pp. 14, 18, 16–17.

28. Ibid., p. 278.

29. Prior to the nineteenth century most children received little formal education. The first compulsory education law in the United States was passed in Massachusetts in 1852. It required all children ages eight to fourteen to attend school for at least three months a year. In 1873 the upper age limit was lowered to twelve and the time requirement was raised to twenty weeks. Over the next several decades, other states adopted similar laws.

30. James H. Baker, "Report of the Committee of Ten," originally written July 9, 1892, http://tmh.floonet.net/books/commoften/mainrpt.html (accessed March 6, 2013).

31. The Odysseus Group, John Taylor Gatto, "Occasional Letter Number One," 1906, http://www.johntaylorgatto.com/chapters/2i.htm (accessed March 6, 2013).

32. National Education Association, "Report of the Committee of Nine on the Articulation of High School and College," 1911, p. 560. Cited in Thomas R. McCambridge, "E. D. Hirsch, Common Culture, and Postmodernism: Implications for School Reform," at http://public.callutheran.edu/~mccamb/hirschdraft.htm (accessed March 7, 2013).

33. For a discussion of NEA reports and related matters, see Richard Hofstadter, *Anti-Intellectualism in American Life* (New York: Vintage, 1963), ch. 13.

34. Cited at *Goodreads*, http://www.goodreads.com/quotes/35754-we-want-one-class-of-persons-to-have-a-liberal (accessed March 7, 2013).

35. Quoted in Gould, *Mismeasure of Man*, p. 190.

36. Quoted in D'Antonio, *State Boys Rebellion*, p. 11.

37. "Secrets of the SAT: Americans Instrumental in Establishing Standardized Tests," *Frontline*, http://www.pbs.org/wgbh/pages/frontline/shows/sats/where/three.html (accessed March 7, 2013).

38. Hoftstadter, *Anti-Intellectualism in American Life*, pp. 332–43.

39. Ibid., pp. 345–46.

40. Quoted in Ravitch, *Left Back*, p. 250.

41. Quoted in Hofstadter, *Anti-Intellectualism in American Life*, p. 18.

42. The National Child Labor Committee began lobbying for legal restrictions in 1904; a bill regulating child labor was drafted in 1906; the US Children's Bureau was established in 1912; and President Woodrow Wilson signed the child-protecting Keating-Owens Act into law in 1916.

43. The Gilbreths were concerned not only with the management goal of increased productivity but also with the benefits of efficiency to workers, both on and off the job. In the larger program of scientific management, however, the latter, more altruistic concerns received less consideration. The Gilbreths and their large family were the subject of the film *Cheaper by the Dozen*.

44. For more information on job instruction training, see The Bilas Group, LLC, at http://www.thebilasgroup.com/twi-learning-center/job-instruction/ (accessed March 7, 2013).

45. Two excellent introductions to W. Edwards Deming and his system are Andrea Gabor's *The Man Who Discovered Quality* (New York: Random House, 1990) and Mary Walton's *The Deming Management Method* (New York: Putnam, 1986).

46. The system was more elaborate, of course, involving the use of statistical measures by employees and management. For an explanation of these measures, see Walton, *Deming Management Method*.

47. Cited in ibid., p. 248.

48. The first advertising agency in the United States was established in 1850.

49. Walter Dill Scott, *The Psychology of Advertising*, 5th ed. (New York: Arno Reprint, 1954, originally published in 1913), pp. 82–83. Quoted in Deborah J. Coon, "Not a Creature of Reason: The Alleged Impact of Watsonian Behaviorism on Advertising in the 1920s," in *Modern Perspectives on John B. Watson and Classical Behaviorism*, ed. James T. Todd and Edward K. Morris (Westport, CT: Greenwood Press, 1994), pp. 44–45.

50. To verify for yourself the accuracy of these statements about attention shifts, make a simple stroke tally while watching some commercial breaks. Keep your eyes focused on the screen and make a tally mark every time the image or the camera angle changes.

51. Occasionally the books that are published have merit, particularly those by conscientious journalists, but the overall quality of nonfiction publishing has been compromised. The preference for celebrity authors has denied the reading public access to informed, expert opinions on a vast range of subjects. See veteran journalist James Fallows, *Breaking the News* (New York: Pantheon Books, 1996), for an insightful discussion of this development.

52. In some cases, unfortunately, business leaders were not prepared for the reality that employees who had been taught to think for themselves often would have ideas different from those of their employers.

53. His original list of "intelligences" consisted of logical-mathematical; linguistic; musical; spatial; bodily-kinesthetic; interpersonal, or knowledge of others; and intrapersonal, or knowledge of oneself. He later added two others to the list: naturalist and existential. Subsequently, Peter Salovey and John Mayer argued for an additional intelligence, that is, emotional intelligence, which involves the ability to perceive, understand, and regulate emotions. Peter Salovey and John Mayer, "Emotional Intelligence," *Imagination, Cognition, and Personality* 9 (1990): 185–211.

54. Howard Gardner, "Multiple Intelligences after Twenty Years" (invited address, American Educational Research Association, April 2003), http://www.pz.harvard.edu/PIs/HG.htm (accessed August 19, 2004).

55. Howard Gardner, *Frames of Mind: The Theory of Multiple Intelligences* (New York: Basic Books, 1983), p. 287.

56. Ibid., p. 69.

57. E. D. Hirsch Jr., *Cultural Literacy: What Every American Needs to Know* (New York: Houghton Mifflin, 1987), pp. 2, 14, 19, 132–33.

58. John Goodlad, *A Place Called School* (New York: McGraw-Hill, 1984). See also the update of this study in John Goodlad, *A Place Called School: Prospects for the Future* (McGraw-Hill, 2004).

59. Rowland Jepson warned against this fallacy many years before Hirsch committed it: "It is a great mistake to regard any of the processes of constructive thought as being the proprietary characteristic of any particular branch of learning or research. Knowledge is

all one: thinking is the interchangeable handle to the tools used in its various branches; and the attainment of human welfare is the common integrating aim." Rowland W. Jepson, *Clear Thinking*, 5th ed. (New York: Longmans, Green, 1967), pp. 28–29.

2. ENTER HUMANISTIC PSYCHOLOGY

1. Cited in R. Murray Thomas, *An Integrated Theory of Moral Development* (Westport CT: Greenwood Press, 1997), ch. 11.

2. Ibid.

3. B. F. Skinner, *Beyond Freedom & Dignity* (Hackett Publishing, March 2002), p 199. (*Merriam-Webster* supports this definition: "[The self is] an individual's typical character or behavior," http://www.merriam-webster.com/dictionary/self.)

4. Expressed by Roy Wood Sellars, *Critical Realism* (New York: Rand McNally, 1916), p. 201.

5. Cited in Peggy Rosenthal, *Words and Values: Some Leading Words and Where They Lead Us* (New York: Oxford University Press, 1984), p. 23. This is a convoluted way of saying that the self is something an individual perceives. But an individual perceives many objects. What we need to know is what this particular object called "the self" *is*. Rosenthal's excellent (and underappreciated) book provides insight into the impact of the language changes wrought by Humanistic Psychology.

6. WitchVox, "Adult Pagan Action Series," http://www.witchvox.com/va/dt_article .html?a=usmn&id=10342 (accessed March 8, 2013).

7. In Karen Horney, *Neurosis and Human Growth: The Struggle toward Self-Realization* (New York: W. W. Norton, 1991), p. 17.

8. Deepak Chopra, *The Way of the Wizard* (New York: Harmony, 1995).

9. See www.siddhayoga.org.in/glossary.html (accessed March 8, 2013). Similarly, in *Your Sacred Self* (New York: Harper Collins, 1995), author Wayne Dyer speaks of taking readers "from a sense of ourselves as sinful and inferior, to an acceptance of ourselves as divine." Among his central claims are, "You are sacred, and in order to know it you must transcend the old belief system you've adopted," and "You are a divine being called to know your sacred self by mastering the keys to higher awareness."

10. The Theosophical Society, http://www.theosociety.org/pasadena/key/key-glo3 .htm (accessed March 8, 2013).

11. Princeton University, WordNet Glossary definition. See http://wordnetweb .princeton.edu/ (accessed March 8, 2013).

12. Garden of Life, a self-described "Eclectic Pagan Temple." See gardenoflifetemple .com/02WhoWeAre/DefinitionsS.html (accessed March 8, 2013).

13. Cited in Thomas, *Integrated Theory of Moral Development*, ch. 11.

14. Carl R. Rogers, *Client-Centered Therapy: Its Current Practice, Implications and Theory* (London: Constable, 1951), cited in http://en.wikipedia.org/wiki/Carl_Rogers (accessed March 8, 2013).

15. Carl R. Rogers, *On Becoming a Person* (New York: Houghton-Mifflin, 1961), cited in http://www.panarchy.org/rogers/person.html (accessed March 8, 2013).

16. Ibid.

17. William Coulson, a close associate of Rogers, maintains that this sentence was Rogers's creed. See "Reflections on the Human Potential Movement," http://narth.com/docs/coulson.html (accessed March 8, 2013).

18. Rogers, *On Becoming a Person*.

19. Carl R. Rogers, *Client-Centered Therapy: Its Current Practice, Implications, and Theory* (Boston: Houghton Mifflin, 1951), pp. 484–85. Subsequent citations in this chapter refer to the Houghton Mifflin edition.

20. Carl R. Rogers, *A Way of Being* (Boston: Houghton Mifflin, 1980), pp. 102, 104.

21. Rogers, *On Becoming a Person*, pp. 22, 189, 325, respectively.

22. Rogers, *Way of Being*, pp. 43, 194–95.

23. William Coulson, interview with Linda Nicolosi. See "Reflections on the Human Potential Movement," http://narth.com/docs/coulson.html (accessed March 8, 2013).

24. A. H. Maslow, *The Farther Reaches of Human Nature* (New York: Viking Press, 1972), pp. 45–46.

25. Abraham H. Maslow, *Toward a Psychology of Being* (Princeton, NJ: D. Van Nostrand, 1962), p. 181.

26. Richard J. Lowry, ed., *The Journals of A. H. Maslow*, 2 vols. (Monterey, CA: Brooks/Cole Publishing, 1979), vol. 1, see entries for February 13, 1962, and January 8, 1966, respectively.

27. A. H. Maslow, "A Theory of Motivation," *Psychological Review* 50, no. 4 (1943): 370–96, http://www.emotionalliteracyeducation.com/abraham-maslow-theory-human-motivation.shtml (accessed October 30, 2008). And A. H. Maslow, "A Preface to Motivation Theory," *Psychosomatic Medicine* 5 (1943): 85–92.

28. In particular, Abraham H. Maslow, *Motivation and Personality*, 2nd ed. (1954; repr. New York: Harper and Row, 1970). It is worth noting that, though the index of this book contains a few dozen listings for *self* used in a compound term, such as *self-esteem*, there is not one reference to *self* as an independent noun.

29. For more on variations of Maslow's hierarchy of needs, see the various images depicting Maslow's hierarchy of needs at http://images.google.com/images?client=safari&rls=en&q=Maslow&ie=UTF-8&oe=UTF-8&um=1&sa=X&oi=image_result_group&resnum=4&ct=title. Also see http://www.businessballs.com/maslow.htm (both sites accessed March 8, 2013.)

30. Maslow, "Theory of Motivation." Maslow's exact words are "Human needs

arrange themselves in hierarchies . . . [and] the appearance of one need usually rests on the prior satisfaction of another, more pre-potent need."

31. See, for example, Viktor Frankl, *Man's Search for Meaning* (New York: Simon and Schuster, 1984; originally published in English in 1959).

32. He wrote: "There are at least five sets of goals, which we may call basic needs. These are briefly physiological, safety, love, esteem, and self-actualization." In Maslow, "Theory of Motivation."

33. A few pages later, he cites the "unexpected finding that the gratification of the basic needs does not in itself automatically bring about a system of values in which to believe and to which one may commit himself." Maslow, *Motivation and Personality*, pp. xii, xiv, respectively. The reader is left wondering: First he says needs and values are synonymous. Then he says values are brought about by needs. Which is it?

34. For example, in "A Theory of Motivation," Maslow writes: "All people in our society (with a few pathological exceptions) have a need or desire for a stable, firmly based, (usually) high evaluation of themselves. . . . These needs may be classified into two subsidiary sets . . . the desire for strength, for achievement . . . [and] the desire for reputation or prestige." In this regard, see also Maslow, "Theory of Motivation," pp. 370–96. After equating needs with desires throughout the article, he adds a summary in which he equates needs with goals: "There are at least five sets of goals, which we may call basic needs."

35. Maslow, *Motivation and Personality*, p. 157.

36. Maslow, *Toward a Psychology of Being*, pp. 184–85.

37. As Michael Daniels has noted, Maslow failed to specify whether he viewed self-actualization as a state of ultimate satisfaction and fulfillment, a state of need, a process, or merely a tendency to this process. See Michael Daniels, "The Myth of Self-Actualization," *Journal of Humanistic Psychology* 28 (1988): 7–38.

38. Rogers's doctoral degree was in psychotherapy; Maslow's, in primate behavior.

39. Paula J. Caplan, *They Say You're Crazy: How the World's Most Powerful Psychiatrists Decide Who's Normal* (Reading, MA: Addison-Wesley, 1995), p. xx.

40. If Rogers's and Maslow's field of expertise had been history, anthropology, or biology, they might still have gained followers, but they would have had relatively little impact on the general culture. What made them so influential was that the aim of psychology is to *counsel others* in the task of living well. Their followers were not only true believers, but they also enjoyed unique opportunities to disseminate those beliefs to a wide audience.

41. To say that morality is objective and impersonal means that the nature of the act determines its rightness or wrongness, regardless of the desire or opinion of the person performing the act. To say that morality is subjective and personal means wanting or believing an act to be moral makes it moral.

42. As William Coulson, a close associate of Carl Rogers, explains, "In the human

potential movement [that is, in Humanistic Psychology], you prove your personhood by having sex in as unconstrained and uncivilized a way as possible. It's, 'I'll have what I want, when I want it.'" See "Reflections on the Human Potential Movement," http://narth.com/docs/coulson.html (accessed March 8, 2013).

43. See, for example, Rogers, *Client-Centered Therapy*, pp. 487–88.

44. Lowry, *Journals of A. H. Maslow*, 1:157. The failure of his audience to realize that his view was not supportive of theirs is understandable. Though Maslow often spoke favorably of spirituality, he did not bother to explain that he viewed it as a natural phenomenon, emanating from within the person, without any supernatural association. See Abraham H. Maslow, *Religions, Values, and Peak Experiences* (Columbus: Ohio State University Press, 1964), pp. 36–37.

45. Of course, given the strength of the sex drive and human vulnerability to temptation, this belief was not always honored in practice. Even when the belief was genuine and deep, lapses were common.

46. See Judith A. Reisman, *Kinsey, Sex, and Fraud* (Lafayette, LA: Huntington House, 1990), especially ch. 1. In this volume, Reisman does an exhaustive critical analysis of Kinsey's works.

47. See Diana E. H. Russell, *The Secret Trauma: Incest in the Lives of Girls and Women*, rev. ed. (New York: Basic Books, 1987), pp. 5–6.

48. Reisman, *Kinsey, Sex, and Fraud*, p. 221. (Note: This page in Reisman's book is an extract from Maslow's letter to a colleague in which he makes the claim I have quoted and reports Kinsey's treatment of Maslow.)

49. Russell, *Secret Trauma*, p. 6.

50. Judith A. Reisman, *"Soft Porn" Plays Hardball* (Lafayette, LA: Huntington House, 1991), pp. 136–37.

51. Ibid., p. 60.

52. Research cited in Victor C. Strasburger, *Adolescents and the Media: Medical and Psychological Impact* (Thousand Oaks, CA: Sage Publishing, 1995), p. 46.

53. Kinsey's twin studies of human sexuality were published in 1948 and 1949. The first issue of *Playboy* magazine appeared in 1950. Rogers's *Client-Centered Therapy* was first published in 1951, and *On Becoming a Person* was first published in 1961. Maslow's *Motivation and Personality* was published in 1954.

54. For these and related statistics, see http://en.wikipedia.org/wiki/Television_set.

55. This expectation was supported by the understanding that a decade or two earlier, when moviemakers challenged those traditions, a strict performance code had been established.

56. In this case, as in certain others, Maslow was more balanced in his thinking than Rogers and Kinsey. Although he accepted the Freudian view that guilt is "recognition of disapproval by others," he acknowledged another sense of guilt, "intrinsic" guilt, "the

consequence of betrayal of one's own inner nature or self, a turning off the path to self-actualization, and is essentially justified self-disapproval," adding that "seen in this way it is good, even necessary, for a person's development [*sic*] to have intrinsic guilt when he deserves to. It is not just a symptom to be avoided at any cost but is rather an inner guide for growth toward actualization of the real self, and of its potentialities." Excellent point, but he unfortunately ties it to the ghostly inner self, where it is all too easily relativized. (See Maslow, *Toward a Psychology of Being*, p. 182.)

57. Matthew McKay and Patrick Fanning, *Self-Esteem* (New York: St. Martin's Press, 1987).

58. Wayne Dyer, *Your Sacred Self* (New York: HarperCollins, 1995).

59. Chopra, *Way of the Wizard*.

60. Quoted in Russell Chandler, *Understanding the New Age* (Dallas, TX: Lewis and Stanley, 1984), pp. 231–42.

61. M. Scott Peck, *The Road Less Traveled* (New York: Simon and Schuster, 1978), pp. 281, 283.

62. David Burns, *The Feeling Good Handbook* (New York: Plume/Penguin, 1990).

63. A more subtle example is the slogan for Celebrex—"Understand the risks, feel the benefits"—which provides cover for the manufacturer by mentioning the risks but then links *feeling* and *benefits* and thus encourages ignoring the risks. (Incidentally, the "risks" include stomach/intestinal bleeding and ulcers, which, according to the official website, "can occur without warning and may cause death.")

64. *Culture*, as I am using the term, may be defined as the most widely accepted ideas, beliefs, attitudes, and assumptions of a country or a civilization. *Mass culture* means the ideas, beliefs, and the like that are disseminated through the communications and entertainment media rather than through home, school, and church.

65. Robert Bork has astutely observed that those who accepted the ideas that opposed traditional beliefs "didn't go just into the universities. . . . They were part of the chattering class, talkers interested in policy, politics, and culture. They went into politics, print and electronic journalism, church bureaucracies, foundation staffs, Hollywood careers, public interest organizations, anywhere attitudes and opinions could be influenced." Robert Bork, *Slouching towards Gomorrah: Modern Liberalism and American Decline* (New York: ReganBooks, 1996), p. 51.

66. Although Kinsey made it possible for the discussion of sex in various courses, especially college social-science courses and high school sex-education courses, his influence on classroom instruction was not as significant as Rogers's and Maslow's. His greatest influence on college education was no doubt in undermining the rules on gender separation in college dormitories.

67. Rogers, *On Becoming a Person*, pp. 300–13.

68. See Lewis Raths, Merrill Harmin, and Sidney Simon, *Values and Teaching* (New York: Charles E. Merrill, 1966).

69. David Lipe offers the following criticism of values clarification: "(1) it fails to distinguish between matters of personal taste and objective moral value; (2) it can be used to justify any ethical position; (3) it has no adequate criteria by which to resolve value conflicts; and (4) it espouses a moral position that is dishonest." David Lipe, "A Critical Analysis of Values Clarification," published online by Apologetics Press, undated. See http://www.apologeticspress.org/rr/reprints/Critical-Analysis-of-Values-Cla.pdf (accessed March 8, 2013).

70. Alfie Kohn, "The Truth about Self-Esteem," *Phi Beta Kappan*, December 1994, pp. 272–83.

71. Joshua Michael Aronson, ed., *Improving Academic Achievement: Impact of Psychological Factors on Education* (New York: Emerald Group Publishing, 2002), p. 19.

72. Robert H. Schuller, *Self-Esteem: The New Reformation* (Waco, TX: Word Books, 1982), pp. 33, 47, 67, 123, 150, respectively. Schuller conveniently ignores such passages as Mark 7:21–23, in which Jesus emphasizes that the things that "defile" us come from within the human heart.

73. My point is not that certain of today's preachers changed the line from St. Luke's gospel themselves, but instead that they chose a Christmas carol variation on that gospel. In "The Angel's Song on Christmas Night," (http://www.bardstown.com/~brchrys/Angelsng.htm [accessed March 8, 2013]), Dr. Emilio Pisani explains that the phrase in the Latin Vulgate version of Luke's Gospel is *et in terra pax hominibus bonae voluntatis*, the English translation of which is "and on earth peace to men of good will." Over the centuries, the authors of some Christmas carols took liberties with Luke; for example in "It Came upon a Midnight Clear," a line reads "Peace on the earth, good will to men."

74. In the gospel according to Carl Rogers, the parable of the Pharisee and the publican would have the publican saying, "Have mercy on the world for its sin." That is very different from Luke 18:9–14, in which the publican said, "Have mercy on me, a sinner." And the difference is precisely why, Luke tells us, the publican "went home justified before God."

75. See Don Matzat's interview with William Coulson, "Meet Dr. Bill Coulson," *Issues, Etc.*, http://www.mtio.com/articles/aissar74.htm. In another interview, Coulson points out that Rogers's own daughter was similarly affected. After she studied in a graduate course with Maslow, Coulson says, "she left her husband and three children to 'become a real person.' Her father's and Maslow's philosophy of self-fascination had persuaded her that marriage and motherhood weren't good enough." Coulson interview with Linda Nicolosi, "Reflections on the Human Potential Movement."

76. William Coulson, interview with Dr. William Marra, "The Story of a Repentant Psychologist," *Latin Mass*, at http://www.cfpeople.org/Apologetics/page51a080.html (accessed March 8, 2013).

77. Malachi Martin, *The Jesuits: The Society of Jesus and the Betrayal of the Roman Catholic*

Church (New York: Simon and Schuster, 1987), pp. 358–59, 377, 406–407, respectively. Martin links the ideas of man's goodness and society's evil to their earlier eighteenth-century champion Jean Jacques Rousseau, but as we have seen, Humanistic Psychology was the chief transmitter of Rousseau's thought in the twentieth century.

78. Ibid., pp. 409, 492–93.

79. Joseph M. Becker, SJ, *The Re-Formed Jesuits: A History of Changes in Jesuit Formation During the Decade 1965–1975*, 2 vols. (1992; repr. San Francisco: Ignatius Press, 1997), 1:250–51, 171, 169, 256, 358, respectively.

80. This endorsement is shown not only in what is said from the pulpit, but also in what is *not* said—in other words, in the tendency of priests to substitute their own position for the Catholic Church's position on moral issues.

81. As sociologist Anne Hendershott notes, two major studies have shown that "students who attend Catholic universities are more likely to disregard Church teachings and lose their faith than to retain or enrich it." Anne Hendershott, *The Politics of Abortion* (New York: Encounter, 2006), p. 109.

82. In the 1967 Land O' Lakes declaration, many Catholic *colleges* embraced this idea by asserting their independence from Rome.

83. Mario Cuomo, "Religious Belief and Public Morality: A Catholic Governor's Perspective" (speech, September 13, 1984, University of Notre Dame), http://www.amber dragonflypress.com/Cuomo-speech.htm (accessed November 12, 2009). At first glance, the speech is a model of thoughtful analysis, but at its core it rests on the historically untenable belief that the Supreme Court's decisions (e.g., *Roe v. Wade*) are sacrosanct and the absurd contention that it is nobler to politicians to legislate *against* their personal beliefs than *for* them.

84. The slogans baby boomers grew up with included "If it feels good, do it," "Do your own thing," and Jerry Rubin's "Don't trust anyone over thirty." The most obvious individuals over thirty were, of course, one's parents.

85. Stepparents, for whom the incest taboo is weak or nonexistent, are more likely than parents to be sexually attracted to the teenagers in their households and to act on that attraction.

86. Ironically, the media lecture parents on responsible parenting even though it is *media dissemination* of the ideas of Rogers, Maslow, and Kinsey that undermine parents' efforts.

87. See Thomas Sowell, "War on Poverty Revisited," *Capitalism Magazine*, August 17, 2004, http://www.capmag.com/article.asp?ID=3864 (accessed February 7, 2009).

88. For a photocopy of the letter, see http://www.scribd.com/doc/3326590/Ted -Kennedy-Abortion-Letter (accessed February 9, 2009).

89. Quoted in Michael Kranish and Jill Zuckman, "Bradley, Gore Feud on Abortion," *Boston Globe*, January 30, 2000, p. A1.

90. See "The Durban Abortion Papers," letter to constituent, August 14, 1989, at http://www.nrlc.org/Judicial/Durbin/index.html (accessed March 8, 2013).

91. See "Joe Biden on Abortion" at http://www.ontheissues.org/2008/Joe_Biden_Abortion.htm (accessed March 8, 2013).

92. Bill Clinton, speech at the Democratic National Convention, August 29, 1996. See http://www.notable-quotes.com/c/clinton_bill.html (accessed March 8, 2013).

93. See the transcript of Kerry's remarks at the NARAL Pro-Choice America Dinner in Washington, DC, on January 21, 2003, http://www.gwu.edu/~action/2004/interestg/naral012103/kerr012103spt.html (accessed March 8, 2013).

94. Quoted at Georgetown's Berkley Center website, http://berkleycenter.georgetown.edu/resources/quotes/john-kerry-on-criticism-from-the-catholic-church-for-his-stance-on-abortion-in-the-third-presidential-debate (accessed March 8, 2013).

95. See Peter J. Wallison, "The True Origins of This Financial Crisis," February 2009, http://spectator.org/archives/2009/02/06/the-true-origins-of-this-finan (accessed March 8, 2013). Also, http://www.factcheck.org/2008/10/who-caused-the-economic-crisis/ (accessed March 8, 2013).

96. The fact that the feelings were noble—compassion for the poor—did not redeem the decision. In the end, the poor, along with everyone else, were injured.

97. As Mark Levin has noted, some justices follow international law rather than the Constitution they are charged with following. See Mark R. Levin, *Men in Black* (Washington, DC: Regnery Publishing, 2005), p. 18.

98. Rogers, *Way of Being*, pp. 106, 194–95.

99. Judge Harold J. Rothwax observed that, "as late as the early 1960s, the Supreme Court did not feel compelled to burden the government with any special duty to inform the suspect that he didn't have to talk. . . . Everyone understood that the government's job was not to counsel a defendant but to question him. Indeed, some pressuring of a defendant was considered absolutely permissible; how else would you get him to confess?" He goes on to note that before the 1960s, defendants' confessions were viewed as "expressions of remorse, not force," but later came to be viewed as "the product of coercion, trickery, or deceit." Harold J. Rothwax, *Guilty: The Collapse of Criminal Justice* (New York: Random House, 1996), pp. 70–71. For the observation about the changing view of confessions, Rothwax cites Professor Gerald M. Caplan, "Questioning *Miranda*," *Vanderbilt Law Review* 38 (1985): 1417–76.

100. Justice Hugo Black said in his dissenting view: "The Fourth Amendment prohibits unreasonable searches and seizures. The Amendment says nothing about consequences. It certainly nowhere provides for the exclusion of evidence as the remedy for violation." See US Supreme Court Center, "Coolidge v. New Hampshire - 403 U.S. 443 (1971)," http://supreme.justia.com/us/403/443/case.html (accessed March 8, 2013).

101. In his dissenting opinion in *Roe*, Justice Byron White wrote: "I find nothing in

the language or history of the Constitution to support the Court's judgment. The Court simply fashions and announces a new constitutional right for pregnant mothers and, with scarcely any reason or authority for its action, invests that right with sufficient substance to override most existing state abortion statutes. The upshot is that the people and the legislatures of the 50 States are constitutionally disentitled to weigh the relative importance of the continued existence and development of the fetus, on the one hand, against a spectrum of possible impacts on the mother, on the other hand. As an exercise of raw judicial power, the Court perhaps has authority to do what it does today; but, in my view, its judgment is an improvident and extravagant exercise of the power of judicial review that the Constitution extends to this Court." Quoted in "Justice Byron White: Dissent from *Roe v. Wade* and *Doe v. Bolton* and Their Progeny," at http://www.endroe.org/dissentswhite.aspx (accessed March 13, 2013).

102. Levin, *Men in Black*, p. 143.

103. They may have been aware, of course. Judicial activism is hardly a new phenomenon; some jurists have regarded it as the proper perspective on the Constitution dates since the earliest days of the republic.

104. Although Kinsey's ideas had a significant impact on the entertainment media, they had little influence on journalism.

105. Bob Kohn, *Journalistic Fraud* (Nashville: WND Books, 2003), p. 27.

106. Cited in ibid., p. 28.

107. Bill Kovach and Tom Rosenstiel, *The Elements of Journalism* (New York: Three Rivers Press, 2001), cited in ibid., p. 31.

108. Bob Baker, *Newsthinking* (New York: Allyn and Bacon, 2001), cited in Kohn, *Journalistic Fraud*, p. 30.

109. Investigative analysts have discovered similar tactics in other news organizations. See, for example, Bernard Goldberg's *Bias* and *A Slobbering Love Affair*, William McGowan's *Coloring the News*, James Fallows's *Breaking the News*, Tammy Bruce's *Thought Police*, and Brent Bozell's *Weapons of Mass Distortion*.

110. Again, Kinsey's ideas greatly influenced the entertainment media but had much less impact on journalism.

111. James Fallows, *Breaking the News* (New York: Pantheon Books, 1996), p. 151.

3. MEANINGS AND CONSEQUENCES

1. For a more detailed account of chaos theory, see James Gleick, *Chaos Theory: The Making of a New Science* (New York: Penguin, 1988).

2. This section, called Cause and Effect among Ideas, is copyrighted by MindPower, Inc. 2009 and is used with permission. Clarification of the term *idea*, as it is used in this

section, may be helpful. In everyday usage, the word *idea* suggests both a subject and a predicate—not just "Sally" or "tax relief," but "Sally still mourns her father's passing" or "tax relief is overdue." If an idea is expressed (not all are), it is referred to as a *proposition*, a *claim*, an *assertion*, or a *statement*. If the idea is formed by reasoning rather than merely heard or read and then accepted, it is called a *judgment* or a *conclusion*. An argument consists of a judgment or conclusion plus the reasoning that produced it or, if in popular parlance, the "reasons" that support it.

3. The mere fact that one idea follows another in time does not establish causation. To make that assumption is to commit the error of false cause, also known as the post hoc fallacy. (A Google search of this term will explain it more fully.)

4. Cited in Robert H. Bork, *Slouching towards Gomorrah* (New York: ReganBooks, 1996), p. 144.

5. The reasons for acceptance or rejection are not necessarily sound. We may base our decision simply on whether the ideas flatter or challenge our prior opinions.

6. For a discussion of how familiarity with an idea invites its acceptance, see Scott A. Hawkins and Stephen J. Hoch, "Low-Involvement Learning: Memory without Evaluation," *Journal of Consumer Research* (September 1992). (This effect was recognized long before research revealed it. The infamous Nazi propagandist Joseph Goebbels wrote: "If you tell a lie big enough and keep repeating it, people will eventually come to believe it.")

7. Carol Tavris, *Anger: The Misunderstood Emotion* (New York: Simon and Schuster, 1982), pp. 131–35.

8. The reason it is probable rather than certain is that, no matter how strong the habit of mindlessness, we never lose the potential to break a habit and choose an uncharacteristic response.

9. Peggy Rosenthal offers a slightly different explanation of the same phenomenon: "Even when we think we are choosing our words with care and giving them precise meanings, they can mean much more (or less) than we think; and when we use them carelessly, without thinking, they can still carry thoughts. These thoughts we're not aware of, these meanings we don't intend, can then carry us into certain beliefs and behavior—whether or not we notice where we're going." Peggy Rosenthal, *Words and Values: Some Leading Words and Where They Lead Us* (New York: Oxford University Press, 1984), p. viii.

10. One example of non sequitur is a child's answer to his teacher's question "Why do you get so dirty during playtime?" He responded, "Because I'm closer to the ground than you are." Another is the conclusion of a medical authority in 1622 about the treatment of a wound: "If the wound is large, *the weapon* [emphasis added] with which the patient has been wounded should be anointed daily; otherwise, every two or three days." The medical quotation is from Christopher Cerf and Victor Navasky, *The Experts Speak: The Definitive Compendium of Authoritative Misinformation* (New York: Villard, 1998), p. 38.

11. David Elton Trueblood, *General Philosophy* (New York: Harper and Row, 1963), p. 9.

12. Newsbreaks began as program interruptions necessitated by events that required immediate reporting. Today they are generally advertisements for the next newscast.

13. To be sure, today's special effects are vastly superior to those of earlier times, but this is the result of *technological* innovation and is largely unrelated to popular culture.

14. See Bernard Goldberg's *Bias*, James Fallows's *Breaking the News*, William McGowan's *Coloring the News*, and Alfie Kohn's *Journalistic Fraud*.

15. See Ray Marshall and Marc Tucker, *Thinking for a Living: Education and the Wealth of Nations* (New York: Basic Books, 1992), p. 80. The organizational structure of the school was revised to match the factory. Principals were managers and teachers were workers—that is, not thinking for themselves but slavishly following what they were told to do. And what was told was what the "Committee of Nine" decided in 1911. They replaced the traditional emphasis on training the mind with an emphasis on citizenship and vocational training. (Both the American Federation of Labor and the National Association of Manufacturers supported these changes.) In order to ensure that these changes would not be challenged, women were preferred over men for teaching·posts and, unlike European and Japanese counterparts, paid relatively little. In 1870, 50 percent of teachers were women, by 1920, 86 percent.

16. It should be noted that Rogers and Maslow did not originate the ideas that human nature is essentially wise and good, evil resides outside rather than within the individual, and other people are responsible for whatever goes wrong in our lives. Jean Jacques Rousseau, the man known as the "father of Romanticism," articulated these same views in the eighteenth century. As his biographer noted, "The assertion of man's natural goodness is plainly something very fundamental in Rousseau, but there is something still more fundamental, and that is the shifting of dualism itself, the virtual denial of a struggle between good and evil in the breast of the individual." He goes on to say that Rousseau "abandoned his five children one after the other, but had we are told an unspeakable affection for his dog." When others disapproved of Rousseau's behavior toward his children, he claimed that *not he but the wealthy class* were responsible for his deeds. See Irving Babbitt, *Rousseau & Romanticism*, introduction by Claes G. Ryn (1919; repr. New Brunswick, NJ: Transaction Publishers, 1991), pp. 130, 143, 155.

17. Carl Rogers, *A Way of Being* (Boston: Houghton-Mifflin, 1980), pp. 43, 194–95.

18. In chapter 2 we noted that the rejection of guilt and shame has been a significant theme in hundreds of self-help books that gave practical application to the Rogers's and Maslow's ideas.

19. In 1950 the *Diagnostic and Statistical Manual of Mental Disorders* (DSM) listed 106 disorders. By 1994 the number had almost tripled to 297. It now includes such conditions as "immature personality disorder," "nicotine dependence," "self-defeating personality disorder," and low sex drive. Moreover, the list of behaviors to which the adjective *compulsive* has been joined continues to grow; at this writing it includes shopping, lateness, drinking, gambling, talking, eating, thumb sucking, bedwetting, and coition.

20. Blaming one's country for all that is wrong in the world is an extension of blaming one's parent and teachers for all that is wrong in one's life. Examples of adulation of alternative political systems include Jane Fonda's support of North Vietnam and, more recently, other celebrities' praising of other repressive societies, notably Venezuela and Cuba.

21. Notable examples include the uncritical admiration celebrities express for such dictators as Fidel Castro and Hugo Chavez.

22. The most dramatic example of such an organization is the Society of Jesus (also called the Jesuits), which not only rejected its original purpose—to serve the pope in his role as the successor to St. Peter—but also abandoned some of its core beliefs. The Jesuit transformation is discussed at some length in chapter 5.

23. For an extended discussion of the evolution of the concept of social justice from its origin to the present day, see Vincent Ryan Ruggiero, "American Catholics and Social Justice," *Catholic Journal*, March 18, 2012, www.catholicjournal.us (accessed January 28, 2013).

24. In addition to resentment of individuals, there is increasing resentment of entire classes of people, notably the resentment of people of higher-than-average income and accomplishment. The reasoning goes, "If I am no less wise and good than they, yet I am less successful, they must be cheating me of what is rightfully mine."

25. The notion that this need is preeminent is usually associated with Maslow's hierarchy, but Rogers held much the same view, writing: "There is one central source of energy in the human organism. This source is a trustworthy function of the whole system rather than some portion of it; it is most simply conceptualized as a tendency toward fulfillment, toward actualization, toward not only the maintenance but also the enhancement of the organism." Carl Rogers, *A Way of Being* (New York: Houghton-Mifflin, 1980), p. 123.

26. Carl R. Rogers, *On Becoming a Person* (New York: Houghton-Mifflin, 1961), pp. 108, 119.

27. This consequence is related to the idea that human nature is inherently wise and good as well as to the idea that self-actualizing is the highest need.

28. Quote beginning "that is own deep impulses" is from Rogers, *On Becoming a Person*, p. 325. Coulson's attribution to Rogers is from Linda Nicolosi, "An Interview with William Coulson," http://narth.com/docs/coulson.html (accessed November 14, 2012).

29. Innumerable books have documented these developments. For a summary of the developments, see Executive Summary, "The Decline of Marriage and Rise of New Families," Pew Research Social and Demographic Trends, http://www.pewsocialtrends.org/2010/11/18/the-decline-of-marriage-and-rise-of-new-families/ (accessed March 9, 2013).

30. The most common form of such aggrandizement is most dangerous because it seems so noble—the argument that it is legitimate to violate one's principles in order to get reelected because reelection will provide greater opportunity to honor those principles.

(In reality, reelection is a recurring challenge, so the "greater opportunity" is perennially deferred.)

31. For a useful discussion of this trend see Myron Magnet, "The Decline and Fall of Business Ethics," *Fortune Classics*, 1986, at http://features.blogs.fortune.cnn.com/2011/04/03/the-decline-and-fall-of-business-ethics/ (accessed March 9, 2013).

32. See Sewell Chan, "Financial Crisis Was Avoidable, Inquiry Finds," *New York Times*, http://www.nytimes.com/2011/01/26/business/economy/26inquiry.html?_r=0&adxnnl=1&adxnnlx=1362841640-949DvUxaoEsVZln8WqrFnA (accessed March 9, 2013). In addition, the self-absorption of management is responsible for extravagant pay raises for CEOs and irresponsible expenditures on airplanes, vacations, and the like for executives, even when companies teeter on the edge of bankruptcy.

33. See Don Matzat, ed., "Meet Dr. Bill Coulson," *Issues, Etc.*, http://www.mtio.com/articles/aissar74.htm (accessed March 9, 2013). An example of an author advocating such self-indulgence is Thomas Moore's claim that narcissism is "not a personality defect, but the soul trying to find its otherness." He goes on to say that "it is wrong to be negative toward the ego and even egotism. The ego needs to be loved, requires attention, and wants exposure. That is part of its nature. . . . The narcissistic person tries very hard to be loved, but he never succeeds because he doesn't realize yet that he has to love himself as other before he himself can be loved." Thomas Moore, *Care of the Soul: A Guide for Cultivating Depth and Sacredness in Everyday Life* (New York: Walker, 1992), pp. 101–103. Many more examples can be found by searching on Amazon.com for "self-assertion" books.

34. Roy Baumeister, "Self-Esteem," *Education.Com*, http://www.education.com/reference/article/self-esteem2/ (accessed March 10, 2013).

35. For statistics on grade inflation, see *GradeInflation.Com*, last major update March 10, 2009, http://gradeinflation.com/ (accessed March 10, 2013). For an example of relaxed discipline, see "New York City's Public Schools Change 'Discipline Code' REDUCING Penalties for Smoking, Cursing AND Cutting Class," *InvestmentWatch*, August 31, 2012, http://investmentwatchblog.com/new-york-citys-public-schools-change-discipline-code-reducing-penalties-for-smoking-cursing-and-cutting-class/ (accessed March 10, 2013).

36. Samantha Cleaver, "Too Much of a Good Thing?" Scholastic Online, http://www.scholastic.com/teachers/article/too-much-good-thing (accessed November 16, 2012).

37. Daniel Patrick Moynihan, "Defining Deviancy Down," *American Scholar*, Winter 1993.

38. Robert W. Reasoner, "Can the Use of Self-Esteem Programs in Schools Actually Reduce Problem Behaviors and Create More Positive School Climates?" *Self-Esteem International*, http://www.self-esteem-international.org/Research/SEPrograms.htm (accessed March 10, 2013).

39. Lucia Zedner and Julian V. Roberts, eds., *Principles and Values in Criminal Law and Criminal Justice* (New York: Oxford University Press, 2012), ch. 18.

40. Examples of such extolling may be found at Russell Chandler, *Understanding the New Age* (Dallas, TX: Word, 1988), pp. 64, 319; M. Scott Peck, *The Road Less Traveled* (New York: Simon and Schuster, 1978), pp. 281, 283; and Robert Schuller, *Self-Esteem: The New Reformation* (Dallas, TX: Word, 1982), pp. 15, 33, 67, 98. Editors even shun projects about self-knowledge and self-respect, the former because they imply that we don't already know ourselves completely, and the latter because they imply qualifications on self-esteem.

41. Harold W. Stevenson and James M. Stigler, *The Learning Gap* (New York: Simon and Schuster, 1992), p. 17.

42. Christopher B. Swanson, "U.S. Graduation Rate Continues Decline," *Education Week*, June 2, 2010, http://www.edweek.org/ew/articles/2010/06/10/34swanson.h29 .html (accessed November 17, 2012).

43. Reported in Brian Moore, "The Worst Generation?" *New York Post*, May 10, 2010, http://www.nypost.com/p/news/business/jobs/the_worst_generation_ZHtISjvJY3Ggl WGTlWa0gO (accessed November 17, 2012). Ron Alsop offers a related view in his book *The Trophy Kids Grow Up*.

44. Except, of course, *my* opinion. This "mine is better" perspective is among the most mischievous of tendencies, as I explain in a later chapter.

45. Peter Shaw describes how the dependability of language came to be questioned on the theory that "nothing makes any sense; everything is relative, anyway; one person's opinion is as good as another's; [and] moral distinctions are useless." This notion, he points out, is central to the phenomenon known as deconstruction. One literary scholar (Harold Bloom) argued, in effect, that all readings of a work of literature are wrong. And another (Stanley Fish) argued that all readings are right. Others have proclaimed "freedom from fact" and the approval of "the manipulation of data" to advance their views. Peter Shaw, *The War against the Intellect* (Iowa City: University of Iowa Press, 1989), pp. 43–44, 61–65.

46. The basic premise of "values clarification" is that there is no objective standard of morality; rather, each person decides on his or her own and whatever is decided is "right for that person."

47. If everyone is wise and good, rather than complex and imperfect, there is no legitimate basis for judging any individual or culture or his/its behavior.

48. Examples of the decrease in language skills include failure of even educated people to distinguish between *phenomenon* and *phenomena*, *amount* and *number* (as in "an amount of people"), glaring mispronunciations, and the use of *like* and *you know* to punctuate ideas.

49. Adam Smith, "Lack of Motivation Part of America's Social Decline," *Collegiate Times*, September 15, 2010, http://www.collegiatetimes.com/stories/15830/lack-of -student-motivation-part-of-americas-national-decline (accessed March 10, 2013).

50. Stevenson and Stigler, *Learning Gap*.

51. In 1961, *Webster's Third New International Dictionary* abandoned its prescriptive philosophy, which presented the correct meanings of words as determined by the usage of

linguistically sensitive, informed people, for a descriptive approach that made no such distinction among users. One example: The word *fact* is now defined as (1) "something known with certainty" and (2) "something asserted as certain." The second means that anything that anyone, no matter how ill-informed, may assert is a fact. Not a viewpoint, a theory, a position, but a fact. The following warning, often attributed to Greek historian Thucydides, is worth pondering in this regard: "A nation falls apart not when men take up arms against each other, but when key words do not mean the same thing to a majority of citizens."

52. T. S. Eliot anticipated this development decades earlier when he said it is unlikely that "the profoundest and most original works," meaning literary works, will gain a wide audience. "The ideas which flatter a current tendency or emotional attitude will go farthest; and some others will be distorted to fit in with what is already accepted. The residuum in the public mind is hardly likely to be a distillation of the best and wisest; it is more likely to represent the common prejudices of the majority of editors and reviewers." T. S. Eliot, *Christianity and Culture* (1939; repr. New York: Harcourt Brace, 1949) p. 162.

53. Bob Kohn, *Journalistic Fraud* (Nashville: WND Books, 2003).

54. For more examples, see Larry Schweikart's *48 Liberal Lies about American History* (New York: Sentinel Trade, 2009).

55. Quoted in John Leo, "Oliver Stone's Paranoid Propaganda," *Frontline,* January 13, 1992, http://www.pbs.org/wgbh/pages/frontline/shows/oswald/conspiracy/jfkleo.html (accessed March 10, 2013).

56. Rogers, *On Becoming a Person*, p. 22.

57. See Jeffrey Thayne, "Rogers and the Modern Worldview," *LDSPhilosopher,* January 5, 2013, http://www.ldsphilosopher.com/tag/carl-rogers/ (accessed March 10, 2013).

58. Babbitt, *Rousseau & Romanticism*, p. 162.

59. See, for example, Paula J. Caplan, *They Say You're Crazy: How the World's Most Powerful Psychiatrists Decide Who's Normal* (Reading, MA: Addison-Wesley, 1995), especially pp. 76–77.

60. The incest taboo still may still be a strong deterrent to child-parent sex, but only a weak one, if it exists at all, with child-*step*parent sex.

61. The expression of this idea has lifted one individual to celebrity in academe and beyond. Peter Singer, author of many books and scholarly articles, including the *Encyclopedia Britannica* article on "ethics," was awarded an endowed ethics chair at Princeton in 1998. Among his ideas is that sex between humans and animals—*his examples include a woman having sex with an octopus and a man with a chicken*—"ceases to be an offence to our status and dignity as human beings." (He also supports euthanasia, sterilization of the poor in third-world countries, and infanticide. He regards killing disabled infants as morally acceptable.) Cited in Daniel J. Flynn, *Intellectual Morons: How Ideology Makes Smart People Fall for Stupid Ideas* (New York: Crown Forum, 2004), pp. 73–76.

62. A dramatic indication of the impact of the idea that all sexual expression is

acceptable is the increase in the number of teachers, notably women teachers, becoming sexually involved with their students.

63. The most common expression of this view is that the victims of sexual assault "want it" or are "asking for it."

64. Conversely, the belief, common to many Asian cultures, that age produces wisdom and the young have much to learn from their elders leads to the respect for elders and eagerness to learn from them that is also common in those cultures.

65. Cited by William Coulson, Rogers's close associate, in an interview with Dr. William Marra, "The Story of a Repentant Psychologist," *Latin Mass*, http://www.cfpeople .org/Apologetics/page51a080.html (accessed March 15, 2010).

66. Abraham H. Maslow, *Motivation and Personality*, 2nd ed. (1954; repr. New York: Harper and Row, 1970), pp. 45–46.

67. Richard J. Lowry, ed., *The Journals of A. H. Maslow*, 2 vols. (Monterey, CA: Brooks/ Cole Publishing, 1979), 1:185–86, see entry for August 19, 1962, specifically.

68. A. H. Maslow, *The Farther Reaches of Human Nature* (New York: Viking Press, 1972) p. 45.

69. Lowry, *Journals of A. H. Maslow*, 1:154–57, see entries for April 15, 1962, and April 17, 1962, specifically.

70. Ibid., 2:1147, see entries for March 31, 1969, and April 30, 1969, specifically.

71. Ibid., 1:581, see entry for January 8, 1966, specifically.

72. Ibid., 2:949, see entry for March 3, 1969, specifically.

73. Ibid., 2:848, see entry for November 12, 1967, specifically.

74. Ibid., 2:1162, see entry for January 6, 1970, specifically.

75. Maslow, *Motivation and Personality*, p. xix.

4. THE FALLACIES EXPOSED

1. Significant authors and works include the following: Henry Hazlitt, *Thinking as a Science* (New York: E. P. Dutton, 1916); J. Boraas, *Teaching to Think* (New York: Macmillan, 1922); Alfred North Whitehead, *The Function of Reason* (Princeton, NJ: Princeton University Press, 1929); Joseph Jastrow, *Effective Thinking* (New York: Simon and Schuster, 1931); Rowland Jepson, *Clear Thinking* (London: Longmans, Green, 1936); C. H. Judd, *Education as the Cultivation of the Higher Mental Processes* (New York: Macmillan, 1936); Richard Weil, *The Art of Practical Thinking* (New York: Simon and Schuster, 1940); and Edward Glaser, *An Experiment in the Development of Critical Thinking* (New York: Columbia University Press, 1941).

2. Graham Wallas, *The Art of Thought* (New York: Harcourt, Brace, 1926), p. 288.

3. Ernest Dimnet, *The Art of Thinking* (New York: Simon and Schuster, 1928), pp. 58–59.

4. John Dewey, *How We Think* (New York: D. C. Heath, 1933), pp. 9, 16, 78, 265. Oddly, Dewey also founded the very Progressive Education movement that *displaced* the traditional academic curriculum and made the child (rather than knowledge) the focus of learning. However, he did not intend for that movement to reject his views on thinking and eventually expressed his disapproval of those who did so.

5. Cited in Michael D'Antonio, *The State Boys Rebellion* (New York: Simon and Schuster, 2004), pp. 15–16.

6. Edward M. Glaser, *An Experiment in the Development of Critical Thinking* (New York: Teachers' College, Columbia University, 1941), pp. 5–6, 69–70.

7. Feuerstein had studied under the famous Swiss psychologist Jean Piaget, author of *The Psychology of Intelligence* (1942) and other works.

8. Reuven Feuerstein, *Instrumental Enrichment: An Intervention Program for Cognitive Modifiability* (Baltimore, MD: University Park Press, 1980), pp. 102–103, 115–17.

9. Reuven Feuerstein, "New Horizons," in *Creating the Future: Perspectives on Educational Change*, comp. and ed. Dee Dickinson (Aston Clinton, Bucks, UK: Accelerated Learning Systems, 1991). Feuerstein's piece also available at http://education.jhu.edu/PD/new horizons/future/creating_the_future/crfut_feuerstein.cfm (accessed March 11, 2013).

10. J. P. Guilford, "Creativity," *American Psychologist* 5 (1950): 444–54. It should be noted that although psychologists had ignored creativity, certain others had not. Significant works on the subject that predate Guilford's 1950 article include Hughes Mearns's *Creative Power* (1935) and *The Creative Adult* (1940), Alex Osborn's *Your Creative Power* (1948), and Eliot Dole Hutchinson's *How to Think Creatively* (1949).

11. Given the Hereditarian bias of psychology prior to Guilford's time, the lack of knowledge of any research on thinking was understandable.

12. J. P. Guilford, "The Structure of Intellect," *Psychological Bulletin* 53 (1956): 276–93.

13. Mary Meeker, *The Structure of Intellect: Its Uses and Interpretation* (Columbus, OH: Charles Merrill, 1969).

14. Jeff Wells, "Biographical Note," E. Paul Torrance Collection, at http://www.gcsu .edu/library/sc/collections/torrance.htm (accessed March 11, 2013). Other researchers who made significant contributions to the understanding of creativity include Erich Fromm, Rollo May, Frank Barron, Calvin Taylor, and Sidney Parnes.

15. Ilma Brewer, *Learning More and Teaching Less* (Guildford, Surrey, UK: Society for Research in Higher Education, 1985).

16. Howard Barrows and Robyn Tamblyn, preface to *Problem-Based Learning: An Approach to Medical Education* (New York: Springer, 1980).

17. Each group was led by a tutor who offered guidance but did not impart information or direct students' efforts. Students changed groups and tutors at specified intervals.

18. For information on the problem-based learning initiative, see http://www.pbli .org/.

19. In comedy, the flaw was a mistake or misunderstanding that created confusion among the characters; in tragedy, it was something more serious such as jealousy, lust, greed, envy, or excessive pride that led to the character's ruin or demise. In classical theater, the main character was a person of high station and regard, reflecting the playwright's and the audiences' shared understanding that weakness and imperfection were present in all human beings.

20. Listed at "Ben Okri Quotes," Brainy Quote, p. 1 of 2, http://www.brainyquote .com/quotes/authors/b/ben_okri.html (accessed February 19, 2013).

21. Richard Nisbett and Lee Ross, *Human Inference: Strategies and Shortcomings of Social Judgment* (Englewood-Cliffs, NJ: Prentice Hall, 1980), p. 287.

22. Stuart Sutherland, *Irrationality: Why We Don't Think Straight!* (New Brunswick, NJ: Rutgers University Press, 1994), p. 29.

23. I. Broveman et al., "Sex Role Strategies and Clinical Judgments of Mental Health," *Journal of Consulting and Clinical Psychology* 34 (1970): 1–7. Cited in Sutherland, *Irrationality*.

24. Quoted in Daniel Goleman, *Vital Lies, Simple Truths* (New York: Simon and Schuster, 1985), p. 98.

25. Stephen Lucas, *The Art of Public Speaking* (New York: Random House, 1983), p. 26.

26. Elizabeth Loftus and Katherine Ketcham, *Witness for the Defense* (New York: St. Martin's Press, 1992), p. 77. See also Elizabeth Loftus, *Eyewitness Testimony* (Boston: Harvard University Press, 1979).

27. David G. Myers offers some interesting data on how memories about ourselves are constructed, terming the process "revising our life histories." He cites several research studies, one of which involved ninth-grade boys who were asked various questions—about discipline at home, intellectual interests, teen sex, and so on. The same people were contacted over thirty years later and asked to recall the views they held and expressed earlier. Myers found that "the men's recollections were astonishingly inaccurate." Another study asked university students to rate their steady dating partners; then, two months later, the same people were asked to rate their partners again. Those who were still in love "recalled love at first sight." Those who had broken up claimed to have spotted the partners' faults from the outset. Similarly, he notes that "emotional memories for positive events often become more positive over time." The process, it seems, involved "minimizing the unpleasant or boring aspects and remembering the high points." Myers, *Intuition*, pp. 69–71.

28. The imperfection of problem solving and decision making has a positive side: it ensures that every generation will have opportunities for intellectual achievement. Perfection may be impossible, but excellence is achievable.

29. Sutherland, *Irrationality*, p. 27.

30. Richard Nisbett and Lee Ross, *Human Inference*, pp. 167, 181–83.

31. The reason was that the medieval church considered charging interest a sin of usury.

32. Cited in Myers, *Intuition*, p. 102.

33. And the legal system has its own examples of human imperfection. As novelist John Grisham trenchantly observed, "Wrongful convictions occur every month in every state in this country, and the reasons are all varied and all the same—bad police work, junk science, faulty eyewitness identifications, bad defense lawyers, lazy prosecutors, arrogant prosecutors." In John Grisham, *The Innocent Man* (New York: Bantam Dell, 2006), p. 430.

34. This is the mainstream Christian view and it is very different from the Calvinist Christian view that human beings are not merely deprived but *depraved*—that is, inherently evil. Failure to distinguish the mainstream from the Calvinist view has led some people to believe that the Christian view of human nature is at odds with the views of other religions, as well as with secular philosophy. In fact, it is at odds with neither.

35. Though Hinduism is commonly considered polytheistic, some forms posit one supreme god and other lesser gods, and others are agnostic or atheistic.

36. Irving Babbitt, *Rousseau & Romanticism*, introduction by Claes G. Ryn (1919; repr. New Brunswick, NJ: Transaction Publishers, 1991), p. 153.

37. From *Mark Twain's Autobiography*, cited in "Cruelty," TwainQuotes.com, http://www.twainquotes.com/Cruelty.html (March 10, 2013).

38. Goodreads quotations from Albert Einstein found at http://www.goodreads.com/quotes/87105-it-is-easier-to-denature-plutonium-than-to-denature-the (accessed March 11, 2013).

39. "Havelock Ellis," Brainyquote, http://www.brainyquote.com/quotes/authors/h/havelock_ellis.html (accessed March 11, 2013).

40. Stanton E. Samenow, *Inside the Criminal Mind* (New York: Times Books, 1984), p. xiii.

41. See, for example, "Feral Child," *Psychology Wiki*, at http://psychology.wikia.com/wiki/Feral_child (accessed March 11, 2013).

42. The only possible response of those who assert inherent human wisdom and goodness is to blame society—that is, parents and other authority figures—for a child's or a student's stupidity and evilness. But that claim does not withstand scrutiny. Today's parents and authority figures were once children and thus can blame their parents, those parents can blame their parents, and so on, back through time until at last we reach the first humans in a garden or, if you prefer, a cave, and whom can they blame?

43. In an interesting critical essay, Professor Michael Daniels argues that a majority of those who write about self-actualization, including Rogers and Maslow, have "concealed" the fact that it is more about "moral philosophy" than "psychological science." See Michael Daniels, "The Myth of Self-Actualization," *Journal of Humanistic Psychology* 28, no. 1 (1988): 7–38.

44. As Maslow himself acknowledged, the term was originally coined by psychiatrist Kurt Goldstein in a different scholarly context. See Kurt Goldstein, *The Organism* (New York: American Book Company, 1939).

45. Maurice Friedman, *Dialogue and the Human Image* (Newbury Park, CA: Sage Publishing, 1992), p. 16.

46. A particularly clear example of Maslow's carelessness and the difficulties this creates for those appraising his work is his treatment of transcendence as it relates to self-actualization. To begin with, his acknowledgement of transcendence came many years after his famous pyramid, and he never revised the pyramid to accommodate it. And when it finally came, in *The Farther Reaches of Human Nature*, he offered fully thirty-five different meanings of self-transcendence, including transcendence of "ego, self, selfishness, ego-centering," and "the basic needs," of which the highest one is "self-actualization." Most significant, he did not address the contradictions of his earlier work suggested by such self-transcendence. Abraham H. Maslow, *The Farther Reaches of Human Nature* (New York: Viking Press, 1972), pp. 270–76.

47. Ibid. Peggy Rosenthal also noted the irony that "those urging us to work at our personal development don't seem to hear the oddness of their calling for self-absorption in the traditional language of self-denial, nor to notice the contradiction of their insisting that we must constantly 'work' at a development process that they claim to be inevitable, 'natural,' and 'spontaneous.'" Peggy Rosenthal, *Words and Values: Some Leading Words and Where They Lead Us* (New York: Oxford University Press, 1984), p. 98.

48. See, for example, L. Geller, "Another Look at Self-Actualization," *Journal of Humanistic Psychology* 24, no. 2 (1984): 93–106.

49. Abraham H. Maslow, *Motivation and Personality*, 2nd ed. (1954; repr. New York: Harper and Row, 1970), ch. 11. Given that Maslow's selection of individuals for his study was largely based on his personal admiration for them, it is not unreasonable to wonder whether his resulting description of the characteristics of self-actualizing people was similarly biased.

50. Ibid., pp. 149–52; and Richard J. Lowry, ed., *The Journals of A. H. Maslow*, 2 vols. (Monterey, CA: Brooks/Cole Publishing, 1979), 1:850, see entry for November 12, 1967, specifically.

51. Lowry, *Journals of A. H. Maslow*, 2:793, see entry for May 25, 1967 specifically.

52. Ibid., 2:628, see entry for May 17, 1966, specifically.

53. Abraham H. Maslow, *Toward a Psychology of Being* (Princeton, NJ: D. Van Nostrand, 1962), p. 190.

54. The phrase is from nineteenth-century French literary critic C. A. Sainte-Beuve. Quoted in Babbitt, *Rousseau & Romanticism*, p. 305.

55. Stephen C. Danckert, comp., *The Quotable [Samuel] Johnson: A Topical Compilation of His Wit and Moral Wisdom* (San Francisco: Ignatius Press, 1992), pp. 127, 111, respectively.

56. Arnold Toynbee, *Surviving the Future* (New York: Oxford University Press, 1971).

57. Arnold Toynbee, *A Study of History*, rev. ed., abridged by the author and Jane Caplan (1972; repr. New York: Portland House, 1988), pp. 347–48.

58. Karl Menninger, *Whatever Became of Sin?* (New York: Hawthorn Books, 1973), pp. 135, 199.

59. For an interesting review of biblical quotations related to self-esteem, see "A Biblical View of Self-Esteem," http://www.rapidnet.com/~jbeard/bdm/Psychology/self-est/key.htm (accessed March 11, 2013).

60. Alfie Kohn, "The Truth about Self-Esteem," *Phi Delta Kappan*, December 1994, pp. 272–83.

61. Martin E. P. Seligman, *Learned Optimism: How to Change Your Mind and Life*, 2nd ed. (1990; repr. New York: Free Press, 1998), introduction and p. 288.

62. Harold Stevenson and James Stigler, *The Learning Gap* (New York: Simon and Schuster, 1992). See also, Nina H Shokraii, "The Self-Esteem Fraud," http://www.lecfl.com/media/pdf/41/ogXE419755.pdf (accessed March 11, 2013).

63. John Marshall Reeve, *Motivating Others: Nurturing Inner Motivational Resources* (Boston: Allyn and Bacon, 1996), p. 152.

64. Roy F. Baumeister, Laura Smart, and Joseph M. Boden, "Relation of Threatened Egotism to Violence and Aggression: The Dark Side of High Self-Esteem," *Psychological Review* 103, no. 1 (1996): 5–33.

65. Thomas Gilovich, *How We Know What Isn't So: The Fallibility of Reason in Everyday Life* (New York: Free Press, 1991), p. 77.

66. Sutherland, *Irrationality*, p. 240.

67. For example, George Orwell, in his 1943 essay "Looking Back on the Spanish War," observed that many people had come to embrace the belief, not just that historians sometimes err, but also that it is impossible to present history truthfully because there are no facts to record. William Barrett says that Aristotle and medieval philosophers defined truth as correspondence between our thoughts and reality. Descartes defined it as consistency between one's idea and one's perception. Thus, he put whole matter within the mind, leaving reality out of the equation. This planted seeds of subjectivism that have flowered in the present age. Barrett suggests the cartoon picture of the lightbulb illuminating in the head nicely depicts Descartes's view. The correct image for the discovery of truth, he believes, would be a spotlight shining on some portion of the world. William Barrett, *The Illusion of Technique* (New York: Anchor/Doubleday, 1979), pp. 155–64.

68. Quoted in "Turning the Intellectual Tide," http://vision.org/visionmedia/article.aspx?id=718 (accessed March 11, 2013).

69. Rosenthal, *Words and Values*, pp. 124–25, 148–50.

70. As Mortimer Adler has noted, the views that "nothing is true or false" and "everything is a matter of opinion" are hardly new. They were present as far back in human history as ancient Greece. Aristotle answered them by pointing out that the first one is self-contradictory and the second is self-defeating because it, too, is an opinion, and therefore

no truer than its opposite. Mortimer Adler, *The Great Ideas: A Lexicon of Western Thought* (New York: Macmillan, 1992), p. 595.

71. What message would avoid this nonsense yet not foster self-defeating thoughts? The message that we don't know our capabilities until we try and that success sometimes occurs after a string of failures; that effort can reveal hidden talent.

72. Philosopher David Elton Trueblood called the principle of contradiction "the necessary condition of intelligible discussion." He also offers two examples of statements that are self-evident (that is, cannot be contradicted): "Knowledge is possible" and "There is error." To deny either, he notes, is to affirm it. David Elton Trueblood, *General Philosophy* (New York: Harper and Row, 1963), p. 88.

73. All quoted material in this paragraph is from the *Oxford English Dictionary* (OED).

74. William G. Perry Jr., *Forms of Intellectual and Ethical Development in the College Years* (New York: Holt, Rinehart, and Winston, 1970).

75. Maxine Hairston, "Required Courses Should Not Focus on Charged Issues," *Chronicle of Higher Education,* January 23, 1991, p. B3.

76. Jodi O'Brien and Peter Kollock, *The Production of Reality*, 3rd ed. (Thousand Oaks, CA: Pine Forge Press, 2001), pp. ix, 578, 586.

77. David Newman, *Sociology: Exploring the Architecture of Everyday Life* (Thousand Oaks, CA: Pine Forge Press, 1995), p. 44.

78. Cited in Peter Shaw, *The War against the Intellect* (Iowa City: University of Iowa Press, 1989), pp. 61–62.

79. Disdain for history is especially damaging to learning because, as Lord Acton observed, "History is not only a particular branch of knowledge, but a particular mode and method of knowledge in other branches."

80. According to A. Quinton, the Romantic movement favors "nature over culture, convention and artifice . . . [and] freedom over constraint, rules and limitations. . . . Mentally, the Romantics prefer feeling to thought, more specifically emotion to calculation; imagination to literal common sense, intuition to intellect." In "Philosophical Romanticism," in T. Honderich, ed., *The Oxford Companion to Philosophy* (Oxford: Oxford University Press, 1996), p. 778. Quoted at http://www.infed.org/thinkers/et-rous.htm (accessed September 18, 2004).

81. Arthur S. Reber, *The Penguin Dictionary of Psychology*, 2nd ed. (New York: Penguin Books, 1995), pp. 284, 246.

82. Compare the definitions of the nouns *feeling*, *emotion*, and *thought* in the *Oxford English Dictionary*, as defined at http://dictionary.oed.com/.

83. We often hear the term *wishful thinking*. But feelings can be even more wishful than thoughts and therefore more distorting of reality.

84. Research psychologist David G. Myers found that though intuition has some advantages, one disadvantage is that it "is prone to err when we evaluate our own knowl-

edge and abilities." He went on to say that "this is most strikingly evident in three robust phenomena: hindsight bias, self-serving bias, and overconfidence." Myers, *Intuition*, p. 88.

85. As Samuel Johnson insightfully explained, "A man is always desirous of being at peace with himself; and when he cannot reconcile his passions to his conscience, he will attempt to reconcile his conscience to his passions." Danckert, *Quotable [Samuel] Johnson*, p. 39.

86. Harry A. Overstreet, *The Mature Mind* (1949; repr. New York: Norton, 1959), p. 106.

87. Richard Weaver reasoned that "if we attach more significance to feeling than to thinking, we shall soon, by a simple extension, attach more to wanting than to deserving." (This frame of mind undermines the motivation to excellence.) Richard Weaver, *Ideas Have Consequences* (Chicago: University of Chicago, 1948), p. 37.

88. The first quote is from English Romantic poet Lord Byron; the second, from the American scholar Irving Babbitt, who also aptly noted the error of the Romantic notion that civilized behavior "gushes up spontaneously from the unconscious."

89. Victor C. Strasburger, *Adolescents and the Media: Medical and Psychological Impact* (Thousand Oaks, CA: Sage Publishing, 1995), 45–47.

90. Anthony J. Cortese, *Provocateur*, 2nd ed. (Lanham, MD: Rowman and Littlefield, 2004), pp. 68–73

91. Kinsey not only thanked these child molesters for their contributions to his research—he *congratulated* them for their "efforts."

92. Information in this paragraph is derived from Daniel J. Flynn, *Intellectual Morons* (New York: Crown Forum, 2004), ch. 2. Flynn cites several sources, chiefly James H. Jones's biography, *Alfred C. Kinsey: A Public/Private Life* (New York: W. W. Norton, 1997).

93. See Judith Reisman and Edward M. Eichel, *Kinsey, Sex, and Fraud* (Lafayette, LA: Huntington House, 1990), pp. 62, 221.

94. Ibid., pp. 45, 48–49, 70, 112. The authors add that Kinsey's coauthor Ward Pomeroy defended Kinsey's view, contending in a later book that "incest between adults and younger children can also prove to be a satisfying and enriching experience" and that boys could have "a loving sexual relationship" with animals and would generally feel good about it until someone told them it was inappropriate. See specifically pp. 45, 70.

95. Errol E. Harris, "Respect for Persons," *Daedalus* (Spring 1969): 113.

96. Harm may be understood in the physical, psychological, or moral sense.

97. The traditional view of homosexual acts (as distinguished from homosexual inclinations or urges) was that they use sexuality in a deviant or "unnatural" way—that is, a way that deviates from the way nature (or God) designed sex organs to be used. This view was not merely philosophical or theological; it was the official view of psychiatry before the third edition of the *Diagnostic and Statistical Manual of Mental Disorders* (DSM) was published in 1973.

98. Arnold Toynbee, letter to the editor, *New York Times*, May 10, 1964.

99. Quoted in Philip Rieff, *Triumph of the Therapeutic* (1966; repr. Chicago: University of Chicago Press, 1987), p. 233.

100. Viktor E. Frankl, *The Unheard Cry for Meaning* (New York: Simon and Schuster, 1978), pp. 35–36.

101. The invitation can, of course, be refused because of a prior vow or commitment, as in the case of a priest or a nun, or someone already married. Also, if the relationship is essentially platonic, the invitation to sexual expression may be so weak as to be almost nonexistent.

102. Other examples of sexual expression leading to love, no less real for being unusual, occur when people who are abducted and repeatedly raped come, in time, to love their abductors; or, even more uncommon, when such abductors progress to genuine love for their victims. The term given to the latter situation is *Lima syndrome*.

103. A logician would rightly point out that if something is inherent, there is no need for it to be "actualized." But logically or not, Rogers and Maslow married these views. In an earlier chapter, we noted Rogers's view that we must *become what we are*. Similarly, Maslow not only believed that self-actualization is the highest need but also that the noblest qualities come from within rather than outside human nature. See Maslow, *Religions, Values, and Peak Experiences* (Columbus: Ohio State University Press, 1964), pp. 36–37.

104. G. K. Chesterton, *Orthodoxy* (1908; repr. Wheaton, IL: Harold Shaw Publishers, 1994), pp. 78, 144. As the date indicates, he described the error a good half century before Humanistic Psychology fell into it.

105. Quoted in Paul C. Vitz, *Psychology as Religion: The Cult of Self-Worship*, 2nd ed. (Grand Rapids, MI: William. B. Eerdmans, 1994), p. 46.

5. MORE VEXING QUESTIONS

1. T. S. Eliot, for example, described how ego affects our view of ourselves and others: "For the most part he [the secular reformer or revolutionist] conceives of the evils of the world as something external to himself. They are thought of either as completely impersonal, so that there is nothing to alter but machinery; or if there is evil *incarnate*, it is always incarnate in the *other people*—a class, a race, the politicians, the bankers, the armament makers, and so forth—never in oneself. There are individual exceptions; but so far as a man sees the need for converting *himself* as well as the World, he is approximating to the religious point of view." T. S. Eliot, *Christianity and Culture* (1939; repr. New York: Harcourt Brace, 1949), p. 74.

2. Thomas Gilovich, *How We Know What Isn't So: The Fallibility of Reason in Everyday Life* (New York: Free Press, 1991), p. 77.

3. Thomas Moore, *Care of the Soul: A Guide for Cultivating Depth and Sacredness in Everyday Life* (New York: Walker, 1992), pp. 101–103.

4. If the metaphor seems extreme, review the facts: Humanistic Psychology tells people who *already have strong egos* that they are inherently wise and good, deserve all the esteem they and others can offer, and can think, say, and do whatever they "feel" without fear of being wrong.

5. Arnold Toynbee, *Surviving the Future* (New York: Oxford University Press, 1971), no page cited, quoted in Karl Menninger, MD, *Whatever Became of Sin?* (New York: Hawthorn Books, 1973), p. 227.

6. When Humanistic Psychology was beginning to gain sway in our culture, Henry B. Veatch noted the contradiction of those who say all morality is relative and then urge others to practice tolerance. (If morality is relative, then tolerance is no better than intolerance.) This contradiction, he went on to point out, lies at the very center of relativism: the moment we say that no action is more moral than another, we make it impossible, logically speaking, to discuss many of the most important questions in life. Henry B. Veatch, *Rational Man: A Modern Interpretation of Aristotelian Ethics* (Bloomington: Indiana University Press, 1962), p. 43.

7. Alan Charles Kors and Harvey Silvergate, in *The Shadow University*, reported by John Leo, "Oh, No, Canada!" *U.S. News*, June 14, 1999, p. 15. For an assortment of examples not limited to colleges and universities, see David E. Bernstein, *You Can't Say That: The Growing Threat to Civil Liberties from Antidiscrimination Laws* (Washington, DC: Cato Institute, 2003).

8. John Stossel, *Give Me a Break* (New York: HarperCollins, 2004), p. 282.

9. James Mursell, *Using Your Mind Effectively* (New York: McGraw-Hill, 1951), p. 217.

10. Deming's remark was shared with me in a private conversation with a man who served as his liaison at a large American manufacturing company.

11. Thomas Sowell, *The Vision of the Anointed* (New York: Basic Books, 1995), pp. 2, 253.

12. This is not to deny the reality (or the shamefulness) of past discrimination or to say that nothing should be done to remedy it; it is to say that more reasonable, noncontradictory approaches should have been chosen. For example, instead of setting aside college entrance requirements for aggrieved minority students, special programs should have been established to help them raise their scores to a level that meets existing requirements.

13. In fairness, it should be acknowledged that Progressivism produced some worthy achievements, for example, the passing of child-labor laws, the extending of the vote to women, and the improvement of working conditions in sweat shops. The case against the movement is that despite such laudable accomplishments, its foremost and largely intended effect was that it compromised individual liberty and created a centralized governmental authority very much like, if not identical to, socialism or communism.

14. Richard Cloward and Frances Piven, "The Weight of the Poor: A Strategy to End Poverty," *Nation*, May 2, 1966.

15. Saul Alinsky, *Rules for Radicals: A Pragmatic Primer for Realistic Radicals* (New York: Random House, 1971), pp. xvii, 3, 195.

16. Pope Leo XIII, *Rerum Novarum, Encyclical on Capital and Labor* (Vatican City: Vatican Press, 1891). See www.papalencyclicals.net/Leo13/l13rerum.htm (accessed March 11, 2013).

17. For an analysis of the changes in papal encyclicals that followed Leo XIII's *Rerum Novarum* and the ways in which they, often inadvertently, invited more progressive lines of thought and thus encouraged the USCCB, see Vincent Ryan Ruggiero, "American Catholics and Social Justice," at www.catholicjournal.us.

18. The link to this document can be found at http://www.usccb.org/issues-and -action/human-life-and-dignity/economic-justice-economy/ (accessed March 11, 2013).

19. For example, Sowell links the "disintegration" of the black family to the growth of the "liberal welfare state." See Thomas Sowell, "Race and Rhetoric," *TownHall*, March 20, 2012, http://townhall.com/columnists/thomassowell/2012/03/20/race_and_rhetoric/ page/full/ (accessed May 11, 2012).

20. The links to all the documents cited in this paragraph can be found at: http:// www.usccb.org/issues-and-action/human-life-and-dignity/economic-justice-economy/ (accessed March 11, 2013).

21. Joseph Cardinal Ratzinger, "Liberation Theology," http://www.christendom -awake.org/pages/ratzinger/liberationtheol.htm (accessed May 7, 2012).

22. Malachi Martin, *The Jesuits: The Society of Jesus and the Betrayal of the Roman Catholic Church* (New York: Simon and Schuster, 1987), pp. 15–22.

6. A WISER PERSPECTIVE

1. Viktor Frankl, *Viktor Frankl Recollections: An Autobiography*, trans. Joseph Fabry and Judith Fabry (New York: Plenum Books, 1997), pp. 52, 60–65.

2. Ibid., pp. 91, 93.

3. Ibid., p. 97.

4. Viktor E. Frankl, *Man's Search for Meaning*, 3rd ed. (New York: Simon and Schuster, 1984; first English publication, 1963), pp. 44, 46, 52–55.

5. Ibid., p. 88.

6. Viktor E. Frankl, *The Doctor and the Soul: From Psychotherapy to Logotherapy* (1955; repr. New York: Vintage Books, 1986), p. xvi.

7. Frankl, *Viktor Frankl Recollections*, p. 97. Frankl adds that "Nardini and Lifton, two American military psychiatrists, found the same to be the case in the prisoner-of-war camps in Japan and Korea."

8. Viktor E. Frankl, *The Unheard Cry for Meaning* (New York: Simon and Schuster, 1978), p. 35.

9. Viktor E. Frankl, *Man's Search for Meaning*, 1st ed. (New York: Washington Square Press, 1963), p. 17.

10. Viktor E. Frankl, *Man's Search for Ultimate Meaning* (New York: Basic Books, 2000), p. 85.

11. Viktor E. Frankl, *The Will to Meaning: Foundations and Applications of Logotherapy* (1969; repr. New York: Meridian, 1988), p. 52.

12. Frankl, *Viktor Frankl Recollections*, p. 56.

13. Frankl, *Man's Search for Ultimate Meaning*, p. 28.

14. Frankl, *Viktor Frankl Recollections*, pp. 64, 129. Frankl's own meaning in life was, he realized, to help others find theirs.

15. Frankl, *Man's Search for Ultimate Meaning*, p. 141.

16. Frankl, *Will to Meaning*, p. 55. In a book written with Frankl's close cooperation (*The Pursuit of Meaning* [Boston: Beacon Press, 1968], p. 33), Joseph B. Fabry adds that, concerning the meaning of life, "each man can answer for himself, and never for more than the moment. For the man and the situation are constantly changing, and with them the meaning that he is required to fulfill."

17. Frankl, *Will to Meaning*, p. 58.

18. Frankl, *Man's Search for Meaning*, 3rd ed., p. 119.

19. Frankl, *Man's Search for Ultimate Meaning*, p. 34.

20. Frankl, *Unheard Cry for Meaning*, p. 66.

21. See Frankl in an interview, "Interview with Dr Viktor Frankl II," YouTube video, 10:28, uploaded by "yecto" on May 6, 2007, http://www.youtube.com/watch?v=KnWETfCaBmo (accessed January 10, 2010).

22. Frankl, *Will to Meaning*, pp. 8, 127–28.

23. Frankl, *Doctor and the Soul*, p. 87. And Frankl, *Will to Meaning*, p. 137. See also Frankl, *Unheard Cry for Meaning*, pp. 47, 55.

24. Frankl, *Unheard Cry for Meaning*, pp. 49–50.

25. Frankl, *Man's Search for Meaning*, 3rd ed., p. 136

26. Frankl, *Unheard Cry for Meaning*, p. 51. Of course, Frankl was speaking of situations in which the guilt feeling was appropriate—that is, deserved. He knew well that overly scrupulous people can feel guilt where there is no good reason to. For more of Frankl's views on the subject of guilt, see Joseph B. Fabry, *The Pursuit of Meaning: Logotherapy Applied to Life* (Boston: Beacon Press, 1968), p. 75.

27. Frankl, *Viktor Frankl Recollections*, pp. 102–103.

28. Frankl, *Man's Search for Meaning*, p. 175.

29. Frankl, *Will to Meaning*, pp. 38–39.

30. See Fabry, *Pursuit of Meaning*, pp. 82–83.

31. Frankl, *Unheard Cry for Meaning*, p. 33.

32. Ibid., pp. 66, 80.

33. Frankl, *Doctor and the Soul*, p. 240.

34. Frankl, *Unheard Cry for Meaning*, pp. 35, 89.

35. Frankl, *Will to Meaning*, p. 59.
36. Frankl, *Man's Search for Meaning*, p. 17.
37. Frankl, *Will to Meaning*, pp. 61, 62.
38. Frankl, *Doctor and the Soul*, p. xxvii.
39. Frankl, *Will to Meaning*, p. 43.
40. Frankl, *Unheard Cry for Meaning*, pp. 81–84.
41. Frankl, *Doctor and the Soul*, pp. 165, 170.
42. Frankl, *Unheard Cry for Meaning*, pp. 81–84.
43. Frankl, *Doctor and the Soul*, p. 173.
44. Ibid., p. 139. See also Frankl, *Unheard Cry for Meaning*, pp. 79–80.
45. Fabry, *Pursuit of Meaning*, p. 11. Fabry wrote this book with Frankl's support and guidance. The aim was to clarify logotherapy for a general audience.
46. This is not to suggest that Frankl's work has not been acclaimed; only that it has never managed to displace the reigning views of Humanistic Psychology in Western culture.
47. Frankl, *Viktor Frankl Recollections*, p. 38.
48. I used *Man's Search for Meaning* as a supplemental humanities text in the 1960s and wrote of its significance. See Vincent Ryan Ruggiero, "Concentration Camps Were His Laboratory," *The Sign*, December 1967.
49. Abraham H. Maslow, *The Farther Reaches of Human Nature* (New York: Viking Press, 1972), pp. 270–74.

7. HUMAN NATURE REVISITED

1. Much of the confusion that, as we saw in chapter 1, befell some very intelligent people can be traced to the mistake of forcing an unnecessary distinction between *self* and *person*.

2. Viktor Frankl introduced the representation of the human being in terms of *dimensions*. His dimensions were the body, the psyche, and decision making or choice (he calls this the "noëtic" dimension). (See Joseph B. Fabry, *The Pursuit of Meaning: Logotherapy Applied to Life*, [Boston: Beacon Press, 1968], pp. 19–20.) My diagram accounts for all the same "parts"; however, I believe it is more precise to speak of choice not as a separate dimension but as part of the metaphysical dimension—that is, as an aspect of mind, specifically, the dynamic application of will.

3. Mortimer Adler notes that under "mind," some thinkers also include sensation and imagination but that all major theorists agree that mind is "the place of ideas." See Adler, *The Great Ideas: A Lexicon of Western Thought* (New York: Macmillan, 1992), pp. 543, 547, 550.

4. G. K. Chesterton, *The Everlasting Man* (1925; repr. Radford VA: 2008), p, 26. Even Humanistic Psychology *inadvertently* acknowledges that humans are not what they ought

to be. For example, Rogers titled one of his books *On Becoming a Person* and argued that we should strive for something we should have but don't yet have, which is personhood.

5. Thomas S. Szasz, *The Second Sin* (London: Routledge and Kegan Paul, 1973), p. 97.

6. *Thought* is not mentioned as part of the behavioral dimension because it cannot be seen or heard but can be only inferred from what we say and do. Strictly speaking, however, purposeful conscious thought is a behavior that results from choice.

7. For those who wonder why *thoughts* are not included with *words* and *deeds*, the reason is that thoughts are manifest only to oneself; words and actions, both to oneself and to others.

8. In a Cherokee legend about the importance of choice, a grandfather was telling his grandson about a battle waged between two "wolves" that live within each person. One, he explained, is Evil and consists of anger, envy, jealousy, sorrow, regret, greed, arrogance, self-pity, guilt, resentment, inferiority, lies, false pride, superiority, and ego. The other is Good and consists of joy, peace, love, hope, serenity, humility, kindness, benevolence, empathy, generosity, truth, compassion, and faith. After thinking about the story for a moment, the grandson asked, "Which wolf wins the battle?" The grandfather replied, "The one you feed."

9. G. K. Chesterton, *Orthodoxy* (1908; repr. Wheaton, IL: Harold Shaw Publishers, 1994), p. 22.

10. Irving Babbitt, *Rousseau & Romanticism*, introduction by Claes G. Ryn (1919; repr. New Brunswick, NJ: Transaction Publishers, 1991), p. 16.

11. "Freedom of Choice Quotes," *ThinkExist*, http://thinkexist.com/quotes/with/keyword/freedom_of_choice/ (accessed March 12, 2013). Two other interesting quotations on free will: Indian statesman Jawaharlal Nehru wrote that "life is like a game of cards. The hand you are dealt is determinism; the way you play it is free will." And Isaac Bashevis Singer made the clever tongue-in-cheek observation: "You must believe in free will; there is no choice."

12. That self-transcendence cannot be achieved once and never lost is documented in everyday experience. We may forget about self at one moment—say, when we feel sympathy or empathy toward others—and in the very next moment slide back into self-preoccupation, even selfishness.

13. The "more or less" is important. We tend to believe the old saying "every day in every way, I'm getting better and better." In reality, though we may be getting better, we may as easily be getting worse. In fact, absent the effort to improve, it is more likely that we will get worse.

14. The discussion of *guilt* and *shame* in this chapter is copyrighted material and is used with the permission of MindPower, Inc.

15. See these definitions from the *Oxford English Dictionary*, www.dictionary.oed.com.

16. Quoted in Philip Chew Kheng Hoe, ed., *A Gentleman's Code: According to Confucius, Mencius and Others* (Singapore: Graham Brash, 1984), p. 36.

17. Wayne Dyer, *Your Erroneous Zones* (New York: William Morrow, 1976), pp. 93, 104, cited in *Self-Help or Self-Destruction? Ten Pop Psychology Myths That Could Destroy Your Life*, by Chris Thurman (Nashville: Thomas Nelson, 1996).

18. David D. Burns, *Feeling Good: The New Mood Therapy* (New York: William Morrow, 1980), ch. 8.

19. Abraham J. Twersky, MD, *Addictive Thinking: Understanding Self-Deception*, 2nd ed. (Center City, MO: Hazelden, 1997), p. 67.

20. Carole Wade and Carol Tavris, *Psychology*, 5th ed. (New York: Longman, 1998), p. 397.

21. Other factors in psychology's disparaging of guilt and shame are its embrace of the ideas that humans are inherently good, that morality is personal and subjective, and that "ought" statements are unsupportable.

22. A notable exception is when the focus is on determining the extent of the person's moral culpability for his or her actions.

23. Allan Bloom, *The Closing of the American Mind* (New York: Simon and Schuster, 1987), p. 121.

24. Quoted in Robyn M. Dawes, *House of Cards: Psychology and Psychotherapy Built on Myth* (New York: Free Press, 1994), p. 235.

25. The view I am proposing may, unfortunately, be relatively unfamiliar to many people born after 1960. However, it is really not new at all but rather much older than the dominant view.

26. I am replacing "need" with "challenge" because the former has become too closely associated with entitlement. The latter more accurately reflects the view, as Viktor Frankl expressed it, that life has expectations of us and the quality of our existence is bound up with how well we meet them.

27. Not only am I reversing the dominant idea—in other words, saying that self-esteem *follows* achievement—I am also adding the qualification "justified" because genuine self-esteem must be earned. (Fairly early in the self-esteem mania, Barbara Lerner drew a valuable contrast between narcissistic "feel-good-now" self-esteem and "earned" self-esteem. See Barbara Lerner, "Self-Esteem and Excellence: The Choice and the Paradox," *American Educator*, Winter 1985, p. 13.)

28. Philosopher William Barrett points out that Aristotle and medieval philosophers defined truth as correspondence between our thoughts and reality, but Descartes defined it instead as consistency between one's idea and one's perception, thus putting whole matter within the mind and leaving reality out of the equation. This change planted seeds of subjectivism that have flowered in the present age. Barrett adds that the cartoon picture of the lightbulb illuminating in the head nicely depicts Descartes's view but that the correct image for the discovery of truth would be a spotlight shining on some portion of the world. William Barrett, *The Illusion of Technique* (New York: Anchor/Doubleday, 1979), pp. 155–57.

29. Chapter 4, you will recall, demonstrates no fewer than ten disadvantages of following feelings rather than reason.

30. Historically, attempts to measure intelligence capacity of individuals or groups have failed. Those that have *seemed* to succeed have been revealed to be, on closer analysis, measuring performance.

31. The word *any* is used advisedly and is meant to exclude the assumptions about intelligence related to race, ethnicity, religion, gender, and socioeconomic status.

32. Everyday experience confirms that anyone can have a "bad day" in thinking just as in playing tennis or golf. The smartest among us behave stupidly on occasion.

33. I use the word *most* to avoid involvement in the argument concerning whether *all* knowledge arrives through the senses (see Plato or Aristotle, Hobbes or Leibnitz, et alia).

34. This word *rescuing* is chosen for its applicability to a variety of contexts. The key point is that, in our imperfection, we humans regularly require extrication from unfortunate circumstances of our own making, but it leaves open the issue of the *agency* and *manner* of rescue. (In a religious context, the word *salvation* would be preferred.) Theological differences should not keep us from agreeing about human imperfection.

35. Why does this chapter speak of "probable consequences" whereas the parallel discussion in chapter 3 spoke of "consequences"? Because here we are speaking of what would likely occur, whereas in chapter 3 we were speaking of what had actually occurred.

36. The attractiveness of liberation theology, with its focus on political revolution, derives from the notion that the faults of the world are caused by government and other institutions rather than individual human beings. The realization that human nature is imperfect undermines that notion.

37. It is hard to imagine someone who is wrapped up in himself rising above himself.

38. It is worth adding that a particular accomplishment warrants feeling good about oneself *for that accomplishment* rather than feeling good about oneself in a more global sense. It follows that I can feel self-esteem for my generous contributions to charity and simultaneously feel ashamed of myself for my tendency to gossip about others.

39. In other words, "that's the way I *feel*" will no longer be an acceptable response; students will be required to present evidence for their judgments.

40. When acting out of feelings, we tend to be self-focused and to take little note of other people's rights, needs, and feelings. In contrast, when acting out of reason, we tend to consider factors outside ourselves.

41. Such behaviors are traceable to deep-seated *emotions*; following our feelings merely intensifies them. In contrast, reason enables us to expose them as inappropriate.

42. Reason enables us to consider the consequences of our actions before we act; impulsiveness, by definition, does not.

43. Because love always considers the good of the other person (as well as oneself), loving sexuality neither harms nor degrades. In sharp contrast, lust considers only self-

gratification and therefore can be, and often is, harmful and/or degrading. This distinction is meaningful because it provides a criterion—the presence or absence of love—for judging the morality of sexual behavior.

44. The fact that some forms and occasions of sexual expression can be harmful suggests the need for considering at what point young people should engage their sexuality. Among the issues that deserve discussion are whether youthful sex can rise above lust to genuine love and whether early sexual experimentation does emotional harm.

45. To say that people should feel guilt or shame over sexual behavior that is harmful or degrading does not answer the question, "Exactly what sexual behavior is harmful and/or degrading?" It does, however, provide a context in which that question can be intelligently discussed.

8. REORIENTING OURSELVES

1. Arnold Toynbee, *A Study of History*, rev. ed., abridged by the author and Jane Caplan (1972; repr. New York: Portland House, 1988), pp. 347–48. He also notes that Mohammed, Zarathustra, the Buddha, and Jesus agreed about the importance of self-surrender, a fact he said was "very striking, because their conceptions of the nature of ultimate reality differed widely."

2. Even people fortunate enough to have grown up in families that resisted the false ideas have nevertheless encountered them in school and in the communications and entertainment media.

3. The order is slightly different here than in chapter 7. That chapter followed the historical order in which the error of Hereditarianism, pessimism about human intelligence, came before the errors of Humanistic Psychology. In the order of self-improvement, the focus of this chapter, overcoming the false idea of self is placed first.

4. The W.I.S.E. approach is copyrighted material and is used with the permission of MindPower, Inc.

5. Husband of Alzheimer's patient, private conversation with the author.

6. Even religions that are not, strictly speaking, theistic (notably Buddhism) share this view.

7. Errol E. Harris, "Respect for Persons," *Daedalus* (Spring 1969): 113.

8. It could be argued that the search for truth about our own personality and character require looking within ourselves, but even in those cases it is necessary to consult other people's observations in order to be sure we are not deceiving ourselves.

9. Rowland W. Jepson, *Clear Thinking*, 5th ed. (New York: Longmans, Green, 1967), p. 81.

10. Ironically, even some who oppose abortion mistakenly consider this term scientifically accurate.

11. The "hunches" quote is from Dr. Joyce Brothers, cited at http://thinkexist.com/ search/searchquotation.asp?search=TRUST+HUNCHES (accessed March 12, 2013).

12. Carol Tavris, *Anger: The Misunderstood Emotion* (New York: Simon and Schuster, 1982), pp. 143, 135–35, 223, 253, respectively.

13. Religions with some form of the Golden Rule include African traditional religion, Baha'i, Buddhism, Christianity, Confucianism, Hinduism, Islam, Jainism, Judaism, Native American religion, Shintoism, Sikhism, Taoism, Unitarian Universalism, and Zoroastrianism. For quotations from each, see Vincent Ryan Ruggiero, *The Practice of Loving Kindness* (Hyde Park, NY: New City Press, 2003).

14. Attempts to define conscience more specifically and concretely have not been very successful. Some have said it is the voice of God whispering to the soul, but they have difficulty accounting for the fact that some people—serial killers, for example—seem to have no conscience. (Their definition would imply that God plays favorites.) Others say conscience is custom or the influence of culture, but they have difficulty explaining how conscience makes some people oppose the dictates of custom or culture. Still others define conscience as a moral sense, but senses are associated with particular organs (the eyes or the ears, for example), but conscience cannot be that kind of sense.

15. Stephen C. Danckert, comp., *The Quotable [Samuel] Johnson: A Topical Compilation of His Wit and Moral Wisdom* (San Francisco: Ignatius Press, 1992), p. 39.

9. REFORMING THE CULTURE

1. I am speaking here not of books specifically designed to teach students how to think—that is, books that present a heuristic (approach) to improve students' production and evaluation of ideas, and that invite students to use it in addressing a variety of problems and issues. Instead, I mean the "standard" textbooks that present the principal subject matter of the courses. Although over the last few decades, some of these texts have encouraged students to think about the subject matter rather than simply commit it to memory, such encouragements have been modest, often consisting of no more than a "thought" question at the end of each chapter. In other words, even these texts for the most part do students' thinking for them.

2. The tragedy is that these crucial problems are ignored while critics and pundits pursue other, considerably less important issues. They propose higher salaries, increased testing, and smaller classes, yet they ignore the pessimism and permissivism that underlie the entire education system.

3. This story was offered by a professor taking part in a workshop I offered some years ago on the teaching of thinking. The professor offered it to me and his fellow participants as personal testimony of the efficacy of providing students with intellectual challenges rather than simply lecturing to them.

4. A book I wrote some years ago, now out of print, is a helpful guide for teachers and administrators. See Vincent Ryan Ruggiero, *Teaching Thinking across the Curriculum* (New York: Harper and Row, 1988).

5. See the following Paideia Program resources by Mortimer J. Adler: *The Paideia Proposal: An Educational Manifesto* (1982), *Paideia Problems and Possibilities* (1983), *The Paideia Program: An Educational Syllabus* (New York: Macmillan, 1984).

6. Adler, *Paideia Proposal*, chs. 4, 6, 7.

7. Ibid.

8. Adler, *Problems and Possibilities*, p. 24.

9. Viktor E. Frankl, *The Will to Meaning: Foundations and Applications of Logotherapy* (1969; repr. New York: Meridian, 1988), pp. 85, 87.

10. Howard Barrows and Robyn Tamblyn, *Problem-Based Learning: An Approach to Medical Education* (New York: Springer Publishing, 1980). For information on second school applications of PBL, search the Internet using the key words "problem-based learning."

11. The W.I.S.E. approach is copyrighted by MindPower, Inc., and is used with permission. For more detailed information, see Vincent Ryan Ruggiero, *Becoming a Critical Thinker*, 7th ed. (Boston: Houghton-Mifflin, 2011).

12. For a detailed discussion of errors in thinking and ways to avoid them, see Vincent Ryan Ruggiero, *Beyond Feelings: A Guide to Critical Thinking*, 9th ed. (New York: McGraw-Hill, 2011).

13. Anyone who has asked scholars to discuss their cognitive strategies knows how awkward this can be. Their responses tend to be halting, vague, defensive, or all three. Discussions about problems and issues in their fields are often more productive in the context of professional challenges but not in the context of teaching materials.

14. For all their impressiveness, these data often tell us little about student understanding of subject matter and even less about the quality of students' thinking about subject matter. To illustrate, I offer an example not from student testing but from students' evaluation of teachers, which underwent the same transformation from essay to objective form. In the 1960s, I was head of the Humanities Department in my college. At the end of each semester, the other professors and I had our students anonymously answer a half dozen or so questions such as "What was the most difficult aspect of this course for you?" and "What suggestions do you have for improving the course?" Many of the responses were unhelpful (especially if the student had been absent numerous times), but many others were very helpful. Alas, within a few years, the college instituted a "nationally normed" standardized evaluation with fifty or so questions. Though it was touted as much more meaningful than our simple evaluation, from a practical teaching standpoint it was worthless.

15. See Jeffrey P. Moran, "Sex Education," *Faqs.Org*, http://www.faqs.org/childhood/Re-So/Sex-Education.html (accessed March 13, 2013).

16. Martin E. P. Seligman, *Authentic Happiness* (New York: Free Press, 2002), pp. 11, 21, 128–29, 132–35.

17. In this section, when speaking of religion, I am referring to the largest US religions, Christianity and Judaism. There are, of course, liberal and conservative forms of both religions, and the former are more susceptible to theological and philosophical change than the latter.

18. Karl Menninger, MD, *Whatever Became of Sin?* (New York: Hawthorn Books, 1973), pp. 45, 134–35.

19. This quotation and others by Schuller are cited in chapter 2.

20. The liturgical revisions of 2011, though modest, reveal a tendency to return to traditional wording.

21. Parishioner, private conversation with the author.

22. The notion of "collective salvation," often invoked by influential people, makes God out to be like the seventh-grade teacher who assigns "project grades" instead of individual grades to a group of students, thereby holding students responsible for matters over which they have absolutely no control—that is, other people's efforts. "Collective salvation" is both absurd and an insult to God.

23. A secondary role of the church is to create structures for practicing the good works its theology inspires. Among the ways churches have done so is the building of schools, hospitals, and homeless shelters.

24. See also columnist Charles Krauthammer's address titled "Defining Deviancy Up," in which he expands Moynihan's observation, claiming not only that bad behavior was redefined as acceptable, but also that good behavior, such as disciplining children, was redefined as bad.

25. Another example of this mentality is the persistent effort, all logic notwithstanding, to treat foreign terrorists as common criminals and extend to them the legal rights and privileges of American citizens.

26. Certain exceptions will be necessary, most obviously, national security matters.

27. It is curious how readily people who deny the existence of objective reality invoke it in defense of their work.

28. They are also, of course, a way of compensating for the decline of people's attention span and, in the case of television, the availability of the remote control to switch channels when sensory stimulation wanes.

INDEX

abilities, 110, 112, 268n71

abortion, 44, 55, 57–59, 61, 141, 176, 196, 241, 278n10

    rate of increasing, 56, 89

    See also Roe v. Wade

absurdity, 10, 129

achievement. *See* justified self-esteem; self-esteem, as a requirement for achievement

Acton, Lord, 268n79

actual guilt, 168

Adam and Eve, 103

Addams, Jane, 107

ADHD. *See* attention deficit/hyperactivity disorder (ADHD)

Adler, Alfred, 149, 150

Adler, Mortimer, 211, 212, 267n70, 274n3

Adlerian psychology, 106, 152

adultery, 37, 122, 124, 202, 218, 223

Adult Pagan Action Series, 34

advertisements, 28–29, 48, 70–71, 257n12

    attention shifts during commercials, 29, 71, 246n50

    first advertising agency in US, 246n48

affirmative action, 139, 271n12

affordable housing, government encouraging, 146

agape, 200, 201

agenda-driven journalism, 72

Aid to Dependent Children, 77

Alinsky, Saul, 11, 143

Allport, Gordon, 33

alternative political systems, 76, 258n21

Alzheimer's patient, care of, 188

American Federation of Labor, 257n15

American Federation of Teachers, 32

American Heritage Dictionary, 33

American Journal of Psychology, 243n2

American Psychological Association, 125, 243n2

American Society of Newspaper Editors, 62

analytical intelligence, 31

Anger: The Misunderstood Emotion (Tavris), 69, 198

antiheroes. *See* villains and antiheroes

Aristotle, 102, 219, 267n67, 267n70, 276n28

Aronson, Joshua Michael, 51

arrogance, 77, 109, 138, 226, 227, 275n8

assumptions, 102, 182

    false assumptions, 224

Atlantic (magazine), 63

attention

    attention shifts during commercials, 29, 71, 246n50

ego requiring attention, 131, 202, 259n33

shortened attention span, 71, 235, 281n28

attention deficit/hyperactivity disorder (ADHD), 71, 257n12

Auschwitz, 150, 153, 156

autoeroticism, 202

awareness, 46, 87, 171, 197, 247n9

"premature awareness of sex," 123, 218

self-awareness, 91

Babbitt, Irving, 104, 165

Bacon, Francis, 135

Baha'i, 279n13

bailout of banks after 2008 financial crisis, 59–60

Balfour, Lord, 21

Balluseck, Fritz von, 121

banks and the 2008 financial crisis, 59–60, 226, 254n96

Barrett, William, 267n67, 276n28

Barrows, Howard, 98–99, 212–13

Baumeister, Roy, 80, 109

Becker, Joseph, 54, 147

behavior. *See* human behavior

behavioral dimension of self, 163, 275n6

Behaviorism, 28, 33, 42, 164, 183, 184, 243n1

beliefs, 46, 59, 68, 111, 129, 130, 193, 194, 253n83

basing on evidence, 96

believing not making something true, 177

basing on first impressions, 102

imposing on others, 10, 127, 134–35

relationship to culture, 163, 251n64

religious beliefs, 129, 134, 189

"cafeteria approach" to, 84–85

Bell, Alexander Graham, 21

Berkeley, George, 34

bias

hindsight bias, 268n84

and intuition, 118, 268n84

and journalism, 62, 63, 72, 230, 240, 255n109, 257n14

self-serving bias, 121, 268n84

Biden, Joseph, 58

Bierce, Ambrose, 128–29

bigot, 129

Binet, Alfred, 16–17

Black, Hugo, 254n100

blacks

discrimination against, 74, 110

intelligence of, 18, 19, 73, 243n3

blame

blamelessness of individuals, but oppression of society, 147

determining who is to blame, 171, 187

government blaming for problems caused by government, 128, 137–38

hostility toward own country, 9, 76, 258n20

not blaming others for own imperfections, 172

rich are blamed for wealth, but poor not to blame for poverty, 145

Bloom, Allan, 168

Bloom, Harold, 115, 260n45

bodily-kinesthetic intelligence, 246n53

Bork, Robert, 251n65

borrowed ideas, evaluating, 181

Boston Globe (newspaper), 63

Bradbury, Ray, 46

brain, 16, 19, 163. *See also* mind

Branden, Nathaniel, 50

Brewer, Ilma, 98

Brigham, C. C., 25

Broca, Paul, 16, 243n3

Brown v. Board of Education, 60

Buck, Carrie, 23

Buck v. Bell, 23

Buddha and Buddhism, 103–104, 108, 132, 219, 220, 278n1, 278n6, 279n13

burden of proof, 183

Burns, David, 46, 167

Burns, Robert, 100

business. *See* industry and business

"butterfly effect," 66

Calvinist Christianity, 183, 265n34

Campbell, Don, 125

Campbell, Stacy, 82

Camus, Albert, 123

capacity, 31, 35, 153, 211, 213
  intelligence as sum of capacity
  and performance, 168, 169,
  180, 277n30

capricious nature of feelings, 117

"Cardinal Principles of Education,
  The" (NEA Commission on the
  Reorganization of Secondary Edu-
  cation), 24

Carnegie family, 23

Carney, Francis, 147

Carter, Jimmy, 59

Castro, Fidel, 258n21

Catholic Church
  changes in reflecting different
    concept of sin, 222
  "Economic Justice for All," 145–46
  impact of Humanistic Psychology,
    53–55, 76, 221, 253nn80–82,
    258n22
  liturgical revisions of 2011, 222,
    281n20
  and social justice, 128, 144–48
  See also liberation theology

cause and effect, 65–66, 67–69, 72,
  118, 255n2, 256n3, 256n8
  causation in the realm of ideas, 177
  difference between hard and soft
    causation, 68
  and false cause, 256n3

change, reality of, 165–66

chaos theory, 66

charity, 144

Chavez, Hugo, 258n21

Cheaper by the Dozen (film), 245n43

cheating, 84

Cherokee legend, 275n8

Chesterton, G. K., 9, 72, 99, 125,
  162–63, 164, 237

children, 205–208, 207–208, 278n2
  child labor, 26, 245n42, 271n13
  See also family; parenting

China, comparison with US education
  process, 82, 84, 109

choice, 153–54, 164, 187
  and dimensions of humans, 274n2
  freedom of, 128, 138, 165, 181

Chopra, Deepak, 34, 46

Christianity, 103, 121, 132, 183, 220,
278n1, 279n13, 281n17
    calling for self-conquest and self-
        surrender, 108
    See also Catholic Church; original
        sin

Churchill, Winston, 21

civility
    decline of, 78, 208
    impact of self-transcendence on,
        172–73
    incivility of those who preach,
        127, 133–34, 271n6
    respect for other people, 189–90

Clinton, Bill, 58

Clinton, Hillary, 143

Cloward, Richard, 142, 143

cognition, 86, 163
    cognitive deficiency, 96–97
    cognitive strategies, 214–15,
        280n13
    cognitive therapy, 46

collective guilt, 154

collective salvation, 281n22

colleges encouraging students to think
    for themselves, 30

Combs, Arthur, 33

comedy, 100, 264n19

commercials. *See* advertisements

Commission on the Reorganization
    of Secondary Education (National
    Education Association), 24

Committee of Nine from the NEA, 24

Committee of Ten from the NEA, 23

common sense, 31, 221, 225, 268n80
    about human nature, 168–78

government not using, 128,
    138–39, 226

communications revolution, 44–45. *See
also* mass culture

Community Action Programs, 77

compassion, 59, 148, 167, 189, 197,
    204, 224, 254n96, 275n8

concentration camps, 39, 121, 149,
    150, 151, 152, 154, 155, 156, 164,
    186

conclusions, hasty, 102, 183

conditioning, 12, 19, 28–29, 68, 124,
    164, 187, 196, 203, 243n1

Confucius and Confucianism, 103,
    219, 220, 279n13

conscience, 154, 165, 168, 268n84,
    269n85, 279n14
    as part of the metaphysical
        dimension, 162
    reviving conscience, 203–204
    voice of, 205

conscious mind (mental activity), 28,
    68, 101

consequences, 189
    of applying Hereditarianism, 73–74
    of applying Humanistic Psy-
        chology, 76–77, 78–79, 80–82,
        83–85, 86–87, 88–90
    beneficial consequences, 106, 177,
        178
    of ideas, 69, 74, 79, 89, 90
    probable consequences, 178, 277n42
    unintended consequences, 70–72,
        225

conservative politics, 128, 141–42
    Catholic Church as conservative
        institution, 144–48

consistency, 183, 267n67, 276n28
Constitutional law, 60, 254n97
    Constitution as a "living docu-
        ment," 84
    judges who uphold Constitution
        rather than political agendas,
        228–29
    reading the Constitution, 240
constructive criticism, 238, 240
contempt
    for own country, 9, 76, 258n20
    treating parents and teachers with,
        10
contradiction, 117, 183
    examples of, 133–34, 165, 271n6,
        271n12
    principle of contradiction,
        112–13, 268n72
Coolidge v. New Hampshire, 61, 254n100
Coulson, William, 37, 53, 78, 80,
    249n42, 252n75
courts. *See* judges and judicial matters
creativity, 50, 97, 237
    as an avenue to finding meaning,
        151
    creative intelligence, 31
    creative thinking, 98, 170, 182,
        210
criminals
    criminal personality study,
        104–105
    intelligence of, 16, 243n4
    making choice to be criminal,
        153, 164
    perceived vs. actual guilt, 168
    treatment of offenders, 10, 77, 89,
        228, 254n99

critical thinking, 96, 97, 108, 137, 148,
    170, 176, 178, 182, 210, 212, 214,
    215, 218
Critical Thinking movement, 12, 30,
    31–32, 49
criticism
    constructive criticism, 238, 240
    discouraging or rejecting, 80, 83,
        118, 132, 184, 185
    and high self-esteem, 110, 173
    self-criticism, 80, 81, 173, 185,
        193
    viewing as positive, 193
Cultural Literacy (Hirsch), 31
culture, 163–64, 208, 251n64
    American culture and Hereditari-
        anism, 28–30
    conscience as the influence of,
        279n14
    encouraging deviancy, 226
    reforming the culture, 209–42
    See also mass culture
Cuomo, Mario, 54–55, 253n83
curriculum, restoring traditional cur-
    riculum, 213

Daniels, Michael, 106, 265n43
Darwin, Charles, 15
Darwin, Leonard, 21
D'Azeglio, Luigi, 144
decision making, 26, 27, 96, 102,
    136–37, 157, 264n28, 274n2
Declaration of Independence, 239
deconstruction, 260n45
default perception, 128
"Defining Deviancy Down"
    (Moynihan), 81, 225

"Defining Deviancy Up" (Krauthammer), 281n24

delusion, 114

Deming, W. Edwards, 27–28, 136–37

democracy, Goddard's view of, 17

Democratic Party on abortion, 57–58

deprivation of humans (not depravity),
183

Der Sturmer (Nazi anti-Semitic newspaper), 68

Descartes, René, 267n67, 276n28

desegregation, 60

deviancy
defining downward, 81, 225
defining up, 281n24

Devil's Dictionary (Bierce), 128–29

Dewey, John, 96, 263n4

dictionaries presenting all usage as
equally correct, 84, 260n51

dimensions of humans, 274n2

Dimnet, Ernest, 96

disagreement with children, anticipating, 207–208

discernment, 114, 116

discipline, 92

discovering truth, 194

discrimination, 74, 86, 87, 114, 139,
176, 271n12

dishonesty, 43, 195–96, 232, 252n69

disorders, growth in numbers of, 76,
257n19

disrespect, 10, 28, 55, 199, 201, 202,
207

distrust, 74

diversity, 83, 115, 133

divinity of the self, 34, 247n9

divorce rates, 10, 78, 87, 172

Doctor and the Soul, The (Frankl), 149

drama that is faithful to reality, 236–37

Durban, Dick, 58

Dye, Harold, 96

Dyer, Wayne, 46, 167, 247n9

dysfunctional family, 9, 76, 153

"Economic Justice for All" (USCCB
position paper), 145–46

education, 210, 279n2
based on idea that wisdom and
goodness not inborn, 103
belief that many not be able to
handle liberal education, 24–25
cafeteria-style curriculum, 115
cognitive strategies of faculty,
280n13
as creation of habit of thinking,
96
Critical Thinking movement's
failure to reform, 31–32
decline in performance despite
bigger budgets, 10
forcing personal views on students,
127, 134–35
growth of compulsory education
in US, 10, 244n29
and Hereditarianism, 23–26,
73–74, 127, 135–37
impact of applying concept of justified self-esteem, 173
impact of belief that intelligence
is sum of capacity and performance (inherited and acquired),
170
impact of belief that truth and
reality are objective, 174

impact of Humanistic Psychology, 49–51, 73, 80–81, 82, 83–84, 257n15

impact of recognizing human nature is imperfect, 171

lower performance standards, 10

Progressive Education movement, 263n4

recognizing teaching opportunities with children, 206

reform of, 209–19, 279n1, 279n3

and relativism, 115–16

restoring traditional curriculum, 213

sex education, 89, 177

teaching what to think rather than how to think, 11, 25

    applied to medical school students, 98–99, 263n17

    finding ways that teach how to think, 279n1, 279n3

thinking vs. subject-matter learning, 32, 280n14

what the average individual can do about, 237–38, 239

See also learning

educational psychology, 16–17, 30–31

effective thinking, 182

egocentrism, 278n2

egotism, 259n33

    ego affecting our view of self and others, 270n1

    egocentrism, 129

    ego factor (perceiving self as better than others), 128–32, 134

    ego needing to be loved, 131

    ego requiring attention, 131, 202, 259n33

    egotist (Bierce's definition), 129

    exaltation of ego, 138

    Humanistic Psychology unleashing the ego, 131, 271n4

    threatened egotism, 110

Einstein, Albert, 104, 107, 111

elders, 76, 78, 89–90, 172, 261n64, 262n64

elected officials. *See* government

Eliot, T. S., 261n52, 270n1

Ellis, Havelock, 104

eminent domain, 61

emotional intelligence, 123, 246n53

emotions

    comparison of intellectual and emotional reactions, 119

    comparison to feelings, 116–17

    deep-seated emotions, 277n41

    emotional memory, 264n27

    unrestrained expression of emotion in mass culture, 237

    See also feelings

employees. *See* workers/employees

encyclicals, 144

entertainment media. *See* mass culture

entitlement, 9, 57, 77, 82, 145, 172, 174, 225, 226, 227, 276n26

envy, 128, 190, 197, 264n19, 275n8

Epstein, Seymour, 101

equality, 140, 227

    of opinions, 83, 112, 260n45, 267n70

erotic love, 200–201

errors, common errors in thinking, 182–83, 214

Essay on Man, An (Pope), 104

esteem, need for, 39, 249n32

ethics, 15, 50, 79, 143, 168, 172–73, 189
   moral and ethical judgment, 50,
     189
   replace values clarification,
     218–19
   sexual ethics, 120, 132, 201
   See also morality
ethnocentrism, 129
Eugenics movement, 11–12, 16,
   21–23, 74, 140, 219
Europe, payments to teachers in,
   257n15
euthanasia, 261n61
evaluate as part of W.I.S.E. approach
   to effective thinking, 182
evidence, basing opinions on, 194
evil, 33, 52, 53, 75, 80, 100, 104, 142,
   162, 236, 265n34
   existence of, 91
   good and evil, 34, 41, 46, 47, 91,
     122, 143, 223, 224
   impact of belief that truth and
     reality are objective, 174–75
   man's goodness and society's evil,
     53, 252n77
   not requiring outside influence,
     171
   residing outside rather than
     within, 257n16, 270n1
   as seen in Cherokee legend, 275n8
   trusting evil impulses means they
     aren't really evil, 80
examinations, design for, 215–17
exclusionary rule, 61
existential intelligence, 246n53
expectations, 27, 50, 76, 80, 171,
   185–86, 194, 197, 276n26

experience, 86, 182, 191, 198, 216
   as an avenue to finding meaning,
     151
   everyday experience, 39, 113, 116,
     125, 168, 275n12, 277n32
   peak experience, 42
   self as product of, 35–36, 37, 100,
     119
   sensory experience, 47
*Experiment in the Development of Critical
   Thinking, An* (Glaser), 96

Fabry, Joseph, 158, 273n16
facts, 114, 231–32
   freedom from fact, 260n45
   and opinions, 10, 72, 82–83, 115,
     175
   thinking skills vs. knowledge of
     facts, 216
fairness, 189, 204
   government not using, 128, 138–39
   in journalism, 231–32
fallacies
   as deception by false ideas, 114
   of feelings being more dependable
     than reason, 12, 36–37, 42, 47,
     85–87, 130, 132
     exposed as false, 116–20
   of human nature as inherently
     wise and good, 12, 41, 75–77,
     99–105, 257n16, 258n27,
     260n47, 265n42
     exposed as false, 130, 131
   of intelligence as fixed and unal-
     terable, 16–19, 21, 30–31,
     73–74
     exposed as false, 95–99

leading to vexing questions, 127–48

negative impact of combining concepts, 124–25

of self-actualization as highest human need, 39, 77–79, 130, 131, 249n32, 249n37, 258n25, 258n27

exposed as false, 106–107

of self-esteem as a prerequisite to achievement, 39, 50, 52, 80–82, 130, 131

exposed as false, 108–11

that people create their own truth and reality, 130, 132

exposed as false, 82–85, 111–16

that sexual expression is natural and wholesome, 47, 87–90, 130, 132

exposed as false, 120–24

fallibility. *See* imperfection in humans

Fallows, James, 63

false assumptions, 224

false cause, 256n3

false ideals, 24

false ideas, 114, 156, 205, 218, 233, 239, 242, 278n2, 278n3

family

dysfunctional family, 9, 76, 153

impact of Humanistic Psychology, 55–56, 76, 78, 80

increase in infidelity, abuse, and divorce, 87

See also children; parenting

Fanning, Patrick, 46

"feel-good-now" self-esteem, 276n27

Feeling Good (Burns), 48

feelings, 197, 277n41

belief in personal feelings, 56, 78

benefits and limitations of, 196–97

comparison to emotions, 116–17

considering rights, needs, and feelings of others, 175, 277n40

dictating handling of 2008 financial crisis, 59, 254n96

distorting perception, 117, 268n83

Frankl on, 157

guilt feelings about sex, 205

more dependable than reason, 12, 36–37, 42, 47, 85–87, 124–25, 130, 132

research to debunk concept of, 116–20

negative feelings, 188, 198–99

reason more reliable than, 169, 175–76, 196–99

shift from moral life to feeling good, 9

supporting assertion of feelings with evidence, 175, 277n39

trusting feelings, 12, 78, 118, 120, 125, 198, 221

valuing more than thinking, 269n87

See also emotions

feral children, 105

fetus, definition of, 196, 278n10

Feuerstein, Reuven, 96–97

financial crisis of October 2008, 59, 146

Fine, Benjamin, 25–26

First Amendment, 60, 61

fiscal conservatism, 128, 141–42

Fish, Stanley, 115, 260n45
Fonda, Jane, 258n20
Food Stamps, 77
foreign terrorists, treatment of, 281n25
fornication, 37, 201
Fourth Amendment, 61, 77, 254n100
Frames of Mind (Gardner), 31
Franciscans, 53
Francis of Assisi, Saint, 39
Frankl, Viktor, 107, 123, 158–59, 186,
　　221, 272n7, 274n2, 274n46, 276n26
　　on education, 212
　　on guilt, 154, 273n26
　　impact of concentration camp on,
　　　149–52
　　on reality and truth, 156
　　on reason and feelings, 157
　　on self, 153–54, 161
　　on self-actualization, 154–55
　　on self-esteem, 155–56
　　on sex, 157–58
　　on what life expects from us, 165
free causes, 66
freedom of choice, 128, 138, 165, 181
freedom of speech, 60, 61, 78, 133
free will, 28, 33, 164, 187, 219, 228,
　　275n11
Freud, Sigmund, 149, 150
Freudianism, 33, 42, 106, 152, 183,
　　243n1, 250n56
Friedman, Maurice, 106
"full humanness," 107

Gable, Clark, 235
Galton, Francis, 16
Garden of Life Temple, 35
Gardner, Howard, 31

Gaylin, Willard, 168
GC31. *See* General Council 31 (GC31)
Gebhard, Paul, 121
General Council 31 (GC31), 53–54
General Education Board. *See* Rock-
　　efeller Foundation
Genesis, book of, 103, 220
Getting What You Want (Ringer), 48
Gilbreth, Frank, 26–27, 245n43
Gilbreth, Lillian, 26–27, 245n43
Gilovich, Thomas, 111, 130
Glaser, Edward, 96
global government, 146
Goddard, H. H., 17, 18, 21
Goebbels, Joseph, 256n6
Golden Rule, 200, 279n13
Goldstein, Kurt, 265n44
Goodbye to Guilt (Jampolsky), 48
goodness, 140
　　education based on idea that
　　　goodness not inborn, 103
　　good and evil, 34, 41, 46, 47, 91,
　　　122, 143, 223, 224
　　human nature as inherently
　　　wise and good, 12, 41, 75–77,
　　　124–25, 130, 131, 221, 226,
　　　229, 257n16, 258n27, 260n47
　　　research to debunk concept
　　　　of, 99–105, 265n42
　　impact of belief that truth and
　　　reality are objective, 174–75
　　and love, 277n43
　　as seen in Cherokee legend, 275n8
　　self-actualization and humans
　　　as inherently wise and good,
　　　124–25, 270n103
Gore, Al, 58

Gould, Stephen Jay, 19

government

blaming industry for problems caused by government, 128, 137–38

curtailing rights and freedoms, 128, 138

democratic government based on idea that rights need to be protected, 103

and generation of employment, 146

global government, 146

impact of belief that intelligence is sum of capacity and performance (inherited and acquired), 170

impact of Humanistic Psychology on, 57–60, 77, 84

impact of self-transcendence on, 172–73

not using common sense or fairness, 128, 138–39

pursuing policies to make self-actualization and success difficult, 128, 139–41

redistribution of wealth as government theft, 196

reforming of, 226–29

and self-aggrandizement, 79, 258n30

serving special interests rather than constituents, 10

what the average individual can do about, 239–40

young people hostile toward, 76, 258n20

See also politics

Grant, Madison, 21

gratification, 249n33

pathology of, 92

self-gratification, 92, 123, 200, 277n43

Gray, Thomas, 192

Great Books Program, 211

Great Society program, 57

greed, 79, 264n19, 275n8

Grisham, John, 265n33

Griswold v. Connecticut, 60

Guilford, J. P., 97–98, 263n11

guilt, 9, 101, 113, 121, 171, 199, 224, 275n8

collective guilt, 154

determining moral culpability, 276n22

Frankl on, 154, 273n26

Freudian view of, 250n56

guilt as recognition of disapproval, 250n56

Humanistic Psychology on, 154

intrinsic guilt, 250n56

under law, 113, 228

perceived vs. actual guilt, 168

rejecting or ignoring guilt and shame, 9, 46, 56, 76, 88, 154, 168, 257n18, 276n21

and sex, 56, 88, 176, 205, 278n45

value of, 166–68

Gutiérrez, Gustavo, 146, 147

Hairston, Maxine, 115

hard causation, 68, 256n5

Harvey, Paul, 82

hasty conclusions, 102, 183

hate crimes, 87

Hefner, Hugh, 44, 120, 200

Heisenberg, Walter, 111

Hereditarianism, 11, 12, 20, 219,
220–21

    and American culture, 28–30

    bias of psychology, 263n11

    conflict with America's founding
        documents, 138

    and education, 23–26, 49

    efforts to overcome, 31–32

    erroneous ideas of, 240

    Humanistic Psychology as a reac-
        tion to, 33

    on human nature as inherently
        wise and good, 12, 41, 75–77,
        257n16, 258n27, 260n47

        research to debunk concept
            of, 99–105

    impact on education, 238

    and industry, 26–28

    on intelligence as inherited and
        unalterable, 16–19, 21, 30–31,
        140, 229, 236

        consequences of belief in,
            73–74

        continued prevalence of
            concept, 127, 134–35

        research to debunk concept
            of, 95–99

    leading to Eugenics movement, 21

    legacy of, 72–74

    negative impact of combining
        concepts, 125

    pessimistic views of, 11, 12,
        15–32, 127, 135–37, 142,
        243n1, 278n3

    replacement for, 149–59, 161–78

Hereditary Genius (Galton), 16

hierarchy of human needs, 38–40,
    249nn32–34, 258n25

    assumption that lower needs must
        be met before higher ones can
        be met, 39, 155

    Maslow's carelessness in devel-
        oping, 106, 266n46

    See also self-actualization, as
        highest human need

hindsight bias, 268n84

Hinduism, 103, 265n35, 279n13

Hirsch, E. D., Jr., 31–32, 213, 246n59

history, disdain for, 115, 268n79

Hitchcock, Alfred, 237

Holmes, Oliver Wendell, 23

Holocaust

    Eugenics movement as model for,
        23

    Frankl on impact of concentration
        camp, 149–52

homosexuality, 37, 43, 81, 89, 120,
    121, 269n97

honesty, 189, 219, 229, 232

Hoover, Herbert, 21

Horney, Karen, 34

human behavior

    and considerations of right and
        wrong, 203

    defining identity, 179

    ease of classifying behavior as
        "compulsive," 175

    effect of ideas on, 67–69

    impulsive behavior, 87, 92, 118,
        176, 277n42

    individuals responsible for
        behavior, 171–72

and responsibility, 187–88,
222–23
Humanistic Psychology, 12–13, 33–63,
127, 189, 220
as a challenge to tradition, 40–42
and the ego factor, 129–32
erroneous ideas of, 233, 240, 242
on feelings as more dependable
than reason, 12, 36–37, 42, 47,
85–87, 130, 132, 237
research to debunk concept
of, 116–20
on human nature as inherently
wise and good, 130, 131, 140,
221, 226, 229, 236
research to debunk concept
of, 265n42
impact on education, 49–51, 210,
238, 279n2
impact on family, 237
impact on government, 57–60,
240
impact on journalism, 62–63, 229
impact on law, 60–61
impact on mass culture, 45–49,
65, 71–72, 235, 236, 242
impact on publishing, 232, 241
impact on religion, 51–55,
221–22, 239
impact on the family, 55–56
legacy of, 74–90
on morality, 201, 203
negative impact of combining
concepts, 124–25
not believing shame or guilt have
purpose, 167
optimistic view of, 140, 142

not replacing Hereditari-
anism, 127, 135–37
on people creating their own truth
and reality, 82–85, 130, 132,
218–19, 223
research to debunk concept
of, 111–16
recognizing human imperfection,
274n4
replacement for, 149–59, 161–78
on self-actualization as highest
human need, 39, 77–79, 130,
131, 229, 249n32, 249n37,
258n25, 258n27
research to debunk concept
of, 106–107
on self-esteem as a prerequisite to
achievement, 39, 50, 52, 80–82,
130, 131, 191
research to debunk concept
of, 108–11
on sexual expression as natural
and wholesome, 47, 87–90, 130,
132
research to debunk concept
of, 120–24
human nature
common sense about, 168–78
guiding children to know right
from wrong, 205–208
is inherently imperfect, 165, 169,
171–72, 177, 183–86, 220–21,
260n47
as inherently wise and good, 12,
41, 75–77, 124–25, 130, 131,
140, 221, 226, 229, 257n16,
258n27, 260n47

debate over truth of, 99–105,
265n42

need for accurate understanding
of, 179

a new look at, 161–78

optimism that divinized human
nature, 127

representation of humans in
terms of dimension, 274n2

restoring traditional view of, 13

Rogers and Maslow's ideas
replacing traditional views,
41–42

self-actualization and humans
as inherently wise and good,
124–25, 270n103

and sexual restraint, 123–24

and will to meaning, 150–52

human needs, hierarchy of. *See* hierarchy of human needs

human potential movement. *See*
Humanistic Psychology

human rights, expansion of, 145

"human triumph," 152

humility, 77, 165, 166, 171

hunches, trustworthiness of, 86, 175

Hussein, Saddam, 85

Hustler (magazine), 44

Huxley, Aldous, 107

"I," 129. *See also* egotism

ideas, 69–70, 233, 255n2, 274n3
accepting or rejecting of, 68,
256n5
can be both true and false, 112–13
cause and effect among, 67–69,
256n3, 256n8

consequences of, 69, 70–72

consistency of ideas and perception, 276n28

false ideas, 278n2

familiarity leading to acceptance,
68, 256n6

kinship of, 69–70, 256n9

realm of, 177

testing of, 112, 181

truth as consistency between idea
and perception, 267n67

ways mass culture influences, 68–69

ideational cause, 67

identity, 35, 92, 153
behavior defining, 179

Ignatius, Saint, 54, 147

IHM. *See* Immaculate Heart of Mary,
Catholic Sisters of (IHM)

illusion, 114

Immaculate Heart of Mary, Catholic
Sisters of (IHM), 53, 56, 90

immigration, 10, 74

Immigration Act of 1917, 20

imperfection in humans, 165, 177
complexity and imperfection of
humans, 100, 171–72, 260n47
Hereditarianism exaggerating, 162
inherent imperfection, 183
overcoming imperfections, 183–86
reaffirm human imperfection,
220–21
recognized in social institutions,
103

impressions, trustworthiness of, 86,
102, 175, 198

improve, efforts to, 165, 183–86, 275n13

impulse voices, 38

impulsive behavior, 87, 92, 118, 176, 277n42

incest, 43, 87, 89, 120, 122, 176, 253n85, 261n60, 269n94

incivility, 172–73, 183
    of those who preach civility, 127, 133–34, 271n6

incurable illness, 152

individuality, 55, 75, 171, 205
    individual rights, 128, 138

industry and business
    excessive risk taking, 79, 259n32
    government blaming for problems caused by government, 128, 137–38
    impact of belief that intelligence is sum of capacity and perfor-mance (inherited and acquired), 170
    impact of Hereditarianism, 26–28, 127, 135–37
    impact of Humanistic Psychology, 79, 84
    impact of self-transcendence on, 172–73
    private companies as examples of human potential, 139
    See also workers/employees

inequality, 224

inherent imperfection, 183

injustice, 77, 148, 224, 227

"inner truth," 85

instrumental causes, 66

intelligence
    assumptions about intelligence based on race, gender, etc., 169, 277n31
    comparison of intellectual and emotional reactions, 119
    emphasize intellect rather than memory, 210–13
    and head size, 16
    increasing intelligence, 180–83
    as inherited rather than acquired, 16–19, 21, 30–31, 140, 229, 278n3
        consequences of belief in, 73–74
        continued prevalence of concept, 127, 134–35
        debate over truth of, 95–99
    intellectual skills, 212
    mass culture as a disparaging view of, 28–30
    measuring intelligence capacity, 277n30
    separate types of, 31, 246n53
    as sum of capacity and perfor-mance (inherited and acquired), 168–70
    testing of army recruits during WWI, 18, 19, 20, 21, 73–74
    See also IQ test

Intelligence Quotient. See IQ test

International Congresses of Eugenics, 21

International Council for Self-Esteem, 81

International Encyclopedia of Psychiatry, Psychology, Psychoanalysis, and Neurology, 34

international law, 254n97

interpersonal intelligence (knowledge of others), 246n53

interruptions, use of in mass culture, 29–30, 70–71, 72, 85, 115, 246n50, 257n12

intimacy, 123, 124, 201, 202, 218

intolerance of those who preach tolerance, 127, 133–34, 271n6

intrapersonal intelligence (knowledge of self), 246n53

intrinsic guilt, 250n56

intuitions, trustworthiness of, 86, 118, 175, 198, 268n84

investigate as part of W.I.S.E. approach to effective thinking, 182

IQ test, 16–17, 24–25, 31, 97–98, 180, 243n5
    on army recruits during WWI, 18, 19, 20, 21, 73–74

Islam, 104, 108, 132, 278n1, 279n13, 287n1

Jainism, 279n13

James, William, 107

Japan
    payments to teachers, 257n15
    and quality control, 27, 30, 136
    US learning gap with widening, 82, 84, 109

Jefferson, Thomas, 107

Jepson, Rowland, 195, 246n59

Jesuits, 53–54, 144, 147, 258n22

Jesus, 278n1

Jews
    historic bias against, 20, 102, 244n17, 264n31
    Jewish immigration to US, 20–21
    killing of in Holocaust, 23, 68
    See also Judaism

JFK (movie), 85

JIT. *See* job instruction training (JIT)

job instruction training (JIT), 26

Johns Hopkins University, 243n2

Johnson, Lyndon, 57

Johnson, Samuel, 70, 108, 203, 269n85

John XXIII (pope), 147

journalism, 234–35
    Alfred Kinsey not influencing, 255n104, 255n110
    extolling importance of the individual, 81
    impact of Humanistic Psychology, 62–63, 72, 84, 175
    impact of mass culture on quality of, 30–31
    objectivity in, 10, 62, 84, 175, 229, 230
    opinions in, 62, 63, 84, 175, 230, 231–32, 240
    as paternalistic and manipulative, 230
    questions to ask journalists, 240–41
    reforming of, 229–32
    traditional rules of, 231–32
    what the average individual can do about, 240–41

Joy of Sex, The (Comfort), 48

Judaism, 103, 121, 132, 183, 220, 279n13, 281n17
    Shema Yisrael (Jewish prayer), 152, 153
    See also Jews

judges and judicial matters
    human imperfection in the legal system, 103, 265n33

judicial activism, 20, 60–61, 74, 228–29, 254n99, 254n101, 255n103

  treatment of lawbreakers, 10, 77, 89, 254n99, 261n63

  uphold Constitution rather than political agendas, 228–29

  See also law

judgment, 114, 118, 180, 209

  different from opinion, 231, 232

  Hereditarian views on, 17, 26

  imperfection of, 102–103

  moral and ethical judgment, 50, 189

  need to be based on evidence, 59, 63, 68, 118, 174, 183, 230, 255n2, 277n39

  reasoned judgment, 50, 189

  value judgment, 37, 60

justice, 115, 219, 224. *See also* social injustice; social justice

justification of mistakes, 166

justified self-esteem, 169, 173–74, 277n38

  achieving, 191–93

Kallikak Family: A Study in the Heredity of Feeble-Mindedness, The (Goddard), 21

Keating-Owens Act (1916), 245n42

Kelo v. City of New London, 61

Kennedy, Edward, 57–58

Kennedy administration, 139

Kerry, John, 58

King, Rex, 121

Kinsey, Alfred, 43–44, 120–24, 157, 200, 251n66

  and Abraham Maslow, 43

  influence of, 49–51, 255n104

  as sexually perverted, 120–21, 269n91

knowledge

  acquiring and applying, 180

  acquisition of organized knowledge, 212

  applying knowledge to problem solving, 98

  arriving through senses, 171, 277n33

  expansion of, 195

  of facts, 215–17

  lies within, 75

  losing motivation to learn, 83–84

Kohn, Alfie, 51, 109

Kohn, Bob, 62, 84

Koran, 219

Krauthammer, Charles, 281n24

Land O' Lakes Declaration, 253n82

language, 195, 212

  avoiding dishonest terminology, 195–96

  decrease in language skills, 83–84, 260n48

  dependability of language, 260n45

  dictionaries presenting all usage as equally correct, 84, 260n51

  limited terminology for love, 200

  loaded language, 63, 231

  slanted language, 241

Laughlin, H. H., 23

law

  impact of Humanistic Psychology on, 60–61, 77, 84

"low self-esteem" defenses, 81, 173

and relativism, 113

See also judges and judicial matters

Lawrence v. Texas, 61

laws proscribing certain sexual behaviors, relaxation of, 88, 89

learning, 171, 215, 216, 217, 263n4, 268n79

emphasize intellect rather than memory, 210–13

learning gap with other countries widening, 82, 84, 109, 174

learning styles, 50, 115

problem-based learning (PBL), 99, 212–13, 238, 263n17

rote learning, 32

steps in that emphasize intellect rather than memory, 210–13

See also education

Learning to Love Yourself (Wegschneider), 48

legal system. *See* judges and judicial matters, human imperfection in the legal system

Leo XIII (pope), 144, 145

Lerner, Barbara, 276n27

Levin, Mark, 61, 254n97

liberal politics, 128, 141–42

liberation theology, 146, 147, 148, 171, 277n36

rejecting, 224–25

life, meaning in, 188, 189

Lima syndrome, 270n102

Lincoln, Abraham, 107

linguistic intelligence, 246n53

literature, lovers of, 233

"litmus test" for judges, 229

loaded language, 63, 231

logic, 70, 83, 114, 118–19, 139, 142, 174, 214

logical-mathematical intelligence, 246n53

logotherapy, 155, 158

Lombroso, Cesare, 16, 243n4

Looking Out for #1 (Ringer), 48

Lord's Prayer, 153

Lorenz, Edward, 66

love

as an avenue to finding meaning, 151

love vs. lust, 88, 89, 176, 201, 277n43, 278n44

need for, 39, 92, 249n32

seeing the good of another, 277n43

self-love, 52, 109

and sexual expression, 124, 200, 270n102

Luke, Gospel according to, 252nn73–74

lust

distinguishing eros and lust, 200–201

vs. love, 88, 89, 176, 201, 277n43, 278n44

Machiavelli, Niccoló, 143

Maidanek, 156

manipulation, 12, 117–18, 230, 260n45

"man's inhumanity to man," 100

Man's Search for Meaning (Frankl), 159

Marriman family, 23

Martin, Clyde, 121

Martin, Malachi, 53–54, 147, 252n77

Marxism, 146–47, 148

Maslow, Abraham, 35, 106–107,
112, 129, 147, 149, 200, 249n40,
251n66, 265n43
and Alfred Kinsey, 43
errors in selecting individuals for
study on self-actualization, 107,
266n49
and the hierarchy of human
needs, 39–40, 249n32, 249n33,
249n 34, 249n 37
carelessness in developing,
106, 266n46
impact of ideas on education,
49–51
reactions to Rogers and Maslow,
40–42
reflecting on involvement with
Humanistic Psychology, 90–93
relationship to Catholics, 42,
250n44
on self-actualization, 154–55
view of self, 37–40
views on guilt, 250n56
and Viktor Frankl, 159
warning to Kinsey, 121
See also Humanistic Psychology

Mason, Jackie, 236–37

mass culture, 44–49, 251n64
decline in attention span, 71, 235,
281n27
as a disparaging view of human
intelligence, 28–30
expectation that it would mirror
traditional values, 45, 250n55
Frankl receiving less attention
from, 159
impact of belief that truth and
reality are objective, 174–75
influence of Hereditarianism on,
65
influence of Humanistic Psychology
on, 45–49, 65, 71–72, 81
influence of on Catholic Church,
54
learning gap between US and
other countries widening, 81–82
opposing traditional beliefs,
251n65
reforming of, 235–37
and special effects, 257n13
view of human nature, 276n25
ways it influences, 68–69
what the average individual can
do about, 242
See also television

masturbation, 202

May, Rollo, 35

Mayer, John, 246n53

McGovern, Arthur, 147

McKay, Matthew, 46

McMaster University School of Medicine, 98–99, 212–13

McWilliams, Peter, 46

meaning
and consequences, 65–93
meaning of life, 188, 189, 273n16
will to meaning, 150–52, 157,
273n16

media
not appealing to intelligence,
29–30

reforming of, 235–37

what the average individual can
do about, 242

See also journalism; mass culture;
publishing

Medicaid, 77

Meeker, Mary, 97–98

memory, 23, 25, 68

emphasize intellect rather than
memory, 210–13, 279n1

subjectivity of, 101–102, 264n27

*Menace of Mental Deficiency from the Stand-
point of Heredity, The* (Goddard), 21

Mencius, 167

Mengele, Joseph, 149–50

Menninger, Karl, 109, 222

"mercy killing" of defective infants, 23,
261n61

Mercy Sisters, 53

metaphysical dimension of self, 162,
163, 165, 274n2

mind, 32, 47, 67, 68, 69, 116, 163,
181, 194, 210, 257n15, 267n67

and the brain, 16, 163, 191

conscious mind, 28, 68, 101

creating truth and reality, 42,
82, 174, 178, 276n28 (*see also*
reality; truth)

human mind as greatest natural
resource, 210

metaphysical mind/soul, 15, 91,
162, 274n2

mind as place of ideas, 274n3

mind building, 49, 170, 211, 238

mind stuffing, 31, 49, 98, 99, 135,
136, 170, 213, 219, 238

unconscious mind, 101

mindlessness, 256n8

MindPower, Inc., 280n11

Miranda v. Arizona, 60, 254n99

mistakes, 82, 184, 193, 212

admitting our mistakes, 187, 188

responsibility for, 142, 166

Model Eugenical Sterilization Law, 23

Mohammed the Prophet. *See* Islam

Moore, Thomas, 130–31, 259n33

moral causes, 66

morality, 54, 86, 105, 118, 203, 218,
219

determining moral culpability,
276n22

of Kinseyan view of sexuality, 123

moral and ethical judgment, 50,
189

moral education, 83

moral ideals, 189

moral opinions can be true or
false, 174

"New Morality," 86

no objective standard for, 260n46

as objective and impersonal, 42,
83, 249n41

as personal and subjective, 42, 83,
84, 203, 249n41, 276n21

personal responsibility for moral
offenses, 222

personal taste vs. objective moral
value, 252n69

relative nature of, 271n6

relevance of to sexual behavior,
201–202

return to moral education, 171

self-actualization as "moral philosophy," 265n43

shift from moral life to feeling good, 9

subjective and personal nature of, 42, 83, 261n52

and values clarification, 260n46

See also ethics; sexual expression, sexual morality

motivation, 38, 97, 269n87

and behaving impulsively, 90

losing motivation to learn, 83–84, 116

in sexual relations, 205, 201–202

movies, 10, 71–72, 84, 85, 175, 236, 250n55

Moynihan, Daniel Patrick, 81, 145, 226, 281n24

multiculturalism, 83

musical intelligence, 246n53

Myers, David G., 264n27, 268n84

NARAL. *See* National Abortion Rights Action League (NARAL)

narcissism, 82, 106, 109, 110, 125, 129, 130, 131, 189, 259n33, 276n27

National Abortion Rights Action League (NARAL), 58

National Association of Manufacturers, 257n15

National Association of Secondary-School Principals, 26

National Child Labor Committee, 245n42

National Education Association (NEA), 23–26

Commission on the Reorganization of Secondary Education, 24

Committee of Nine, 24

Committee of Ten, 23

National Intelligence Test, 25

national security, 281n26

Native American religion, 279n13

"native intelligence," 19

Natural Born Killers (film), 67–68

naturalist intelligence, 246n53

NEA. *See* National Education Association (NEA)

necessary causes, 66

needs

considering rights, needs, and feelings of others, 175, 277n40

equated with goals, 40

human needs (*see* hierarchy of human needs)

replacing word *need* with *challenge*, 276n26

seeing needs as rights, 78

self-actualization as highest human need (*see* self-actualization, as highest human need)

transcending basic needs, 92

negative feelings, 188, 198–99

"Negro Family: The Case for National Action, The" (Moynihan), 226

Nehru, Jawaharlal, 275n11

Newman, David, 115

New York Times (newspaper), 26, 62–63, 84, 223

New York Zoological Society, 21

noblesse oblige, 186

non sequiturs, 70, 102, 256n10

non-thinking, 28–29. *See also* conditioning

Obama, Barack, 143
objectivity
    in journalism, 10, 62, 84, 175,
        229, 230
    objective exams, 25, 49, 135, 216,
        280n14
    objective reality, 36, 40, 42, 50,
        111, 114–15, 116, 130, 156,
        174–75, 177–78, 281n27
obligation, 138, 144, 189, 224
    moral obligation, 202, 203–204,
        224
    to others, 78, 172–73, 189, 231,
        234
        neglect of, 56, 79, 131
        parental obligations, 56, 79,
          175
observation, subjectivity of, 101
Okri, Ben, 100
On Becoming a Person (Rogers), 36,
    274n4
On the Origin of Species (Darwin), 15
opinions, 48, 129, 133, 134, 194, 195,
    242, 246n51, 256n5
    equality of opinions, 83, 112,
        260n45, 267n70
    and facts, 10, 72, 82–83, 115, 175
    false opinions, 174, 178
    in journalism, 62, 63, 84, 175,
        230, 231–32, 240
    my opinion is better, 83, 260n44
    seen as truth, 112, 114, 174,
        267n70
optimism that divinized human nature,
    127, 135–37
original sin, 52, 103, 104, 162–63,
    184, 220, 265n34

Orwell, George, 195, 267n67
outside influences, 181
overconfidence, 268n84
overgeneralization, 102, 183
overindulgence, 91
oversimplification, 63, 102, 107, 176,
    183, 214, 232, 235
Overstreet, Harry, 118–19

Paideia Program, 211–12, 213, 238
paradox, 115
    paradox of self, 186–87
parenting, 10, 207, 208, 253n86
    anticipating disagreement with
        children, 207–208
    children growing up in households
        that resist false ideas, 278n2
    and concept of human nature
        as inherently wise and good,
        265n42
    guiding children to know right
        from wrong, 203, 205–208
    impact of Humanistic Psychology
        on, 55–56, 89
    parents derided as out of touch,
        237
    See also children; family
pathology of gratification, 92
PBL. *See* problem-based learning (PBL)
peak experience, 42
Peck, M. Scott, 46
pedophilia, 122
Penguin Dictionary of Psychology, The
    (Reber), 116
penmanship, capacity for, 180
Penthouse (magazine), 44
perception, 108

consistency of ideas and perception, 267n67, 276n28

ego factor (perceiving self as better than others), 128–32

feelings distorting, 117, 268n83

guilt-as-perception, 167–68

imperfect nature of, 100, 101, 193, 198

and reality, 36, 114

self as object of, 34, 35, 101

performance

improving, 169–70

intelligence as sum of capacity and performance, 168, 169, 180, 277n30

permissiveness, 50, 55, 204, 279n2

Perry, William, 115

personal agendas in classroom, 219

personal growth, 119, 166

personal limitations, acknowledging, 230–31

personal responsibility. *See* responsibility

personhood

authority is within each person rather than society, 75, 76

Cherokee legend of two wolves within a person, 275n8

Maslow's daughter searching for real self, 252n75

mistake of forcing distinction between self and person, 274n1

need to work on finding, 266n47

search for truth about own personality, 278n8

sexuality as proof of, 249n42

See also self

pessimistic views of Hereditarianism, 11, 12, 15–32, 127, 135–37, 142, 243n1, 278n3

philia, 200

physical causes, 66

physical dimension of self, 162, 163

physiological needs, 39, 249n32

Pisani, Emilio, 252n73

Piven, Frances, 142, 143

plagiarism, 84, 174

Planned Parenthood, 22

Planned Parenthood v. Casey, 61

Playboy (magazine), 44, 200

politics

alternative political systems, 76, 258n21

and liberation theology, 277n36

See also government

"Politics and the English Language" (Orwell), 195

Pomeroy, Wardell, 121, 269n94

Pope, Alexander, 104

positive atmosphere, 207

Positive Psychology group, 219

potential, 42, 49, 80, 106, 107, 112, 136, 139–40, 180, 224, 250n56

and dimensions of self, 162–63

potential human being (fetus), 59, 196

poverty

causes of, 145

limited success of war on poverty, 85

rich blamed for wealth, but poor not blamed for poverty, 145

power, drive for, 150

practical intelligence, 31

practice, importance of to learning, 32

praise, not being concerned about, 192–93

prejudice, 111, 118, 130, 243n3, 261n52

pride, 9, 27, 41, 51, 109, 165, 166, 185, 191, 195, 264n19, 275n8

Prince, The (Machiavelli), 143

principal causes, 66

prisoner-of-war camps, 272n7

private property, inviolability of, 144

probable consequences, 178, 277n35

problem-based learning (PBL), 99, 212–13, 238, 263n17

problem solving, 30, 67, 98, 102, 264n28

    involving employees in, 27, 136, 137

pro-choice, 57–59

Production of Reality, The (O'Brien and Kollock), 115

Progressive Education movement, 263n4

Progressivism, 10–11, 13, 16, 19–21, 74, 140, 141, 148, 220, 228

    achievements of, 271n13

    "Economic Justice for All" (USCCB position paper), 145–46

    resurgence of, 12, 23–24, 128, 142–43

pro-life, 57–59

promiscuity, 56, 89, 118, 123, 124, 157, 176, 202, 218

proof, burden of, 183

Prosser, Charles, 25

proximate causes, 66

psychology laboratories, 243n2

psychopaths, 91, 110

public discussion/debate and relativism, 114–15

publishing, 81, 214–15

    decline in, 48

    failing to encourage quality nonfiction, 30, 246n51

    reforming of, 232–35

    what the average individual can do about, 240–41

Pure Food and Drug Act, 20

quality control, 27, 136–37, 245n46

Quinton, A., 268n80

quota system for immigration, 20

Race Betterment Society, 23

racial discrimination, 74, 139, 271n12

radicalism, 143

rape, 110, 270n102

Raths, Louis, 50

rationalization, 102

Ratzinger, Joseph, 146

reading, decline in, 48

Reagan administration, 139

reality, 114

    and creating own truth and reality, 42, 82–85, 130, 132, 156, 174, 178, 218, 223, 276n28 (*see also* relativism)

        research to debunk concept of, 111–16

    drama that is faithful to, 236–37

    episodic grasp of, 96–97

    Frankl on, 156

    and perception, 36, 114

reality as objective, 36, 40, 42, 50,
  111, 114–15, 116, 130, 156,
  169, 174–75, 177–78, 281n27
 self-determining, 36
 thoughts and reality, 276n28
 traditional reality, 235
 truth and reality created by
  human mind, 42
reason, 102
 common reasoning errors, 102
 exposing inappropriate feelings,
  277n41
 feelings more dependable than,
  36–37, 42, 47, 85–87, 124–25,
  130, 132
  research to debunk concept
   of, 116–20
 Frankl on, 157
 more reliable than feelings, 169,
  175–76, 196–99
 reasoned judgment, 50, 189
 reasoning for errors, 214
 seeing consequences of actions,
  277n42
Reasoner, Robert W., 81
rebellion against authority, 9
Reber, Arthur, 116
recognition, 187, 192–93
 guilt as recognition of disapproval,
  250n56
redistribution of wealth, 76–77, 128,
  139–41, 142, 144, 195–96, 227,
  281n25
reflection, 189
Reisman, Judith, 44
relativism, 92, 112, 113–16, 271n6. *See
  also* reality

religion, 189, 281n17
 "cafeteria approach" to, 84–85
 and the Golden Rule, 200, 279n13
 impact of Humanistic Psychology,
  51–55, 76, 252nn72–74
 impact of recognizing human
  nature is imperfect, 171
 need to create structures for practicing good works, 225, 281n23
 purge clerical training of Humanistic Psychology, 221–22
 reforming of, 219–20
 salvation, 277n34
 and sexual behavior, 88
 shift from moral life to feeling
  good, 9
 See also names of specific religions
remorse, 167, 203, 254n99
remote causes, 66
repentance, 185–86, 197, 224, 275n8
Rerum Novarum (1891 encyclical), 144
rescuing, need for, 171, 277n34
resentment, 77, 258n24
respect, 28, 133, 170, 194
 expecting respect from others, 132
 for others, 122, 133, 189–90, 201–
  202, 203, 262n64
  teaching children about, 208
 self-respect, 9, 201, 260n40
 See also disrespect
responsibility, 54, 57, 151, 186, 205,
  208, 219–20
 abdicating responsibility, 110, 224,
  234
 and guilt, 154, 166
 people not responsible for actions,
  76, 165, 222, 236

taking personal responsibility, 187–88, 219, 222–23
"Richard Cory" (Robinson), 190
right and wrong, 51, 165, 167, 203, 204, 218
rights of others, 277n40
risk, 251n63
    excessive risk taking, 79, 259n32
    and sex, 56, 122, 201
    unnecessary risk, 118
Robinson, Arlington, 190
Rockefeller, John D., 23–24
Rockefeller family, 23
Rockefeller Foundation, 23–24
Roe v. Wade, 58, 61, 253n83
    dissenting opinion, 254n101
Rogers, Carl, 35–37, 77–78, 85, 86, 106–107, 112, 129, 147, 165, 200, 223, 249n40, 251n66, 265n43, 274n4
    impact of ideas on education, 49–51
    reactions to Rogers and Maslow, 40–42
    reflecting on involvement with Humanistic Psychology, 90
    See also Humanistic Psychology
Romantic movement, 111, 116, 193, 268n80
Roosevelt, Eleanor, 107
Roosevelt, Franklin D., 13, 20–21
Roosevelt, Theodore, 20, 21–22
Roper, Elmer, 21
Rosenthal, Peggy, 256n9, 266n47
rote learning, 32
Rothwax, Harold J., 254n99
Rousseau, Jean Jacques, 111, 193, 252n77, 257n16

Rubin, Jerry, 253n84
Rules for Radicals (Alinsky), 11, 143
Russell, Bertrand, 23, 111
Russell, Diana, 43

sadism, 122–23
safety needs, 39, 249n32
safety net, 145
Salovey, Peter, 246n53
salvation, 76, 224, 277n34
    collective salvation, 281n22
Samenow, Stanton, 104–105
Sanger, Margaret, 22
Santayana, George, 12
SAT. *See* Scholastic Aptitude Test (SAT)
Scholastic Aptitude Test (SAT), 25
Schuller, Robert, 52, 222, 252n72
Schweitzer, Albert, 107
science and relativism, 113–14
scientific management system, 26–27, 74, 245n43
scientific method, 114
Scott, Walter Dill, 28
Segundo, Juan Luis, 147
self, 33–34, 247n5, 247n9
    Abraham Maslow's view of, 37–40, 91
    Carl Rogers's view of, 35–37
    confusions about in Humanistic Psychology, 161
    culture as a factor influencing, 163–64
    determining reality, 36
    dimensions of, 161–65
    expecting more of self than others, 185–86

forgetting about, 275n12

Frankl on, 153–54

intrapersonal intelligence (knowledge of self), 246n53

Maslow's daughter searching for real self, 252n75

mistake of forcing distinction between self and person, 274n1

not used as an independent noun by Maslow, 248n28

paradox of self, 186–87

See also personhood

self-absorption, 12, 48, 109, 128, 151, 172, 189, 190, 232, 259n32, 266n47, 277n37

self-acceptance, unconditional, 116

self-actualization, 38–39, 41, 105, 265n44

books reflecting the idea of, 46

different from self-transcendence, 165

ending pursuit of, 187

Frankl on, 154–55

government pursuing policies to make difficult, 128, 139–41

as highest human need, 39, 77–79, 124–25, 130, 131, 229, 249n32, 249n37, 258n25, 258n27

research to debunk concept of, 106–107

and humans as inherently wise and good, 124–25, 270n103

Maslow's errors in selecting individuals for study on self-actualization, 107, 266n49

as "moral philosophy," 265n43

selflessness as a characteristic of, 91

self-adoration, 109

self-adulation, 130

self-aggrandizement, 79, 219, 258n30

self-assertion, 9, 80, 81, 259n33

self-awareness, 91

self-centeredness, 78, 109, 130, 132, 222

self-contentment, 81

self-control, 9, 80, 81, 92, 110, 172, 173, 204

self-criticism, 80, 81, 173, 185, 193

self-deception, 118, 198, 236, 269n85

self-demeaning, 202

self-denial, 81, 266n47

self-disapproval, 250n56

self-discipline, 80, 81, 151, 173

self-distancing, 151

self-enhancement, 110

self-esteem, 9, 38, 41, 50–51, 78

abolishment of programs on, 217

achievement leads to justified self-esteem, 169

and antisocial activities, 109–10

banning acts that cause loss of, 133

Bierce's definition, 129

books reflecting the idea of, 46

as a byproduct of achievement, 173

correlation to self-actualization, 107

"feel-good-now" self-esteem, 276n27

Frankl on, 155–56

Humanistic Psychology unleashing the ego, 271n4

justified self-esteem, 169, 173–74, 191–93, 277n38

most people have high self-esteem, 111

need to earn, 276n27

and pride, 51

as a requirement for achievement, 39, 50, 52, 80–82, 124–25, 130, 131, 169, 173–74, 277n38

    research to debunk concept of, 108–11

as stable and healthy only when deserved, 90

and a "tyranny of the should," 46

use of concept of to understand the Bible, 52

self-fascination, 252n75

self-focus, 277n40

self-fulfillment, 78

self-gratification, 92, 123, 200, 277n43

self-help books, 46, 48, 56, 234

self-improvement, 38, 80, 166, 171, 232, 234, 241

self-indulgence, 80, 81, 106, 151, 172, 173, 202, 224, 232–33, 259n33

self-interest, 78, 187

selfishness, 103, 109, 125, 266n46, 275n12

selflessness, 91

self-love, 52, 109

self-preoccupation, 275n12

self-reproach, 167

self-respect, 9, 201, 260n40

self-restraint, 80, 172

self-sacrifice, 51, 81, 173

self-serving bias, 121, 268n84

self-surrender, 108, 179

self-transcendence, 151, 158, 266n46, 277n37

    achieving, 186–90

    different from self-actualization, 165

    as greatest human challenge, 169, 172–73

    need to repeatedly gain, 165, 275n12

self-worship, 81

self worth, 52

Seligman, Martin, 109, 219

senses, 29, 47, 279n14

    knowledge arriving through senses, 171, 277n33

    sensory experience, 47

sequiturs, 70

Sermon on the Mount, 223

sex education, 89, 217–18

sexual expression

    age when young people might engage in sex, 278n44

    and Alfred Kinsey, 43–44

    any partner is acceptable, 88, 261n61

    being responsible about sex, 199–205

    choosing not to have sex, 270n101

    control of sexual impulses, 204

    feeling guilt or shame about, 176, 278n45

    Frankl on, 157–58

    and Freudianism, 243n1

    homosexuality, 269n97

    inappropriate sexual conduct, 89, 121, 122–23, 261n62, 269n94, 269n96

and love, 124, 200, 270n102
and motivation, 201–202, 205
natural and wholesome, 42,
   87–90, 124–25, 130, 132
   only when it neither harms
      nor degrades, 169, 176–77
   research to debunk concept
      of, 120–24
"premature awareness of sex,"
   123, 218
as a proof of personhood, 249n42
revise sex education classes,
   217–18
sexual ethics, 120, 132, 201
sexual harassment, 87, 133, 176
sexual morality, 43, 44, 120, 161,
   201–202, 203, 204, 250n45,
   277n43
television increasing sexual
   content of programs, 10
Sexuality in the Human Female (Kinsey),
   43
Sexuality in the Human Male (Kinsey), 43
Sex without Guilt (Ellis), 48
shame, 9, 277n38
   over sexual behavior, 88, 176,
      278n45
   psychology disparaging, 168,
      276n21
   rejection of, 46, 56, 76, 88,
      257n18
   value of, 9, 37, 166–68, 171, 176,
      185
Shaw, George Bernard, 23
Shaw, Peter, 260n45
Shema Yisrael (Jewish prayer), 152, 153
Shintoism, 279n13

Siddhayoga, 34
Sikhism, 279n13
sin, 37, 76, 222–23
   Catholic concepts of, 222, 264n31
   original sin, 52, 103, 104, 162–63,
      184, 220, 265n34
   perception of in Humanistic Psy-
      chology, 51, 53, 252n74
Singer, Isaac Bashevis, 275n11
Singer, Peter, 261n61
Sisters of the Providence of Charity, 53
Skeels, Harold, 96
Skinner, B. F., 33–35
slogans, 28–29, 48, 251n63, 253n84
Smelser, Neil, 109
Smith, Adam, 84
Snygg, Donald, 33
social behavior, 81
social conservatism, 128, 141–42
Social Darwinism, 11, 15–32, 127. *See
   also* Hereditarianism
social injustice, 77, 148
social justice, 76, 128, 143, 144–48,
   227
Society for Individual Psychology, 149
Society of Jesus (Jesuits), 53–54, 144,
   147, 258n22
Socrates, 108, 125, 163, 212
sodomy, 61
soft causation, 68, 256n5
SOI. *See* structure of intellect model
   (SOI)
Sowell, Thomas, 138, 145
spatial intelligence, 246n53
Spearman, Charles, 95
speculate as part of W.I.S.E. approach
   to effective thinking, 182

Spinoza, Benedict, 107
spirituality, 239, 250n44
spontaneous behavior/spontaneity, 40, 50, 85–86, 118, 266n47
stepparents, 253n85
sterilization, 22–23, 74, 261n61. *See also* Eugenics movement
Stern, Wilhelm, 243n5
Sternberg, Robert, 31
Sternberg v. Carhart, 61
Stevenson, Harold W., 81, 84
Stigler, James M., 81, 84
Stone, Oliver, 85
storge, 200
Stossel, John, 133
"straw man," 183
"street smarts." *See* practical intelligence
structure of intellect model (SOI), 97
subjectivism, 267n67, 276n28
subject-matter learning, 32, 280n14
success, 9, 15, 77, 84, 108, 128, 191, 227, 239
    coming after string of failures, 268n71
    government pursuing policies to make difficult, 128, 139–41
suffering, changing attitude toward, 151–52
Supreme Court, 22, 91–92
    judicial activism of, 60–61, 253n83, 254n99, 254n101
surrender, 68, 164
    self-surrender, 108, 278n1
susceptibility, 162
swearing, 235
Szasz, Thomas, 163

Taiwan, US learning gap with widening, 109
talk shows, 47–48
Talmud, 219
Tamblyn, Robyn, 98–99, 212–13
Taoism, 279n13
Tavris, Carol, 69, 198
taxation, 139, 226
Taylor, Frederick, 26–27
television, 29–30, 44–45, 46–47, 70–71, 85
    decline in quality of, 71–72
    using newsbreaks as advertisements, 257n12
    See also mass culture
Ten Commandments, 223
Ten Days to Self-Esteem (Burns), 48
Teresa, Mother, 39
Terman, Lewis, 17, 18, 24–25
textbooks that stuff minds rather than stimulate, 214–15
Theosophical Society, The, 34
thinking, 280n13
    be alert to errors in, 182–83
    before expressing negative feelings, 198–99
    common errors in, 182–83, 214
    complimentary thoughts, 183–84
    consistency in, 183
    creative thinking, 98, 170, 182, 210
    critical thinking, 96, 108, 137, 148, 170, 176, 178, 182, 210, 212, 214, 215, 218
    education as creation of habit of thinking, 96
    effective thinking, 182

good mental habits, 166

guidelines for, 213–14

having a "bad day" in thinking, 277n32

ideas and perception, 276n28

overcoming cognitive deficiency, 96–97

restraining from thought, 28–29 (*see also* conditioning)

students learning to ignore reason and create "personal reality," 49–50

teaching what to think rather than how to think, 181–82, 210, 213, 279n2

    applied to medical school students, 98–99, 263n17

    finding ways that teach how to think, 211, 279n1, 279n3

    replacing textbooks that stuff minds rather than stimulate, 214–15

testing thinking, 215–17

thinking skills vs. knowledge of facts, 216

thinking vs. subject-matter learning, 32, 175, 280n14

thought not included in behavioral dimension of self, 275n6

thoughts and reality, 276n28

thoughts manifest only to the self, 275n7

training in thinking skills leading to more intelligence, 98

valuing feelings more than, 269n87

wishful thinking, 268n83

Thomas Aquinas, Saint, 219

Thorndike, Edward, 18

time and motion studies, 26, 245n43

Tinker v. Des Moines School District, 60

tolerance, 83, 133–34, 271n6

    intolerance of those who preach tolerance, 127, 133–34, 271n6

Torrance, E. Paul, 98

torture, 110, 224

toxic loans and the 2008 financial crisis, 59

Toynbee, Arnold, 108, 123, 132, 165, 179, 218, 278n1

traditional reality, 235

tragedy, 100, 264n19

transcendence. *See* self-transcendence

transference of knowledge, 32, 246n59

Treblinka, 156

Trueblood, David Elton, 70, 268n72

trust, 40, 49, 80, 138, 142

    trusting feelings, 12, 78, 118, 120, 125, 198, 221

    trustworthiness, 36–37, 85, 117, 258n25

        of impressions, hunches, or intuitions, 86, 175, 198

truth, 114

    belief in something not making it true, 177

    as consistency between idea and perception, 267n67

    and creating own reality, 83, 260n45

    and creating own truth and reality, 42, 82–85, 130, 132, 174, 178, 218, 223, 276n28 (*see also* relativism)

        research to debunk concept of, 111–16

discovery of, 276n28

Frankl on, 156

ideas can be both true and false, 112–13

"inner truth," 85

more dependable than reason, 124–25

as objective (discovered rather than created), 169, 174–75, 177

opinion seen as, 112, 114, 174, 267n70

personal truth trumps other person's truth, 134

search for, 194, 278n8

as subjective, 56, 65, 82

valuing truth, 193–96

Twain, Mark, 104

Twenge, Jean, 82

Twersky, Abraham, 167

unconditional self-acceptance, 116

unconscious as God, 46

unconscious mind, 101

underserved self-esteem or praise, 173

unintended consequences, 70–72, 225

Unitarian Universalism, 279n13

University of Leipzig, 243n2

University of New Hampshire, 82

unwarranted assumption, 102, 182

USA Today (newspaper), 30

USCCB. *See* US Conference of Catholic Bishops (USCCB)

US Conference of Catholic Bishops (USCCB), 145

US Supreme Court, 23

usury, 264n31

values, 40

absolute code of, 92

value judgment, 37, 60

values clarification, 10, 50, 83, 171, 218, 252n69, 260n46

Vatican Council II, 147

Veatch, Henry B., 271n6

victims, 57, 228

villain and criminals as victim, 47, 77, 84

villains and antiheroes, 10, 47, 77, 84, 175, 236

violence, 29, 71, 72, 110, 123, 232, 236–37, 242

voting extended to women, 271n13

Walker, Francis, 18–19

Wallas, Graham, 95–96

war on poverty, 57

Watson, Goodwin, 96

Watson, John, 28

Watson-Glaser Critical Thinking Test, 96

"Ways of Defeating Guilt" (Burns), 167

wealth

redistribution of wealth, 76–77, 128, 129, 139–41, 142, 144, 195–96, 227, 281n25

rich are blamed for wealth, but poor not to blame for poverty, 145

Weaver, Richard, 269n87

Webster's Third New International Dictionary, 260n51

welfare liberals, 141

"welfare mentality," 57

Wells, H. G., 23
White, Byron, 254n101
will, 242
　free will, 28, 33, 164, 187, 219,
　　228, 275n11
　will to meaning, 150–52
Will, George, 67
Wilson, Woodrow, 13, 20, 23, 24,
　245n42
wisdom, 114
　education based on idea that
　　wisdom not inborn, 103
　human nature as inherently
　　wise and good, 12, 41, 75–77,
　　124–25, 130, 131, 140, 221,
　　226, 229, 257n16, 258n27,
　　260n47
　　　research to debunk concept
　　　　of, 99–105, 265n42
　self-actualization and humans
　　as inherently wise and good,
　　124–25, 270n103
W.I.S.E. approach to effective thinking,
　182, 214, 280n11
wishful thinking, 85, 105, 268n83

wonder as part of W.I.S.E. approach
　to effective thinking, 182
WordNet, 35
workers/employees, 26, 79, 144,
　172–73, 245n43
　feeling sense of entitlement, 82
　improved working conditions,
　　271n13
　intelligence of, 11, 17, 27
　rights of as seen by Catholic
　　Church, 144
　and scientific management system,
　　26, 27, 74, 136–37
　treating teachers as workers/prin-
　　cipals as managers, 275n15
　worker loyalty, 79
wrong. *See* right and wrong

"yellow" journalism, 72
Yerkes, Robert, 18, 19, 20, 21, 25, 28
Your Sacred Self (Dyer), 48

Zarathustra, 108, 278n1
Zoroastrianism, 200, 278n1